Masculinities in Mathematics

EDUCATING BOYS, LEARNING GENDER

Series editors: Debbie Epstein and Maírtín Mac an Ghaill

This timely series provides a well-articulated response to the current concerns about boys in schools. Drawing on a wide range of contemporary theorizing, the series authors debate questions of masculinity and highlight the changing nature of gender and sexual interactions in educational institutions. The aim throughout is to offer teachers and other practitioners grounded support and new insights into the changing demands of teaching boys and girls.

Current and Forthcoming titles include:

Louise Archer: *'Race', Masculinity and Schooling*
Madeleine Arnot: *Boy's Work: Teacher Initiatives on Masculinity and Gender Equality*
Martin Mills: *Challenging Violence in Schools*
Leonie Rowan et al.: *Boys, Literacy and Schooling*
Christine Skelton: *Schooling the Boys*

Masculinities in Mathematics

Heather Mendick

Open University Press

Open University Press
McGraw-Hill Education
McGraw-Hill House
Shoppenhangers Road
Maidenhead, Berkshire
England SL6 2QL

email: enquiries@openup.co.uk
world wide web: www.openup.co.uk

and Two Penn Plaza, New York, NY 10122289, USA

First published 2006

A catalogue record of this book is available from the British Library

ISBN 10: 0335 21827 X (pb) 0335 218288 (hb)
    13: 9780 335218 271 (pb) 9780 335218 288 (hb)

Library of Congress Cataloging-in-Publication Data
CIP data has been applied for

Typeset by BookEns Ltd, Royston, Herts.
Printed and bound in Poland by OZGraf. S.A.
www.polskabook.pl

Contents

List of figures and tables	*vi*
Series editors' foreword	*vii*
Acknowledgements	*ix*
Introduction: a quick guide	1
Part 1 Scene setting	**5**
1 Engendering mathematics	7
2 Introducing the study	25
Part 2 Sex by Numbers	**43**
3 Being/doing 'good at maths'	45
4 Proving something to others	69
5 Proving something to themselves	87
6 Changing directions	105
Part 3 Queering gender and maths	**119**
7 Making choices social: refusing essences in the classroom	121
8 Supporting gender transgression: being and acting different in maths	140
9 Opening up mathematics: living with uncertainty	155
References	167
Index	181

List of figures and tables

Figure 1.1   Participation in A level maths by gender   8

Table 2.1   Grafton examination results   27
Table 2.2   Westerburg examination results   29
Table 2.3   Sunnydale examination results   32
Table 2.4   How is it that people come to choose maths?   39

Series editors' foreword

Educating boys is currently seen – both globally and locally – to be in crisis. In fact, there is long history to the question: what about the boys? However, it was not until the 1990s that the question of boys' education became a matter of public and political concern in a large number of countries around the world, most notably the UK, the USA and Australia.

There are a number of different approaches to be found in the literature to troubling questions about boys in schools. The questions concern the behaviours and identities of boys in schools, covering areas such as school violence and bullying, homophobia, sexism and racism, through to questions about boys' perceived underachievement. In *Failing Boys? Issues in Gender and Achievement*, Epstein and her colleagues (Epstein et al. 1998) identify three specific discourses which are called upon in popular and political discussions of the schooling of boys: 'poor boys'; 'failing schools, failing boys'; and 'boys will be boys'. They suggest that it might be more useful to draw, instead, on feminist and profeminist insights in order to understand what is going on in terms of gender relations between boys and girls and amongst boys. An important question, they suggest, is what kind of masculinities are being produced in schools, in what ways, and how do they impact upon the education of boys. In other words, there is an urgent need to place boys' educational experiences within the wider gender relations within the institution and beyond.

This series is one that falls squarely within the last of these broad categories. In the plethora of rather simplistic and often counter-productive 'solutions' (such as making classrooms more 'boy-friendly' in macho ways) which are coming from governments in different part of the English-speaking world and from some of the more populist writers in the area (e.g. Steve Biddulph), there is an urgent need for a more thoughtful approach to the issues raised by what are quite long-standing problems in the schooling of boys. Approaches by policy makers for advice and by teachers and principals responsible for staff development in their schools to researchers in the field of 'boys' underachievement' are an almost daily event, and many have already tried the more simplistic approaches and found them wanting. There is, therefore, an urgent demand for more along the lines suggested here.

This is not a series of 'how to do it' handbooks for working with boys. Rather, it draws upon a wide range of contemporary theorising that is rethinking gender relations. While, as editors, we would argue strongly that the issues under discussion here require theorising, it is equally important that books in the area address the real needs of practitioners as they struggle with day to day life in schools and other places where professionals meet and must deal with the varied, often troubling, masculinities of boys. Teachers, youth workers and policy makers (not to mention parents of boys – and girls!) are challenged by questions of masculinity. While many, perhaps most, boys are not particularly happy inhabiting the space of the boy who is rough, tough and dangerous to know, the bullying of boys who present themselves as more thoughtful and gentle can be problematic in the extreme. We see a need, then, for a series of books located within institutions, such as education, the family and training/workplace and grounded in practitioners' everyday experiences. These will be explored from new perspectives that encourage a more reflexive approach to teaching and learning with reference to boys and girls.

We aim, in this series, to bring together the best work in the area of masculinity and education from a range of countries. There are obvious differences in education systems and forms of available masculinity, even between English-speaking countries, as well as significant commonalties. We can learn from both of these, not in the sense of saying 'oh, they do that in Australia, so let's do it in the UK' (or *vice versa*), but rather by comparing and contrasting in order to develop deeper understandings both of the masculinities of boys and of the ways adults, especially professionals, can work with boys and girls in order to reduce those ways of 'doing boy' which seem problematic and encourage those which are more sustainable (by the boys themselves now and in later life). Thus books in the series address a number of key questions. How can we make sense of the identities and behaviours of those boys who achieve popularity and dominance by behaving in violent ways in school, will find themselves in trouble when they are young men out on the streets? How can we address key practitioner concerns about how to teach these boys? What do we need to understand about the experiences of girls as well as boys in order to intervene effectively and in ways which do not put boys down or lead them to reject our approaches to their education? What do we need to understand about gender relations in order to teach boys and girls more effectively? How can we make sense of masculinities in schools, through multi-dimensional explanations, which take into account the overlapping social and cultural differences (of, for example, class, ethnicity, dis/ability and sexuality) as well as those of gender? What are the impacts of larger changes to patterns of employment and globalisation on the lives of teachers and students in particular schools and locations? The series, as a whole, aims to provide practitioners with new insights into the changing demands of teaching boys and girls in response to these questions.

As editors, we have been fortunate to be able to attract authors from a number of different countries to contribute to our series and *Masculinities in Mathematics* makes a very welcome addition to the series. Heather Mendick makes a useful and original contribution to debates not only about masculinities in schools but also about the choices and identity work involved for young people pursuing mathematics post-16. Mathematics, she argues, is identified as masculine within the curriculum. As a 'hard' subject, both boys and girls need to relate to it through allegiances to specific forms of gendered performance that can be seen as masculine and, amongst the girls, as demonstrating a kind of 'female masculinity' (Halberstam, 1998). The book is theoretically nuanced but, at the same time, intensely empirical and practical. In the first part of the book, Heather draws on her fieldwork to develop her ideas about doing mathematics as a way of doing masculinity in order to make sense of the very gendered rates of participation in post-compulsory mathematics. She then turns to the role of teachers and possibilities for change, advocating the making of a wider range of identities available to both boys and girls in order to move away from binary and oppositional notions of what boys and girls might be and do and how they might relate to mathematics. There is, in this book, then, both a detailed, richly nuanced account of mathematical masculinities for both boys and girls and a clear discussion of how this understanding might fruitfully impact on the practice of teachers in mathematics classrooms.

References

Halberstam, J. (1998) *Female Masculinity*. Durham and London: Duke University Press.

Debbie Epstein
Maírtín Mac an Ghaill

Acknowledgements

Writing is always difficult and there were many people who helped me – directly and indirectly – to write this book. It is impossible to thank all of them by name but, in best Gwyneth Paltrow fashion, I'll have a go.

Masculinities in Mathematics is adapted from my PhD so massive thanks go to all the people who supported me with that. First and foremost my three amazing supervisors: Dennis Atkinson, Debbie Epstein and Leone Burton. Thanks also to Lesley Jones and to Rosalyn George my supervisors for the first two terms. Many people, in addition to my supervisors, read and commented on all or part of either my thesis or this book. There's Carrie Paechter and Rosalyn George who reviewed my work when I upgraded from MPhil to PhD; Meg Maguire and Hilary Povey who were my examiners; Chris Hockings and Graham Mendick who acted as PhD critical readers; Chris Breen and Liz Bills who made my first experience of 'anonymous' peer reviewing such a positive one; Anne Watson, Carrie Paechter and Leone Burton who were nice about the proposal when Open University Press sent it to them; and last but not least, Anna Callan, Steve Dempster, Jo Warin, Tamara Bibby, Alison Phipps, Diane Reay, Graham Mendick and Anne Watson who all read and commented upon various versions of various chapters of this book and, in this way, allayed at least some of my many anxieties about the project. The series editors, Debbie Epstein and Máirtín Mac an Ghaill, and my editor at Open University Press, Fiona Richman, have also been encouraging throughout.

I was fortunate in going to Goldsmiths to do my doctorate and in recently coming to work at the Institute for Policy Studies in Education (IPSE) at London Metropolitan University. These have been good places in which to research and to teach. My colleagues and my students, at these places and elsewhere, have been a huge help in developing the ideas in this book. In particular, IPSE have been generous in making time available for me to finish this book and my office mates there, Nicola Rollock, Sarah Smart and Katya Williams, have helped me to extend my understanding of popular culture (especially of *that* scene with the bottle in Big Brother 6). I have also been lucky to find some welcoming groups of researchers with whom to share thoughts and anxieties. Thanks to the Mathematics and Identity Group (Laura Black, Margaret Brown, Melissa Rodd and Yvette Solomon), and all the members of the Critical Mathematics Education Group, the Gender Reading Group, the Gender and Education Group at King's, the Birmingham Science Education Research Group, and many more.

My dad died during the first term of my PhD and this was a difficult time for my family. My mum, Ruth Mendick, and my brother, Graham Mendick, have always shown their constant support and belief in me and without these I do not think this book could have happened. My family and friends have graciously tolerated me going on about gender and mathematics in an increasingly obsessive manner. I am indebted to them for their patience and understanding, and for lots of fun. I must mention at least Andrew Rhodes, Anna Callan, Gary Callan, Farah Lalljee, Mary Yacoob, Rajko Vujatovic and Susan Shamash.

Finally, I am inordinately indebted to Goldsmiths and to the Economic and Social Research Council for supplying the funding that made this research possible, and to the staff and students at the places that I have called Grafton, Westerburg and Sunnydale who allowed me into their classrooms and into their lives. I have learnt so much from watching, listening to and talking with them, and I hope that comes through in this book. I also hope that they will be happy with it.

Bits of this book have appeared in other forms elsewhere. Earlier versions of Chapters 3, 4 and 5 were published respectively as:

Mendick, H. (2005) A beautiful myth? The gendering of being/doing 'good at maths', *Gender and Education,* 17(2): 89–105.
Mendick, H. (2003) Choosing maths/doing gender: a look at why there are more boys than girls in advanced mathematics classes in England, in L. Burton (ed.) *Which Way Social Justice for Mathematics Education?* Westport, CT: Praeger.
Mendick, H. (2005) Mathematical stories: why do more boys than girls choose to study mathematics at AS-level in England? *British Journal of Sociology of Education,* 26(2): 225–41.

The original publishers have kindly given permission for this material to be used again here. In addition Jeannette Chavez at Hippy Chix enthusiastically allowed me to use an extract from her website in Chapter 8.

A quick guide

This book is organized around the question: *How do people come to choose maths and in what ways is this process gendered?* It is in three parts ...

Part 1: Scene setting

In this part I deal with why the question matters and how I went about coming up with an answer.

There are two chapters in Part 1. The first chapter provides a framework for thinking about masculinities and mathematics and the connections between them. Key elements of this are that gender is something we do, not something we are, and that masculinity and femininity are constructed in opposition to each other, with maths firmly fixed on the masculine side of the divide. The second chapter introduces the research study. There are sections on how I collected the data and ones that give a flavour of each of the three research sites. The concluding section of the chapter focuses on how I grouped the stories, generated from the interviews with my 43 participants, and on how I draw on these in Part 2.

Part 2: Sex by numbers

In this part I answer the question, building up the answer in stages using interview data from maths students.

I develop the framework for thinking about masculinities and mathematics introduced in the first chapter of Part 1 through analysis of data. There are four chapters in this part. Each of the first three is based around a set of mathematical positions occupied by and practices engaged in by students within the study. My answer, as to why choice of maths is gendered, is that through doing mathematics people are doing masculinity and that this introduces more tensions for girls and women, than for boys and men, since they are more invested in their feminine identity. This understanding then makes sense of the gendered pattern of participation in maths and other fields. The final chapter in Part 2 draws together the ideas from the study and begins to explore their implications.

Part 3: Queering gender and maths

In this part I deal with what the answer means in practice.

There are three chapters in Part 3 each of which roughly pursues one of the directions for change identified at the end of Part 2: making choices social, supporting gender transgression and opening up mathematics. The ideas here are focused around subverting the binary structures that define maths and gender and that connect them together or, in other words, around queering gender and maths.

The English education system

Much of the action of the book takes place in England. As a result I thought it would be helpful to collect together some information about how education is organized t/here . . .

Education is compulsory between the ages of 5 and 16. Most children begin attending school, in the Reception class, a little before their fifth birthday. After this years are numbered sequentially from 1 (ages 5 to 6) to 11 (ages 15 to 16).

The first three years of schooling from Reception to Year 2 inclusive are spent in an infant school, the following four years in a primary school and the final five in a secondary school. After compulsory schooling ends young people can choose to continue in full-time education, in Years 12 and 13. For historical reasons this is still often referred to as sixth form. They can study in a, usually small, sixth form attached to a secondary school, in a larger sixth form college oriented around the age group or in a larger still further education college providing a range of academic, vocational, full-time and part-time courses.

Young people are subject to national testing in Years 2, 6, 9 and 11. The first three sets of tests are called Standard Assessment Tasks, or

SATs for short, and are assessed against the levels of the National Curriculum. Maths and English are the only subjects tested at every level. At the end of compulsory schooling, in Year 11, young people sit their General Certificate of Secondary Education exams, or GCSEs for short. Most receive a grade from A to G; a special A* grading identifies exceptional performances and a U grading identifies failures. Although all grades except for U are officially passes there is an 'A to C economy' (Gillborn and Youdell 2000) in which only grades of C and above count for purposes of progression to further education and for securing employment.

Most GCSE exams are tiered in that they can be entered at more than one level, with not all grades being available at each level. Maths is unique in having three rather than two tiers (although this is soon to change). These are: the Foundation tier with grades G to D available; the Intermediate tier with grades F to B available; and the Higher tier with grades D to A* available. Since the different tiers have different syllabuses, decisions about which tier a student will be entered for are taken early, usually at the start of Year 9.

In sixth form young people can follow academic courses, vocational courses or a combination of these. Academic courses have higher status and more currency in applications for university places or employment. Students following an entirely academic programme normally take four subjects in their first year, sitting for AS level qualifications in each of these, they then continue with A2 courses in three of these, sitting for A level qualifications in them at the end of the second year.

Part 1

Scene setting

We are subject in daily life to a continuous dressage of gender. In this continuous drill, each individual's every move is weighted with gendered meaning: vocal inflection, watch size, heel height, hair length and overall musculature. We habitually consider whether we stand with our feet together or apart, sit with our legs or ankles crossed, hold a glass with a pinkie up or down. We monitor our choice of cigarettes, whether our shirts and belts fasten from left to right or right to left, what colours we choose, what sports we play, whether we prefer to eat a thick piece of red beef or lightly steamed veggies. We observe whether we tend to ask questions or make statements, inspect our nails with the fingers bent or extended, point with our wrists broken or firm.

We do this in public where – conscious of others watching us and our continuous visibility – we join then in watching and judging ourselves. And we do it in private, policing and regulating our own behaviour just as avidly as if we were on display.

Gender conformity is made possible through a sense of permanent visibility, a strong consciousness of shame before others, a rock-solid belief in what our bodies mean and that meaning's utter transparency, and the continuous dance of gender that attaches binary meaning to every facet of our waking lives.

(Wilchins 2004: 69)

chapter one

Engendering mathematics

My name is Heather and I'm a mathematician

While not a health endangering addiction, being a mathematician is a
culturally and socially marked category of identity. It is something that
is difficult to admit. It has the power to impress, intimidate and alienate
others; its mention often evokes in them painful memories of their own
experiences of school mathematics. (Perhaps you are feeling something
of that as you read this.) In short, doing mathematics and being a
mathematician make you *different*. This book is about that difference
and about its relationship with another difference that organizes our
lives, gender.

The starting point for my investigations is the fact of the male
domination of maths. In the not too distant past boys outperformed
girls in maths exams every year. Now, in England at least, few
differences remain between the attainment of males and females in
GCSE, AS or A level maths exams taken at ages 16+, 17+ and 18+
respectively (Gorard et al. 2001; *Guardian* 2002a, b, 2003a, b).
Although boys are still a bit more likely to secure the top grades, the
differences are small and getting smaller. However, in stark contrast to
these shifting patterns of results, the choice to study maths once it
becomes optional remains highly gendered. In fact, as the graph in
Figure 1.1 shows, from 1994 to 2004, the proportion of the total
number of 17- and 18-year-olds entered for A level maths in England
who are male changed little, dropping only slightly from 65 percent to
63 percent (DfES 2004, 2005; Government Statistical Service 1995, 1996,
1997, 1998, 1999, 2000, 2001, 2002, personal communication). This
male dominance increases as you progress through the levels (from
AS level to A level, to undergraduate and then to postgraduate) and is

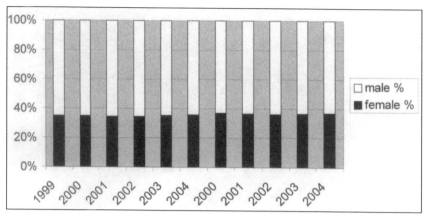

Figure 1.1 Participation in A level maths by gender

reflected in the larger number of men than women working in maths related jobs. This is not just some English quirk, the male dominance of maths can be found, to a greater or lesser extent, in the majority of countries in the world (Hanna 1996; Boaler 2000; Blattel-Mink 2002). This is also not a quirk of maths; boys and girls, men and women make different choices, not just of school subjects and careers, but also of music, reading matter, hobbies and much more.

However, there is something not quite honest about my presenting clean cut graphs and statistics as the starting point for this book. Statistics have to become significant for a person and numbers have to be noticed. So I would like to share something about how I first became aware of the male dominance of maths. This happened when I went to King's College, Cambridge, to study the subject. Up to that point I'd had a pleasurable, successful and largely untroubled relationship with maths. At Cambridge this all changed. The difficulty of the material combined with other (male) students' lack of honesty, or perhaps over-confidence, about how they were coping with the course, led me to experience a sense of failure. I found myself spending hours struggling with seemingly impossible questions. The night before the first year exams began, a friend of mine (now a maths lecturer) came round and made a list of all the 13 first year undergraduate maths students at King's, detailing how many questions he thought each of us was going to complete over the 12 hours of assessment. He put me at the bottom with 8 and him at the top with 18 (actually I got 10 and he got 14). He later said he had intended this to improve my motivation. This incident shows something of the competitive nature of the Cambridge educational experience that fed the process through which my sense of failure was formed. Of course, there is competitiveness, not only in his actions, but also in my telling of them here.

In making sense of the problems I had becoming a mathematician at Cambridge, I have come to see them as being inextricably connected to gender. These experiences transformed my experiences of being female for, as Monique Wittig (1992: 3) says, before conflict 'there are no categories of opposition but only of difference'; in other words some differences make a difference while others do not. It was at university that I first came to see gender as one of those that does. I saw the importance of gender in constructing social life, and that male–female relationships are characterized by inequalities of power. This was the political starting point for this book, an awakening to the politics of the everyday and to the ways that our personal interactions are inflected by and infused with power relations. Since then, the possibility suggested by Wittig, that *difference can operate outside categories of opposition*, has become central to how I think about gender, maths, teaching and life in general. This is a theme that recurs through this book.

This sudden awakening to the salience of gender was perhaps brought on by the transition from an all-girls school to King's College, where I was the only woman among the 13 first year mathematicians. In lectures the ratio was a little better due to the two all-female colleges. Among lecturers the ratio was much, much worse; in fact, during my three years there, I only had one woman lecture me. There was little blatant sexism; although two tutors were not allowed to supervise women, rumour had it that one broke pencils in the presence of female students while the other was distracted by a short skirt; and I doubt that the friend who asked how my then boyfriend was taking it when I got a first to his second would have felt the need to inquire had things been the other way round. However I did feel that, as a woman, I had to do more to prove myself academically with some of my peers. Perhaps this was simply due to the impression I gave of not being able to cope with the work. Looking at it now, I see this as a gendered response, a performance of femininity and an attempt to maintain my gender identity as a woman in spite of my associations with the masculine field of maths. Since gender difference is structured in terms of oppositions, where being female/feminine means being not-male/masculine, there are tensions involved for women in doing maths. These tensions are not the same for all such women, but they are always there. This book sets out to explore how such tensions are lived and how understanding them can help us to make sense of the fact of the male dominance of maths and to think about what we might want to do about it.

At the heart of this book is a qualitative study of young people learning maths, involving interviews with 43 young people and about 120 hours of lesson observations. Through this study I set out to answer the question: *How do people come to choose maths and in what ways is this process gendered?* The young people were studying in seven classes across three different sites. All of them had chosen to continue learning maths once it had become optional. My discussion of this study starts in the next chapter. In the rest of this chapter I introduce three of my central concepts: gender, maths and choice.

Gender!

In the fragment of autobiography above, I make a lot of use of gender. Gender features traditionally as a noun, an aspect of the social world, and as an adjective, pinpointing a particular strand of identity. However, its most important use is as a verb. In other words, gender, as with all differences between people, is something that we do and are done by not something that we are. This unusual usage needs explaining. At birth the question 'Is it a boy or a girl?' is repeatedly asked and answered. Later, although this question is rarely uttered out loud, it is continually being asked and answered in our daily interactions with others. We dress, talk, sit and move in ways that display whether we are male or female; in these ways we show that we have got our gender right (and, occasionally, that society has got our gender wrong); we show this, not just to other people, but also to ourselves. For, as Bronwyn Davies (1989) points out, to not be gendered or to get our gender wrong would be, in some sense, to fail as a human being. This takes constant work, although we are so good at it that it is only occasionally that it rises to the level of our conscious awareness and we notice that we are doing it. In this book I want to raise our awareness of this by investigating the ways in which choosing and doing maths can become part of our daily gender work.

My approach to gender is not original. I have borrowed it from the work of many people but particularly from Bob Connell (1987, 1995). Connell is mostly interested in masculinities but his ideas apply more generally to gender. Here is Connell's (1995: 71) definition of masculinity: ' "Masculinity", to the extent that it can be defined at all, is simultaneously a place in gender relations, the practices through which men and women engage that place in gender, and the effects of these practices in bodily experience and culture'. So masculinities, and femininities, are places, practices and effects within systems of gender that Connell calls gender regimes. This is a very compacted definition and its meanings need unpacking. Two key aspects of this definition that are central to what I want to say in this book are:

- To understand gender difference we need to start from *social* contexts, processes and actions.

This first point contrasts my approach with versions of gender that start from *biological* processes and *individual* actions. Versions of gender that start from biological processes are usually based on evolution and genetics, brain lateralization, hormones or some combination of these. Versions of gender that start from individual processes include ideas about how each individual is socialized into their sex role, influenced by parents, teachers and the media, among other things. I will say more about both of these sets of explanations later in this chapter.

● To understand gender difference we need to see it as *relational*.

This second point contrasts my approach with understandings that start from ideas of *oppositional* gender difference. This idea of male and female as in opposition to each other is shared by approaches that, at first glance, seem to have little in common. For example there is the popular psychology line that 'Men are from Mars, Women are from Venus', and the idea that there is some inner essence shared by all women that is found in some radical feminist writing (for example, Daly 1987; Greer 1999). I am not trying to say that oppositions of masculine against feminine have nothing to do with how gender works. Such oppositions do structure our imaginings of gender. What I am trying to say is that gender does not have to be oppositional and, more than this, that oppositional versions of gender cannot account for much of what happens in the world. Gender oppositions only make sense within a system in which heterosexuality is naturalized, or 'compulsory' as Adrienne Rich (1983) famously put it, and in which gender is seen to operate independently of class, race/ethnicity and other dimensions of difference. In contrast with oppositional approaches that align masculinity with men and boys and femininity with women and girls, within a relational model of gender, we can explore how men and boys do femininity and women and girls do masculinity and also explore how inequalities of class and race/ethnicity interact with gender.

In the next two sections I elaborate further this model of gender, contrasting it with other approaches. What I want to show is how the relationships between various pairs of terms work within this approach. The four pairs of terms that I focus on are:

Social/Biological
Gender/Sex
Individual/Social
Masculine/Feminine

Normally the terms in each of these pairs are seen as opposites, with no overlaps; for example, with reference to the social/biological pairing we argue about whether things are nature *or* nurture, as if we can have one without the other. I want to show how blurring these distinctions can help generate new understandings of the messiness of everyday life in general and of the relationship between mathematics and masculinities in particular. If you are a reader who likes to look at data before discussing theories, then you might prefer to jump over the rest of this chapter and return to it at some point during Chapter 4 or 5. Such an ordering would echo how I developed these ideas through my struggles to make sense of my data.

Y-chromosomes, penises, testosterone and all that jazz

> Scientific and medical authority have provided the ongoing justification to naturalize and pathologize women's emotions, particularly through the growth of psychiatry. An early version of eugenics, 'hysteria' was diagnosed as a female disease whose symptoms included hyper-emotionality and absence of reason. Scientists argued that hysteria was caused by education. The stress of using her mind caused her womb to tear free from its moorings and float about the body. Education thus rendered women useless for childbirth. The fear of hysteria thus justified excluding her from education and enforcing her place as wife and mother.
>
> (Boler 1999: 44)

Megan Boler here is pointing out that biology has a long history of being used to exclude women from education, employment and many other activities. We now know that educating a woman's mind does not sterilize her body; we can see that, within the biological theories Boler is discussing, anatomy is dangerously intertwined with social factors, and we accept that such past scientific research on sex differences was ideologically motivated. However, as Paula and Jeremy Caplan (1997: 55) point out, we have a choice.

> We can smugly laugh at this, attributing the obviousness of their motives to their having lived more than 100 years before research sophisticates such as ourselves, or we can honestly assess the extent to which we have or have not progressed beyond the motives and the sloppy science that characterized so much 19th-century research into sex differences.

What I am proposing is that we don't look at past science as the product of distortions which we have now moved beyond, or that we might ever move beyond, but instead as a result of the way that biology is always figured through the lens of the social. In other words, you cannot separate bodies and biology from culture and society; it may carry an aura of neutrality, but the biological or the natural is *never* innocent; when we think about biology we do it through the words, images, practices and categories available within our social context. This is a context in which gender is understood as binary (there are only two genders), and as oppositional and polarized, and in which the masculine is, generally, more highly valued than the feminine. In an obvious but significant example, active sperm are depicted as penetrating passive and receptive eggs in everything from biology textbooks to Woody Allen comedies, rarely do we find depictions of active eggs engulfing confused and expectant sperm.

Anne Fausto-Sterling (1985) cites another useful example, the study *Eye of the Beholder*, in which researchers showed videotape of a baby reacting to different stimuli, to male and female college students. In one sequence a baby becomes startled, then agitated and then starts to cry when confronted by a jack-in-the-box:

> Those students who thought the baby to be a boy described the baby's tears and screams as anger. In contrast, those who thought the baby to be a girl said 'she' responded fearfully. In other words, the behaviour, crying took on the emotional significance of anger or fear depending only upon the observer's belief about the baby's sex.
>
> (1985: 151)

So, seeing gender difference as natural and oppositional means we attach different labels and ascribe different motivations to what could be seen as identical behaviour.

So where does that leave biology, bodies, hormones and such? Initially second wave feminism (the wave which started in the late 1960s) handled biology by introducing a distinction between sex and gender. Sex, the biological difference between men and women, was detached from gender, the sociological difference, so making change in gender roles possible. This approach sets up the idea of the interaction between the biological and the social in the construction of individuals. This approach, mixing nature and nurture, is attractive. However, it raises many unanswerable questions, such as:

- What exactly is it that is supposed to be interacting (Birke 1999)? And, where are these interactions supposed to taking place (Blackman 2001)?
- How can we tell whether something, such as boys' preference for rough-and-tumble play, is natural or not and, anyway, what relevance does that have for determining what we should do about it?

Underlying all these unanswerable questions is a problem with the whole idea of interaction: the 'model of interaction (however complex an interaction is asserted) leaves the idea of an unmediated biology unchallenged' (Henriques et al. 1984: 21). In other words, in this approach biology is still seen as something that can be separated from the social world rather than something horribly and beautifully intertwined with it. So basically the social/biological dualism operates in much the same way in these feminist explanations as in the more obviously biologically determinist ones; that is, as a pair of nonoverlapping terms with the latter as the more fundamental.

This gender/sex approach, then, closes off possibilities of building new ways of understanding the role of biology in making us who we are. It simultaneously forgets about, or even rejects, biology while keeping it firmly in place. In this book I do not want to abandon biology, just to start thinking about it in more complex ways. With Lisa Blackman (2001: 211), I am concerned that 'what is often overlooked is that "biology" as an object, shifts and changes in meaning and cannot pass as a stable, constant category, which we can simply reject' and so we delegate to biology all discussions of what goes on beyond the surface of the body. I don't want to delegate anything to biology. Instead I view biological processes 'as generative potentialities, which can be transformed through the strategies and practices we develop to identify and act upon these processes' (Blackman 2001: 226).

I want to see biology, and sex in particular, as something that takes work and must be manufactured. One of the more graphic examples of this is how our oppositional gender regime is enforced daily using the scalpel, 'about five intersexed children have their genitals cut into in U.S. hospitals every day for cosmetic reasons, a procedure performed by accredited surgeons and covered by all major insurance plans' (Wilchins 1997: 226), and, in the UK, available free from the National Health Service.

That sex, far from being natural, actually takes work was a point provocatively made by Judith Butler in her landmark book *Gender Trouble* (1999). If gender is socially constructed and radically distinct from sex, she asks: Why then are there only two genders? And, why do sex and gender line up so neatly? Why are there so few masculine women, feminine men and everything else in between?

> Are the ostensibly natural facts of sex discursively produced by various scientific discourses in the service of other political and social interests? If the immutable character of sex is contested, perhaps this construct called 'sex' is as culturally constructed as gender; indeed, perhaps it was always already gender, with the

consequence that the distinction between sex and gender turns out to be no distinction at all.

(Butler 1999: 10–11)

In this way Butler deconstructs the tidy binary:

Gender/Sex

Sex itself is gendered; the supposedly presocial category of sex is actually produced as an effect of the systems of social and cultural construction that we call gender. Among other things, Butler is raising here the role of power in the making of gendered bodies and the possibility that there are more than two genders. Both these points are central to the analyses in this book and I will return to them later, but first there is more to say about the gender/sex opposition.

One is not born a man, one becomes one

The feminist separation of sex and gender was also accompanied by a theory of sex role socialization, the process whereby sexed bodies became gendered individuals. My point in the last section was that in this move 'the biological basis of sexual difference is assumed, and the "roles" that children are taught by adults are a superficial social dressing laid over the "real" biological difference' (Davies 1989: 5). In other words, there is an assumed pre-existing essence of the person on which the social makes its mark. This way of thinking thus maintains the possibility of separating an individual from their context, creating this opposition:

Individual/Social

Again, I want to imagine a more complex relationship between these two terms, one in which the individual, like the biological, is always already social. To do this I will briefly examine sex role socialization and some problems with it.

Bronwyn Davies (1989: 5) provides a useful characterization of this process:

Within the sex-role socialisation model of the world the child is taught her or his sex-role by, usually, one central adult, but is also 'pressed' into maintenance of that role by a multitude of others (peers, media etc.). There is no room in this model for the child as active agent, the child as theorist, recognising for him or herself the way the social world is organised. Nor is there acknowledgement of the child as implicated in the construction and maintenance of the social world through the very act of recognising it and through learning its discursive practices.

The child is positioned as passive, and as acted on, within the story of their socialization. Moreover, there is a simple model of cause and effect operating here, in which certain aspects of the social world are seen to be directly causing gendered behaviours in children (Henriques et al. 1984; Connell 1987; Walkerdine 1998).

Recently, feminist challenges to the model of sex role socialization have pointed out that the social world is far more complex and contradictory than the sex role socialization account allows for. Investigations into the effects of sexist images in books illustrate where the simple cause and effect approach fails to engage with the complexity of what is going on and highlight the problems with positioning girls and boys as passive receivers of social messages. Early research on the effects of sexist images in books, for example that discussed by Dale Spender (1980c), focused on the ways that in picture books women were invariably shown in some kind of domestic role while in fairy tales they lived out clichéd romantic storylines. These analyses assumed:

- The passive receipt of these images by boys and girls.
- 'That sexist images in texts are unreal, as though the "real" existed outside the pages of books, and the books themselves had no productive effect' (Walkerdine 1998: 151).
- That non-sexist images would help to produce feminist young women.

However, more recent research has focused on the ways in which the content of textbooks and storybooks is actively taken up by young people. Probably the most famous example is Bronwyn Davies's (1989) account of how young children reading *The Paperbag Princess*, a feminist fairytale, prefer the wimpish prince to the assertive princess who rescues him. As Alison Jones (1993: 162) remarks, this 'offers a rather pessimistic caution to those who believe that non-sexist curricular material might create major changes for girls'.

The writers discussed above, Bronwyn Davies, Valerie Walkerdine and Alison Jones, all take a poststructural approach to understanding how people become gendered. This is the approach I take in this book. Such approaches imagine a very different relationship between the individual and the social from that assumed within sex role socialization:

> Poststructuralist theory argues that people are not socialised into the social world, but that they go through a process of *subjectification*. In socialisation theory, the focus is on the process of shaping the

individual that is undertaken by others. In poststructuralist theory the focus is on the way each person actively takes up the discourses through which they and others speak/write the world into existence *as if it were their own*.

(Davies 1993: 13, original emphasis)

In the next two sections of this chapter I begin applying these ideas to understanding people's relationships with maths. In this way I introduce the key concepts of discourse, subjectification and power, on which the analyses in the rest of the book are based. I look at how these ideas make sense of the relationship between the individual and the social, and continue my exploration of the binary construction of gender through some initial discussion of the ways that maths fits into this.

Mathematical stories

When thinking about maths, just as when thinking about gender, what I am interested in is not what maths is or is not, in some ultimate sense (for how could we ever know that), but the stories that we tell about it and the positions these make available to teachers and learners. Another word, currently in vogue in academic circles, for social stories about an object of knowledge, such as maths, is *discourses*. It came up in the two quotes from Bronwyn Davies in the last section. While trying to keep this book relatively jargon free, I do want to use the term 'discourse'. This is because the word 'discourse' carries meanings that the word 'story' does not, meanings that are central to what I am trying to say. Discourses are structures of language and practice through which objects come into being. Discourses are knowledges about objects which are powerful because they determine what can be said about something as well as who can say it, and even what can be thought or imagined; they are, of course, imbued with values. Or as Michel Foucault (1972: 49), on whose version of discourse I am drawing here, succinctly put it: they are 'practices that systematically form the objects of which they speak'.

For example, some of the discourses of maths variously frame it as:

- A route to economic and personal power within advanced capitalism.
- A key skill, a source of knowledge necessary for the successful negotiation of life in a scientifically and technologically sophisticated society, and thus as a source of personal power.
- A process for discovering a body of pre-existent truths.

- The ultimate form of rational thought and so a proof of intelligence.
- Associated with forms of cultural deviance where, particularly in the media, mathematicians are depicted as 'nerds', a species apart.
- A skill linked to a particular portion of the human genome.

You will hear a lot more about all of these discourses in the pages to come; they recur within the words and actions of the young people I observed and interviewed and of their teachers. Taking a poststructuralist approach means that these discourses are seen as operating within regimes of truth, not because of their power to *describe* reality but because of their power to *produce* it. They are 'fictions functioning in truth' (Walkerdine 1990).

So, it is within a range of discourses of maths, femininity, masculinity and schooling, among other things, that each person's educational choices and experiences come into being. What a focus on discourses does is to produce a figure/ground switch, whereby the problem of gender and maths is not located within *individual girls* who make the 'wrong' choices or who understand their performance 'wrongly', but in the *discursive context* of gender, schooling and maths. This context makes the patterns of identifications that produce these girls' choices and performances possible and indeed sensible. Instead of asking, 'Why do girls engage in specific practices?' the question is reversed to ask, 'How do specific practices do girls?' (Flax 2002). As I said earlier, this is a very different way of imagining the relationship between the social and the individual. However, it raises many questions. Notably:

- How do individuals become part of discourse at all?
- Why do they take up/are they taken up by one particular discursive position rather than another? (The slash in this question signals the double-edgedness of this process in which we are both acting and acted upon.)

These questions are discussed in the next section.

Absolute power?

In the last section I suggested that we start to think about maths as neither more nor less than that which it is constituted as in and through discourse. This approach to maths is not a standard one. More often, among those who think of themselves as experts in maths *and* those who see themselves as failures, maths is viewed as a body of external truths that are discovered by mathematicians, perhaps the only example of absolute knowledge. It is a matter of right and wrong, black and white, indisputable answers. Early 20th century Cambridge mathematician, G. H. Hardy's (1969: 130, original emphasis) view is typical:

> A chair or a star is not the least like what it seems to be; the more we think of it, the fuzzier its outlines become in the haze of sensation which surrounds it; but '2' or '317' has nothing to do with sensation, and its properties stand out the more closely we scrutinize it … 317 is a prime, not because we think so, or because our minds are shaped in one way rather than another, but *because it is so*, because mathematical reality is built in that way.

Within absolutist thinking about maths knowledge, the pinnacle of rationality is the pure maths method of proof; claims for mathematical certainty rest on this. However, as Morris Kline (1980: 306) shows, 'no proof is final'; the acceptable standards of proof depend both on the time period and on the mathematical school in which one is working. Kline describes four schools which differ in the axioms and principles of reasoning that they deem acceptable for use in proofs and consequently disagree dramatically about the validity of different areas of maths. He concludes that, 'history supports the view that there is no fixed, objective, unique body of mathematics' (1980: 320). As Sal Restivo (1992: 102) says, 'this does not mean we do not and cannot know anything; it means that what we know is always social through and through'. This is directly related to what I was saying earlier about biology being social through and through.

Once you start looking for it, there is a huge array of material available that challenges the absolutist version of truth in maths (for example, Lakatos 1976; Ernest 1991; Skovsmose 1994; Burton 1995). So the obvious questions are why this body of work has not had greater impact and why it is still met with vehement denials (particularly from professional mathematicians, for example, Goldin 2002). Why is the notion of an absolute, objective maths so appealing? In thinking about such questions in this section we are returned to the issue of how people take up a position within a discourse, such as this one of maths as absolute knowledge, and of the role of power in this process of subjectification so I will discuss that before returning to look at Hardy's version of maths in more detail.

The thing about discourses is that they position people within networks of power. They discipline us into certain ways of being and acting and create within us a certain relationship to self. This mode of operation of power was labelled biopower by Foucault (1977): 'I have always found this idea of Foucault's very important because … it presupposes not an ideology foisted upon but separate from subjects, but practices of disciplining and regulation which are, at the same time, practices for the formation of subjects' (Walkerdine 1997a: 15). So power inhabits us shaping us from the inside as well as from the outside. Foucault (1980: 119) writes:

> If power were never anything but repressive, if it never did anything but to say no, do you really think one would be brought to obey it? What makes power hold good, what makes it accepted, is simply the fact that it doesn't only weigh on us as a force that says no, but traverses and produces things, it induces pleasure, forms knowledge, produces discourse. It needs to be considered as a productive network which runs through the whole social body, much more than as a negative instance whose function is repression.

So discursive practices are imagined as negative and positive, oppressive and productive, simultaneously and always. Power is 'not something that is acquired, seized, or shared. Something that one holds on to or allows to slip away; power is exercised from innumerable points, in the interplay of nonegalitarian and mobile relations' (Foucault 1976: 94). Power is in relationships that exist in workplaces, families and schools, and 'major dominations are the hegemonic effects that are sustained by all these confrontations' (Foucault 1976: 94). Thus power is exercised locally and that is also where it is resisted. The Foucauldian idea that wherever there is power there is also resistance is important because it captures the double-edgedness of power. It also makes clear that we have no choice about whether to become part of discourse or not. *To be human is to be discursively constituted.* So the self is contradictory, it owes its existence to the power/knowledge nexus that it is simultaneously resisting.

Now let's go back and apply all this to Hardy's version of maths. After a quick game of 'spot the binaries' (MacLure 2003), it is clear that this view of maths relies on a series of oppositions. Some of those directly invoked are:

> Exactness/Fuzziness
> Mathematical reality/Sensory reality
> Mind-independent/Mind-dependent

This process of unravelling the binary logic on which a text relies is called deconstructing or, more colloquially, troubling. Going a bit further, this passage also relies on other binaries about knowledge that are part of the background of our thinking. Notably:

> Absolute/Relative
> Objective/Subjective

And, of course, the central binary of this book:

Masculine/Feminine

Although binaries move and shift, their overall structure does not. The important things, from a gender point of view, are that:

- The two terms are seen as mutually exclusive.
- In each pair the two terms are unequally valued.
- The term with the higher value is associated with masculinity.

The underlying logic of this background means that new pairs are easy to incorporate into what is a mutually reinforcing system. For example, computing, the recent addition to the curriculum, has fallen in with maths and sciences rather than languages and arts, and some entries have changed sides, such as Latin, which was once on the masculine side of the divide, and has now crossed over, without disturbing the overall structure (Spender 1980b).

So our attachment to absolute maths is inseparable from our attachment to binary gender. Valerie Walkerdine's (1990: 143) work contains a psychoanalytic way of making sense of why such a pattern of binaries might be such a powerful draw for Hardy and others:

Mathematical reasoning presumes mastery of a discourse in which the universe is knowable and manipulable according to particular mathematical algorithms. This, along with the production of 'hard facts', is usually understood as the very basis of certainty. However, conversely we might understand it as the fear, the necessity of proof against the terror of its Other, that is, loss of certainty, control and attempted control of loss. We might understand it as the impossibility of the object of desire, 'woman', and elaborate fantasies to control consequent desire and avoid dependency or powerlessness.

In invoking psychoanalysis here I am using it as a toolkit that can provide thought experiments that move us beyond commonsense explanations. Walkerdine's reading, of investment in mathematical certainty as a desperate defence against the terror of loss and an attempt to control desire, is disturbing. It disturbs the idea of the pursuit of reason as an objective endeavour. It captures the role of power and the unconscious within subjectification, the process through which we become our-selves, through being stitched into the social fabric of interconnected discourses.

So far in this chapter I have concentrated on introducing you to the ways that I will be thinking about *gender* and *maths* in the pages that follow. Basically I am exploring these by focusing on the discourses through which they come into being. It is in and through these discourses that we position ourselves/are positioned relative to gender and maths. The slash in the last sentence suggests the tension between the role of social structures and individual agency. Mixed up in this tension is the notion of *choice*, another key idea in this book.

Choosing subjects

As a neurotic, yet heroic, ant says at the end of animated feature, *Antz*, 'I finally feel like I've found my place. And you know what? It's right back where I started. But the difference is, this time I chose it' (*Antz* 1998). And this, of course makes all the difference. Allowing people to make their own choices is important in our society; it functions as a kind of symbol of our freedom. So, if girls and women simply do not want to do maths then surely that's their free choice? What right have I to suggest trying to manipulate or change their options? These questions are important ones but they only make sense if we can exist outside of society, as individuals free from its influence. If instead we are subjects formed in discourse then no choices are free (or all of them are), and the same goes for manipulation. The autonomous choosing individual assumed by the questions has gone, to be replaced by a subject forever trapped within power relations. It is those power relations, with their constraints and possibilities that we need to focus on.

> It is not the case that there are no choices, but those choices are heavily circumscribed and shot through with conscious and unconscious emotions, fantasies, defences. It is the complexity of the production of the intersection of subject and subjectivity that I [am] exploring.
>
> (Walkerdine 1997b: 171)

Since individual agency to act is generally understood as being exercised through choice, what does agency look like with this understanding of choice? At first the idea that we can never escape power seems to foreclose possibilities for agency. However, I would agree with Judith Butler (1999: 187, original emphasis) that 'para-doxically, the reconceptualization of identity as an *effect*, that is, as *produced* or *generated*, opens up possibilities of "agency" that are insidiously foreclosed by positions that take identity categories as foundational and fixed'. So the un-fixing of women, men, maths and so on is to 'give [them] play as site[s] where unanticipated meanings might come to bear' (Butler 1995: 50). Thus agency exists in the possibility for variation in the repetitive performances, the discourses, through which 'women', 'maths' and other objects, come to exist. If gender and maths are something that we do then they *can* be done differently. In other words, what matters is unpicking the ways in which our choices are formed so that we can decide what, if anything, we want to change about these.

This framework for understanding choice and agency that I have developed so far presents the self as multiple, fractured and contradictory. These are aspects that the word 'identity' does not capture. 'Identity' sounds too certain and too singular, as if it already exists rather than being in a process of formation. So in this book, I will generally use 'identity work' or Stuart Hall's (1996) term 'identification' rather than the word 'identity'. In this way I am trying to capture some new meanings:

- Who we are is always in a process of formation and is never complete. However, we are not 'going forward to meet that which we always were' (Hall 1991: 47), that 'originary essence' is also always being worked on. Another way of thinking this is to read identity, like gender, as a verb rather than as a noun. It is the product not the source of our actions; something we do, not something we are.
- Processes of identification are also psychic ones. For example, we are establishing patterns of sameness and of difference which can be understood as happening through 'splitting between that which one is, and that which is the other' (Hall 1991: 48). The idea of the unconscious being used here is a socially embedded one, in which the discursive environment becomes a 'melting pot of psychical conditions of possibility' (Walkerdine 1997a: 185).
- Our notions of who we are are always narrativized: '[Identity] is always within representation. Identity is not something which is formed outside and then we tell stories about it. It is that which is narrated in one's own self' (Hall 1991: 49).

Above all, 'identity work' positions our choices as producing us, rather than being produced by us.

Conclusions

This chapter has introduced the question that this book seeks to answer: *How do people come to choose maths and in what ways is this process gendered?* I have told you something about why this question matters personally and why it matters politically. I have also introduced gender, maths and choice, three ideas that are at the centre of this book. Summing up, I have suggested that:

- *Gender* is an ongoing process, or better a collection of ongoing processes. Gender congeals onto things but never in a fixed and finished sort of way; it is always on the move. We are all constantly and actively engaged in the social work of doing gender but our choices within this are severely constrained. In particular they are constrained by oppositional ways of thinking.
- *Maths* is a social practice defined by the stories we tell about it. These stories are very powerful and affect how we think about maths and how we can act. Because of their power, I use the word *discourses* to refer to them. Oppositional discourses about maths as objective not subjective, rational not emotional, and so on, tie it to masculinity.
- Making a *choice* has been conceptualized as becoming part of discourse. This is neither an entirely free nor an entirely determined process; we *both* are positioned by discourses *and* position ourselves in them. This process is called *subjectification* and is both psychic and social. I also raised the question of how and how far we can exercise *agency* with respect to our subjectification.

The strand that links gender, maths and choice is *identity work*. I view subject choice as one of the key sites where young people make themselves: 'When we choose subjects we are obliged to redefine ourselves and make a public statement about what sort of person we are, or hope to be. It is perhaps the first significant choice of identity' (Shaw 1995: 113). It is this idea of identity work, the continual process of making our-storied-fractured-selves, which I put into practice in the analyses of the interviews that begin in Part 2. Before that, the next chapter goes into more detail about how, why and where I collected and analysed my data.

chapter / **two**

Introducing the study

In this chapter I set up the research study findings on which I draw throughout the rest of the book. There is information here not just about how I went about collecting and analysing my data and about the issues and problems that arose, but also about the student participants and about the three places where they were learning maths. Collecting data involves making a lot of choices, some conscious and carefully considered, others unconscious, made in a moment, ones that you do not even realize are choices until later. It is these choices that I want to illuminate in this chapter. Just as young people's subject choices are linked to their 'identities' so my own choices about how to do research connect to my 'identity' as a researcher. They, whether conscious or unconscious, enact what kind of researcher I want to be and what kind I do not want to be. So, as well as being an opportunity to meet the characters who populate the rest of the book, this chapter is about me.

To begin, I look at the outcome of one very important choice: where to do my research. I had different relationships with each of my three London research sites which I have called Grafton School, Westerburg Sixth Form College and Sunnydale Further Education (FE) College. At Grafton I identified as a teacher, at Westerburg I identified as a researcher and at Sunnydale I identified both as a researcher and as a student (of Spanish). Below I describe these three organizations: their buildings, their ethos, their populations, their approaches to A level maths teaching and learning, and the different tensions operating there. The aim is to give you a flavour of each place and to help you to make sense of the stories in the rest of the book.

Grafton School

Grafton School is an inner city 11–18 comprehensive with a multi-cultural, mainly working class intake of about 1200 pupils. Over half of Grafton's pupils are eligible for free school meals and about one-third speak English as an additional language; it is located in an area that the school inspectorate, Ofsted, described as 'deprived'. However, Grafton has a respected headteacher and a hard-working staff. Ofsted inspected the school during the research period and judged it 'a good school that has several impressive features, particularly the successful cultural and racial mix of the school community and its citizenship initiative'.

Grafton has about 150 sixth formers and operates as part of a consortium with two local schools; most students also take courses at Sunnydale College. Grafton sixth formers have a common room and are identifiable by not having to wear uniform. They are aware that being in a school rather than a college has advantages and disadvantages. As Simon puts it 'college is more independent' and 'a lot more grown up than in here' where they are 'monitoring you all the time, seeing when you come in and when you haven't'. 'College' signifies Sunnydale to Grafton students, and their generally negative impressions are based on their own experiences of doing courses there and on those of friends and family members. For example, Simon describes how 'my friend was doing maths in college and he doesn't go to any of the lessons now because he found out that the teacher was just like, arrive at that time . . . leave at when you're supposed to be leaving, just teaching what he had to teach and not teaching anything else, like, say you didn't understand how to do something basic, he wouldn't explain it to you, he would like teach you what he's got to do, basically get his money'. Simon was typical in concluding that 'they don't really care that much'.

James had taken business studies at Sunnydale during the previous year and had struggled with the course 'the teachers weren't helpful. I find that at college a lot'. He relates this to the relationship between teachers and students 'whereas at sixth form you know the teachers', he pauses, 'or you've had them at GCSE so they know what you can and can't do, they know your weaknesses and strengths so they can help you'. (For more about Simon and James see Chapter 4.)

The students involved in my research were part of a larger than expected cohort of AS level maths students at Grafton. As a result, although they were originally taught in one group, after three weeks they were divided into two based on their 'ability' as judged by their GCSE maths result. Since GCSE maths can be entered at one of three different tiers – higher, intermediate and foundation – each associated with a different syllabus, the entry level as well as the grade attained were crucial in this setting process. The 'top' set included all those who obtained an A*, A or high B on the higher level exam and it continued to be taught by the same three teachers as the original group, although by the second term, when a member of staff left and department timetables had to be rearranged, they were taken by only one teacher, Matt Delling. This group contained five girls and nine boys. The 'bottom' set consisted of six students who had obtained an intermediate grade C and three who had a higher grade B. I took them for all their lessons, until Easter when the groups were merged. This group contained six boys and three girls. These groups developed different identities, with the 'top' set being quieter and all but two students working and sitting individually; the 'bottom' set had more students who worked cooperatively and, by my design, all students sat around the same table. It is evident from the interviews that the setting created tensions for some students (see Michael's and Julie's stories in Chapters 4 and 5 respectively). The results, during the research period, are shown in Table 2.1.

Table 2.1 Grafton examination results

Level	AS						A					
Grade	A	B	C	D	E	U	A	B	C	D	E	U
2000/01	3	0	2	3	2	6	–	–	–	–	–	–
2001/02	3	0	1	0	2	15	3	1	0	0	0	2

My involvement as a teacher at Grafton makes it more difficult to describe the teaching there. The lessons that I observed were relaxed and structured around preparing students for the exams. There are a number of tensions for all Grafton teachers in their classroom practice. A central tension lies in their desire to protect students from negative learning experiences but to avoid spoon-feeding them (perhaps related to the tension in the student talk about college vs. school, between a desire for autonomy and a desire to feel cared for). This is evident in the way that one teacher I observe, Trisha, talks about the tests that she sets for her AS and A2 groups. She explains that the tests are to 'scare them' into taking a more 'proactive' approach to their work and to make them aware of what they will face in the end. But she then moderates this by offering students help after about 30 minutes. Another tension is illustrated by her refusal to allow students to use textbooks or notes, or to collaborate on these tests, but instead she makes herself the only source of help. This tension is between ceding control of the learning process to the students and keeping it in the hands of the teacher, between positioning students as adults who can take responsibility for their own learning and as children in need of monitoring and regulation; this is not only a tension for Trisha at Grafton but is central to the culture at Westerburg.

Westerburg Sixth Form College

Westerburg educates approximately 800 ethnically diverse, largely middle class young Londoners. It is located, over an hour's underground journey from Grafton and Sunnydale, around the corner from a busy high street whose cafes and takeaways provide lunch for many of the college's students. A large hall functions as the students' social space although they also hang out in other smaller spaces around the buildings and, when it is sunny, flood into the college grounds, leaving behind the customary teenage debris (to the equally customary disapproval of the staff). Westerburg has two entry policies. Although oversubscribed, it guarantees places to applicants from local partner schools and allocates the remaining (majority of the) places competitively. Its curriculum is largely academic, although some vocational courses cater for the less qualified partner school entrants.

Westerburg has formal disciplinary systems. During my observations I encountered students on report for poor attendance, in one case for five months, and others who had been given detention. Attendance was monitored through an electronic registration system and punctuality was an ongoing point of tension. Typically in one of Andy Rhodes's lessons straight after lunch several students were missing at 13:15 when the class started. Mark arrived at 13:20. Mr Rhodes pointed out that this was not the first time he had been late and asked him why. Mark was unsure. Craig followed at 13:21, and seconds later Deji. Mr Rhodes told Craig that this was his fourth instance of lateness and asked why. Craig blamed his watch. For Deji, Mr Rhodes explained: 'constant lateness is a disciplinary offence' leading to application of the disciplinary procedures and ultimately perhaps to exclusion from college.

'I was only six minutes late', protested Craig, apparently thinking the punishment disproportionate to the crime.

Analia (who is always punctual) argued that bells were needed so 'you'd know where you're going and when'.

Their teacher refuted this, drawing on notions of personal responsibility, and the discussion ended. This incident suggests a tension that exists for Westerburg students, caught between discursive practices that position them as adults, free to make their own choices, and that demand they take responsibility for their own learning, and ones that position them as children in need of constant control.

Westerburg's maths department has over 350 students being taught advanced courses by six full-time teachers and one part-timer. To qualify for entry to an AS maths course students must have at least a higher grade B at GCSE (although occasional exceptions are made). Students with an A or A* grade have the option to study further maths. I observed the further maths group, an AS group studying modules in pure, mechanics and statistics and an AS group studying modules in pure, statistics and decision maths. All the Westerburg interview participants were drawn from these groups. These groups consisted of two girls and 18 boys, four girls and 12 boys, and nine girls and ten boys, respectively. The results during the research period, 2001/02, are shown in Table 2.2.

Table 2.2 Westerburg examination results

Level	AS						A					
Grade	A	B	C	D	E	U	A	B	C	D	E	U
Maths	41	33	42	25	14	25	63	51	17	25	9	2
Further	4	0	0	0	1	0	5	2	2	0	2	1

The department has a small suite of dedicated classrooms and a staff office with individual workspaces, a kettle, two computers, a printer and comfy chairs. The office is meticulously organized with copies of past examination papers in colour coded drawers and a whiteboard where agenda items for the weekly department meeting and other work related information are written up. Most conversations in this office relate to maths teaching. The classrooms have impressive displays of posters, including many focusing on careers and university courses involving maths, the UK series *Mathematics on the Underground* and a mathematical timeline entitled *Men* (sic) *of Mathematics*. Teachers prepare lessons carefully and provide excellent web- and paper-based resources for students; they always welcome students who come to the department office seeking help and offer drop-in workshops. However, the idea of the accessibility of maths is in tension with the idea of its exclusivity, for this support happens within an environment in which certain assumptions are made. These assumptions – about what maths is, about how it is best taught and learnt, and about the role of examinations – are explored in detail in Chapter 7. Some of them, in particular that maths is more demanding than other subjects, are evident in a sign pinned to the noticeboard in the foyer between the classrooms:

MATHS IS HARD!

Independent research shows that Mathematics is the most challenging subject at A level. Nationally, last year's AS results in maths were far worse than any other subject.

If you don't really enjoy Maths and if you're not genuinely good at it, don't do it! Two years of struggling and constantly being 'stuck' is not an experience we would wish on anyone.

Success at A level Mathematics usually depends on:

Positive attitudes. Do you enjoy solving problems? Do you *like* Maths?

Persistence. Do you give up easily and ask for help? Or do you prefer to get the answer for yourself?

Independence. Do you need spoon-feeding every step of the way? Can you learn it by yourself?

A student could not be blamed for gaining the impression that some subjects, other than maths, would be recommended for those who 'give up easily' and 'need spoon-feeding every step of the way'.

In many ways Westerburg is a typical representative of the sixth form college tradition. John Robinson and Colin Burke (1996) argue that the very different histories of sixth form and FE colleges meant that they responded differently to the 1992 Further and Higher Education Act which removed post-16 providers from Local Education Authority control. Sixth form colleges had, in 1992, a tradition of combining comprehensive ideals and academic excellence; their teachers came from schools and were employed on the same terms and conditions; they 'had a history which was imbued with an elitism which was both academic and social' (1996: 7) and which was visible in their adapted grammar school buildings (grammar schools were the upper tier of an older system of selective state education). FE colleges, by contrast, had been associated with the education of working class men and had been more closely allied with polytechnics than with schools. They, more than sixth form colleges, are populated with the 'new sixth' created by the massive expansion of the numbers entering postcompulsory education. This alternative FE tradition is exemplified by Sunnydale College.

Sunnydale Further Education College

Sunnydale is one of England's first beacon colleges and has about 13,000 students of whom about a third are full-time and more than a third are studying for qualifications at entry level or level one. The college also attracts a large number of foreign students; of the 13 maths students whom I interviewed, six had nonBritish nationalities and all could be described as from ethnic minorities. The average age of students is about 30. Sunnydale thus caters for different needs than either Grafton or Westerburg, and most of the courses are part-time and/or vocational. The top floor of one of Sunnydale's two campuses forms an Academic Centre, offering a range of AS and A2 daytime courses designed for 16- to 19-year-olds with only a few mature students enrolled. Thus the Academic Centre's intake, location and programmes of study mark it out from the rest of the college and this creates certain tensions for its teachers and students. The mix of students at Sunnydale means that it has a more informal, less hard-working feel about it than either Grafton or Westerburg. In fact, Toni (I tell her story in Chapter 4) thinks the college contains a large number of 'useless boys' and while some boys are 'really into their work' most are 'more like into girls'. She complains, 'I don't even know why they come to college. You see some of them walking down the corridor ... their trousers half way down, with their boxers. No books with them'.

For some students the FE ethos is an advantage. Nefertiti tells me, 'my parents didn't, didn't want me to come to Sunnydale College because you see like, there's a lot of higher learners, older people in this college, coz it's not like sixth form' and they wanted her to go somewhere that has got 'more people straight from secondary school and like you can interact more, like teachers help you more'. She rejected this advice because college 'is more open, if you do you do, if you don't you don't'.

Sunnydale College is within walking distance of Grafton School. The college was inspected during the research period, and the report (like that for Grafton) describes the local area as 'deprived', citing as evidence:

> Unemployment in the area is 11.7%, which is about three times higher than the average for Greater London ... In 2000, only 34.8% of Year 11 students from [local] schools gained five or more General Certificate of Secondary Education (GCSE) grades at C or above, compared with 49.2% nationally.

As both an evening class student and a researcher at Sunnydale I am aware of the chaos circulating through the college. Alex's desk in the maths office, by April, has every inch of it covered with books and papers to a depth of about a metre; it takes me four hours to enrol for one GCSE evening class; the computer printed maths class lists bear little resemblance to who shows up; the wrong people are entered for the GCSE Spanish exam; and at my first meeting with Nick Bennett, the Head of Department, I wait over an hour for him. This chaos means that it is easier for students to get lost. Because of timetabling clashes some students are splitting their maths lessons between the two AS groups. Their teachers are unaware of the details of these arrangements, and it is up to the students to decide which, if any, of the homework assignments set they will do. When I go to collect the exam results it is apparent that the A2 group teachers are unaware of their students' AS results. In contrast, at Grafton and Westerburg, students' first year results are used to determine who is allowed to progress to the A2 course. This laissez-faire approach is perhaps one reason for the poor punctuality and attendance, although these are also systemic features of FE life (Wallace 2002).

There were two AS groups and one A2 group. Each group's three teaching slots were shared between two teachers. I observed both AS groups as they covered modules in pure maths, mechanics and statistics. The groups contained 18 boys and six girls and six boys and ten girls respectively. The imbalance was due to the second group being scheduled against physics. With only four and a half hours per week and a later start and earlier finish to the year, Sunnydale allocates the least teaching time for the AS level of all the three research sites. The examination results for 2001/02 are shown in Table 2.3.

Table 2.3 Sunnydale examination results

Level	AS						A					
Grade	A	B	C	D	E	U	A	B	C	D	E	U
Maths	1	1	0	3	6	9	0	2	2	1	0	0

The Academic Centre has one dedicated maths classroom, containing four computers, an overhead projector, a whiteboard and several maths themed posters including a series of photographs of everyday objects (Toblerone, Cornetto, Cornflakes) accompanied by an isometric drawing of the solid shape that they exemplify. Adjacent to this classroom is an office where the five department members have desk space and access to a computer. The office is small and narrow and the contrast with the Westerburg office, which is over three times the size, is stark. Discussions here between staff rarely focus on teaching maths and are usually general conversations, jokes or complaints about the poor pay and management in the college.

Sitting in maths lessons at Sunnydale, I often feel as if I am in a lecture with the teacher working at the board for most or sometimes all of the 90 minute session. Few students' names are used, and I never see Alex, who teaches more than half of the advanced maths lessons, call or mark a register; instead he uses a signing-in sheet. As someone who had always worked in sixth form colleges and schools, I was shocked the first time I saw a student leave the room, to take a mobile phone call or to talk to a friend, signalling them first through the classroom windows, without any comment to or from the teacher. The teachers also normally ignored late arrivals. However, occasionally tensions were evident, for example, when one teacher, Abdi, jokes to a student whose mobile phone has just gone off for the second time, 'Popular man, I must remember to shoot your friends'.

These features of classroom life matter to the maths that is learnt, to the ways in which learners come to relate to the subject and to whether they choose to continue studying it at the end of the course. However, few studies of maths teaching and learning consider their impact. 'It seems presupposed that noise in the classroom, students making obstructions, students not turning up in schools, etc. do not reveal adequate information for researching the learning of mathematics' (Skovsmose and Valero 2002: 9). I wanted to collect data and produce analyses that highlighted some of these disappeared features. In the rest of the chapter, I aim to give you a sense of how I went about doing this.

Researcher identity work

The portraits above of Grafton, Westerburg and Sunnydale contain data drawn from my classroom observations, student interviews and general just hanging around, at all three places. They were produced through a process at once exciting and tedious of transcribing, coding, searching, writing, re-writing and imaginative invention. As I said earlier, choices are at the heart of all these processes and these choices are part of my researcher identity work. So before giving specifics about those methodological choices I say something about that, about what kind of researcher I was, and am, being and becoming.

Within traditional approaches to research, researchers are required to make choices so as to be objective and detached, in the same ways as in the natural and the physical sciences. In that way we will, supposedly, find the truth. I do not want to be an objective researcher. This is first of all because I think it is impossible. Doing research, like teaching and all aspects of living, is messy: 'If nothing else, we would insist on the absolute reality of this: that being alive involves us in having emotions and involvements; and in doing research we cannot leave behind what it means to be a person alive in the world' (Stanley and Wise 1993: 161). Emotions and relationships are an important part of how we come to know things and our truths are always situated in the contexts in which we live; denying this is not helpful. However, more than this, I want to join with Jane Flax in asserting that denying this is dangerous; 'I believe that four of the greatest tragedies of modern Europe – slavery, the oppression of women, Nazism and Stalinism – were potentiated by our collective wish that innocent and universal positions are possible and desirable' (Flax 1993: 32).

However, I do not want to be a subjective researcher either. This would be to accept the terms of the opposition:

Objective/Subjective

As you are probably not surprised to learn by this point, I want to refuse the terms of the opposition completely, to deconstruct or trouble it. To label myself as subjective would require the existence of an objectivity that I am setting myself up against and so ironically would reinforce the notion of objectivity and the whole gendered binary framework of which it is part.

So if there are no absolute truths out there waiting to be discovered, about maths, about learning or about anything else, how do we decide what to believe? Like Ann Seller (1988: 181), I think that we do this through collective discussions.

> What peace and equality are discovered to be will depend on the decision that various communities have taken. Through our decisions with a community, we decide how we want to belong to the world, how we want to set about understanding it, living in it and changing it, we have nothing else to rely upon except each other in taking these decisions.

Through these collective discussions we decide which stories we feel to be convincing and which not. So one of the aims of the remaining sections in this chapter, on collecting and analysing my data as well as those just gone, on the research sites where I worked, is to help to make the stories in the later chapters convincing for you. Integral to this is for me to explain and be ethically accountable, to the communities of teachers, students and researchers to whom I write, for the choices I made during the research process. The other central aim is to begin to put into action the ideas about identity work discussed in the last chapter, through myself as a researcher and also through the students and teachers with whom I worked.

Collecting the data

Although subject choices do not happen at a single point, the end of compulsory schooling forces a crystallization of young people's views about themselves, their futures, their education and their relationships with maths, and provides a useful place to start exploring these. As a result, I chose to focus on those students on AS level courses who were still quite close to this structurally enforced moment of decision making.

With my emphasis on student choices and 'identities', it seemed that interviews would be the most direct way to access these. I view 'the processes of interviewing and of being interviewed [as] not simply about the giving and receiving of information but at least as much about speaking identities into being, solidifying them and constantly reconstituting them through the stories we tell ourselves and each other' (Epstein and Johnson 1998: 105). Unconscious factors form an important part of this process, 'the elements of phantasy, the rush of desire and/or disgust, of who we desire and who we wish to be – in psychoanalytic terms, the cathexis of object choice and identification' (Epstein and Johnson 1998: 116).

I interviewed 42 maths students aged between 16 and 19 and one mature student. The interviews varied widely both in length, ranging from 15 to 40 minutes, and in formality. Students were asked:

- To describe a typical maths lesson, and what they had enjoyed most and least during the year.
- About the different learning styles used in their classes and about which of their subjects was most similar to maths and which most different from it.
- To give the reasons for their subject choices and for what they hope to do when they leave the sixth form.
- About their feelings on gender.

The interviews were semi-structured and started with a very open question to describe a 'typical maths lesson' to allow students some role in directing the interaction.

Because I believe research is messy, I was not overly concerned with appearing detached in the interviews. Anyway, I was a teacher at Grafton and my class there, and some other participants, already knew something of where I stood on the gender issues that I asked them about. In several cases students asked me about my own views and discussions ensued. I felt that by not trying to project myself as an objective interviewer, I was making the interview a bit more democratic than it might otherwise have been. However, I was still in a powerful position compared to my interviewees, not least due to the age difference between them and me. Miriam David and her colleagues

(2001) argue that any adult in a school is inevitably identified by students with the teachers and benefits from this power.

In Grafton I worked as a teacher, while in Westerburg and Sunnydale I occupied an in-between state. In all classes, I sat with the students, obeyed instructions from the teacher, took notes (although of course very different ones from the other students), and was occasionally used by students to subvert the teacher's intentions. Sometimes when I talked to students about things other than maths I felt as if I were being naughty. I also adopted some teacher-like practices: assisting students with their work and even teaching a few lessons in Westerburg, hanging out in the maths staff office and, although I encouraged students to call me 'Heather', I often found they addressed me as 'Miss'.

I acknowledge that in the age stratified organizations where I researched I benefited from the way students identified me with their teachers. However, I think there were also important distinctions between the ways that the students related to me compared to how they related to their teachers. For example, Michael's willingness to disclose to me the personal information that the parents he lives with are not his biological ones, something he rarely tells teachers (and did not tell me as his teacher), does suggest that he saw the interview as a different space from the classroom. It is also important to remember that there is not just one version of the teacher/student power relation and that other divisions, such as class and gender, combine with age in complicated ways to produce fluid contours of power in the interview.

As well as seeing 'identities' in practice in the interviews I saw these in practice in relation to others in participants' maths lessons. I observed three weeks of lessons in each of the groups containing students whom I interviewed. These classroom observations gave me a sense of the environments in which my participants were learning maths, they also provided me with opportunities for students to get to know me and to get used to me before I asked to interview them and for me to participate in the life of the colleges by working with them in their classes.

Traditionally the combined use of interviews with observations has been thought of in terms of triangulation:

> In the B movie, the exact position of the damaged bomber limping back from Germany is always found by triangulation. The direction of its radio signal is assessed by two geographically separated receivers, allowing an exact fix to be made on its position. In the same way, it is thought that the researcher can use discourse collected from different sources to 'home in' on the facts of the matter and thus show up some accounts as distorted or rhetorical.
>
> (Potter and Wetherell 1987: 63)

This approach assumes that there is a truth out there to be targeted and so relies on ideas of objectivity. However, as Jonathan Potter and Margaret Wetherell (1987: 64) go on to point out, detailed study of data from a range of sources increases rather than reduces the variability; 'indeed, in the course of attempting to triangulate the result is more often than not "homing out", resulting in the proliferation of more and more inconsistent versions'. So I was not using observations to get closer to the 'truth'. Instead I hoped the 'homing out' would enable more complex analyses of the students' accounts of self within the interview, opening out multiple possible meanings.

Issues of power entered into my relationships with staff as well as with students. It was stressful negotiating my role in classes with nine teachers each with different expectations of me. I felt comfortable in the groups in Grafton. I knew the teachers, Matt and Trisha, well and both related to me as a teacher and sometimes asked for my assistance in class. In Westerburg, where I acted as a sort of sub-teacher/observer hybrid, my position felt less secure. Although access was agreed in advance, this was subject to some ongoing negotiation. Twice I was excluded from sections of Veronica's lessons, once when she gave students a talk about the stress they were under and again when she nagged them about their key skills assignments. In the first case she got Alan, the head of department, to tell me that she wanted to be alone with the group and in the second case she told me that this would be something that I would not be interested in because it was not related to maths. In Sunnydale, where classes were more like lectures, I had a more passive role, often spending the entire 90 minutes sitting at the back taking notes, although even during such periods the students nearby often used me as a mathematical resource.

At the end of the data collection process I had masses of stuff. Only a small fraction of which appears in this book. The rest of this chapter deals with what I did to get from one to the other and how I built up this book's story about gender and maths.

Making sense of the data

I make less direct use of the observations than of the interviews in this book. This is partly because their diversity made them difficult to stitch into a coherent picture, but mainly because they seem to be less obviously about 'identity' than do the interviews. As a result I will say something very brief about how I analysed the observations before focusing on the interviews in the rest of this section.

I organized the observations thematically concentrating on the practices engaged in by students and teachers. I worked through my notes identifying and classifying incidents according to themes that emerged from the data. I do not see the process of these themes' emergence as one of my discovery of the intrinsic truth embedded within my data but as one of creative invention on my part. Although, as with the interviews, this was a process of invention that often surprised me.

As for the interviews, I started my analysis with a similar thematic approach. However, I then abandoned this approach in favour of a more holistic one that involved writing a story for each interview. Using stories rather than codes better captured the distinctiveness of each account and the way students, through a complex process of negotiation and identification, were positioning themselves relative to maths. Experience exists through our attempts to make sense of it by telling stories. Stories impose order and structure and patterns of cause and effect; they attempt to explain why things happened as they did, and to decide what did happen.

> It's a way of explaining the universe while leaving the universe unexplained, it's a way of keeping it alive, not boxing it into time. Everyone who tells a story tells it differently, just to remind us that everybody sees it differently. Some people say there are true things to be found, some people say there are things to be proved. I don't believe them. The only thing for certain is how complicated it all is, like string full of knots. It's all there but hard to find the beginning and impossible to fathom the end. The best you can do is admire the cat's cradle, and maybe knot it up a bit more.
>
> (Winterson 1985: 93)

After completing the individual stories I developed connections between them. In the search for patterns in my data I grouped the 43 students by their main reason for choosing maths. Table 2.4 shows the outcome of this process.

There are some overall patterns:

- There are more middle class students (86 percent, 18 out of 21) than working class students (36 percent, 8 out of 22) in the top row of the table, which is occupied by those who chose maths because they enjoy it.
- There are more girls (42 percent, 8 out of 19) than boys (17 percent, 4 out of 24) who chose maths because of specific career goals. However, male students dominate the employment related category: 'To prove something to others'.
- One group, 'To prove something to themselves', is entirely female (16 percent, 3 out of 19).

Table 2.4   How is it that people come to choose maths?

For chosen career and for enjoyment			For enjoyment		
Ashley	Hina	*Jonathan*	**Rachel**	*Yasser*	*Graham*
Nazima	Ling	*Kanton*	**Nefertiti**	*Salvador*	*Desmond*
	Priya	*Matthew*	**Analia**	*Darren*	*Peter*
		Vijay	**Natasha**	*Deji*	*Saldon*
			Maryam	*Sam*	*Phil*
					Kiriakos

For chosen career and not for enjoyment

Vicky	Mei Jin	*Imran*
	Niamh	

To prove something to others			To prove something to themselves
Mika	*James*	*AJ*	Julie
Toni	*Jean*		Lucy
	Lee		**Claudia**
	Michael		
	Simon		

Unclear

Melanie	*Jingki*
	Kenjin

Note: The unmarked, plain text, names belong to working class women, while italicized names belong to boys and bold names to members of the middle class. (So bold italicized names belong to middle class men.) I have used information on parental employment and educational background to make divisions into middle class and working class.

- In the right-hand column of the group who enjoyed maths I have put those who evidenced the strongest identifications as mathematicians. This group is exclusively male (25 percent, 6 out of 24).

Such patterns are fascinating and I could go on in the rest of the book to offer 'representative' quotes from each group. However:

- These generalizations obscure the variations of gender and class within the groups and the ways that there are no simple relationships between someone's demographic profile and their identification with maths.
- Classifications were not easy to craft and I had to make choices about which factor I felt emerged most strongly from their interview. So students in the same section of the table may tell very different stories.

- While divisions into male or female are relatively straightforward, divisions into working or middle class are much less so. Additionally, as work on educational pathways shows (Walkerdine et al. 2001; Power et al. 2002; Brooks 2003), there is huge variation within classes.
- Many important elements, notably family, friends and teachers, are absent from the table. These featured in most interviews but were rarely given as the explicit and never, in my readings, as the main reason for a student's choice of maths (although Rachel, featured in Chapter 4, gets closest to doing this).

These points raise questions about what is lost in an analysis based on grouping data in this way, so 'reducing complexity to single scores' (Hollway and Jefferson 2000: 109).

The purpose of the second part of the book is to increase complexity, to open out some of these groupings; I aim to complicate these apparently clear cut mutually exclusive categories of difference by looking for differences as well as similarities *within* them. In doing this, I use detailed stories of six of the boys and four of the girls and draw on the stories of many others.

- Chapter 3 starts from differences within the group who chose maths *for enjoyment*, exploring differences and similarities between those who identify as 'good at maths' and those who do not and between those who identify as mathematicians and those who do not.
- Chapters 4 and 5 look in turn at those who chose maths *to prove something to others* and those who chose it *to prove something to themselves*. The starting point is the male dominance of the first group and the female dominance of the second group.

Before I launch into these stories I finish this chapter by explaining how I came to present them as I do. I sent each student a copy of my story of our interview. Most students did not provide me with any feedback, but that which I did get was generally positive. For example, Peter emailed: 'Thanks for the report :-) it made amusing reading. You've really got my personality down, it's scary'. I got most feedback from students at Grafton because I was still teaching there a few hours each week. These students' two main concerns were the names that I had given them and the way their words had been presented, repetitions, hesitations, deviations and all. The first was easily changed the second was not. 'We tend to think we speak like characters in a play, but actual or natural verbatim speech is not at all like play dialogue' (Potter and Wetherell 1987: 13). I worried a lot about this. On the one hand, there was my commitment to respond to interviewees' concerns, to present them in a way that they considered fair and not to exploit my power over their words. On the other hand, there were considerations of how far I could edit their words free of the conversational features that were often central to my analysis. My partial resolution is to abandon the long indented extracts from transcripts that featured in my initial stories in favour of using shorter extracts incorporated, like the speech in novels, into this book. This is an idea that I have borrowed from Michael Billig (1992: 29):

> The reconstructions use literary devices for representing dialogue: 'He said ..., then she said ..., then he said', and so forth. These devices are more usually found in fiction or journalism than in social scientific writing. There is a theoretical reason for using this style ... each individual is unique ... The conversations represent unique moments in their lives. The heavy theoretical categories, so commonly encountered in social psychological and sociological texts, can easily obscure this sense of individuality. It is necessary to use a style which conveys that the remarks made in this course of unfolding were moments occurring in the course of lives being led. Moreover, the participants often had very funny things to say. Social scientists should not plod along with their serious concepts, spoiling all the fun.

Billig aims to present accessible and populated social research, to write research that is readable and filled with the people who took part in it. So do I ...

Part 2

Sex by numbers

Feminism had focused on winning for women the same rights as men in terms of access to opportunity, pay, and so on, but not the right to masculinity itself. This was not a problem of 'separate but equal' so much as 'different but equal.'

Actually ... plenty of the rights sought by feminists involved things that were considered masculine: entering management jobs, playing sports, not wearing girdles, and dressing in pants.

However, the argument was not that women had the right to masculinity, but rather that such activities were not intrinsically masculine, and in any case women could do them *and still be feminine*. This established the gender ground rules under which much of mainstream feminism (but not lesbian-feminism) has continued to operate: women could do anything men could do and still retain their femininity. Womanhood and femininity were still entwined in this particular set of assertions. Women's femininity was offered as the guarantor that feminism wouldn't go too far. *Too far*, in this case meant going after gender.

(Wilchins 2004: 7–8, original emphasis)

Being/doing 'good at maths'

Peter: Well, I chose double maths and computing because I want to be a computer programmer. And because maths is what computers do, it's all they really do. And it's just, so maths is really, and I'm quite good at maths, so. And computing, obviously, coz I want to be a computer programmer. And I did physics because I need another subject and I'm really good at physics, so it's what I did.

Saldon: What I found most interesting though was when we had to do investigations or courseworks. Those were the things I really liked because then it was my own work, and I could work it out myself. That's the main part I like about maths is I can work it out and figure it and it's like a challenge for me to do. I'm very good at investigations coz I can sort of imagine the shapes or the puzzles in my head and then see what will fit in well.

These statements are taken from the transcripts of two interviews with Westerburg further maths students. They are interesting for many reasons, but above all because they contain rare examples of students identifying as 'good at maths'. Of the 43 maths students I interviewed only five located themselves in this way (although more spoke about idyllic past times when they *were* 'good at maths', about being good at *other things* or about *other people* being 'good at maths'). As someone who, although well qualified mathematically, has always felt embarrassed admitting this in public, I am jealous of these few students' apparent ease at describing themselves as 'good at maths' and so, given the social stories that attach to the subject, as de facto clever.

In this chapter I explore what makes it possible for someone to claim a position as 'good at maths' and what are the effects of this, first by re-telling the stories the students told me and then by exploring the identity work done in these stories. In telling tales of student choices, I am interested in the ways they locate themselves within discourses of difference or sameness between maths and nonmaths people and practices, and the connections between these and their identification as 'good at maths' or 'not good at maths'. Again I am analysing discourses here, I am *not* interested in whether any of their claims to possess or not possess 'mathematical ability', whatever that may be, are right. I do not think that this question is answerable, and luckily find it neither interesting nor relevant to understanding either success and failure within the subject or enjoyment and hatred of it. My starting point is that such things are socially constructed. However, as Nikolas Rose (1999b: x) points out:

> The language of social construction is actually rather weak. It is not very enlightening to be told repeatedly that something claimed as 'objective' is in fact 'socially constructed'. Objects of thought are constructed in thought: what else could they be? So the interesting questions concern the ways in which they are constructed.

Thus in this chapter I explore the questions:

- How do young people position themselves, as 'good at maths' and 'not good at maths', within their talk?
- What are the discourses they draw on to do this and that make these positions possible?

However, these questions give a one-sided impression of young people engaged in a pick and mix construction of self. There is no 'voluntary free fall through the social positions that are available to people to inhabit, this study demonstrates how restriction on access is central to subjective constructions' (Skeggs 1997: 12). In particular, I argue that the sociocultural constitution of gender as oppositional, and the connection of this to the series of binary relations through which maths is constructed, makes it more difficult for girls and women to identify as 'good at maths'. As a result, I want to rewrite these questions as:

- How are young people positioned – as 'good at maths'/'not good at maths' – within their talk?
- What are the discourses that do this to them and that make these positionings possible?

These questions do not replace the earlier ones. All four remain active in a constant and, it is hoped, productive tension throughout this and subsequent chapters of this book. This is the same tension within choice, between social structures and individual agency, which I discussed towards the end of Chapter 1.

I begin this chapter by looking in detail at the experiences of the further maths students since three of the five students who identified as 'good at maths' were in this group. Among this group this identification was clearly gendered since all three of these students were male and the two female further maths students did a great deal of work in their interviews to deny the possibility of their being thought 'mathematically able'. However, looking overall, the pattern was not oppositional since the overwhelming majority of both the girls and the boys whom I interviewed thought of themselves as 'not good at maths' and the other two students to identify as 'good at maths' were a boy and a girl at Grafton (Salvador and Julie, more about them in Chapter 5). However, the starkness of the contrast in the further maths group struck me as worth exploring and was the starting point for this chapter. After these stories I explore and question the sociocultural context that makes these stories, with their oppositional discourses about maths, possible. In looking at this wider context, I focus on the gendering of rationality within Western Enlightenment thinking and within contemporary popular culture. I will show that these discourses socially construct 'mathematical ability' as natural, individual and masculine, in such a way as to disappear that process of construction. But first the stories . . .

Peter's story

Peter is studying for AS levels in double maths, physics and computing, as he puts it 'very mathematical stuff'. He wants to be a computer programmer and already knows a considerable amount about this from books and magazines. I got to know him better than the other Westerburg students because we chatted when I sat next to him during my initial two weeks of observations. He is white and his mother and father are a teacher and a surgeon respectively.

Peter's identification with maths is structured through his division of the world into 'two different people. People that can do maths and people that can't do maths'. In his discussion of what other people, not doing maths, think about the subject, he explains: 'People that can't do maths just don't, find it really boring and they don't enjoy it and they just don't really bother with it, because they don't like it much. And people that do do maths like it and they do it'. He elaborates when I ask how he thinks people become one type or the other: 'because they got, their mind works in a certain way or is ordered' so 'to be creative, it's very difficult to be mathematical at the same time'. He offers the example of writing poetry, 'even when you read poetry you find some poetry is like quite mathematical and it's ordered . . . and some of it isn't, and it's much more emotional. And I obviously prefer the emotional one coz that's the point of poetry'. The possibility that order can express emotion and creativity is precluded here and the two domains, of ordered activities and of creative ones, are constituted as mutually exclusive. When I ask whether maths can be creative, Peter develops his argument to incorporate the idea of mathematical activity as governed by rigid, unambiguous rules, 'all very strict and defined . . . and to be creative you follow, you just look at different rules'. Even when mathematicians 'find a creative solution . . . they're still looking at all different things that have happened in the past and following the rules still. When in English it's not like that at all. It's really working with things, there's rules, but there aren't really any proper [rules], none of them are rigid'. He sums things up thus: 'They always say the best artists are, they learn rules and break them, and that's true. There aren't so many rules in English. And they aren't rigid'. In these sections Peter is drawing on the oppositions:

> Maths people/Nonmaths people
> Ordered and Rule-based/Creative and Emotional
> Mathematics/English and Art

Peter sees mathematicians as different from other people but equal with them and positions himself within this group. This is enabled via his identification as dyslexic and the way that this facilitates his location within a series of oppositions:

> Fast/Slow
> Competitive/Collaborative
> Learning by rote/Learning how things work

Peter was diagnosed as dyslexic, 'I think when I was about 8 or 9 . . . What happened was my school, I went to special needs at my school, and they said "No, you're not dyslexic", I was like, because I was at the bottom of everything, I literally, I didn't finish any work for a year and . . . I was doing really badly, and they said, "No you're not dyslexic"'. This provoked some scepticism 'because obviously I'm quite articulate . . . but I was doing at the bottom of everything'. After a year in special needs 'my mum took me out of school for a day . . . to the Dyslexic Institute and paid, like, 500 quid for a test or something, and they said, "Yes, he's dyslexic", like after five minutes! So, I went to the Dyslexic Institute once a week and I went to a tutor and I just spent a lot of time just getting over it. So now, like my spelling is almost as good as most people's'. This identification as dyslexic is central to how Peter constructs himself. As Tony Cline and Rea Reason (1993: 30) point out, it is classed, for dyslexia is unique within special education since 'it offers additional and targeted help without carrying a significant social stigma' and so is acceptable to middle class parents. Since dyslexia is defined by the exclusion of other disabilities, socioeconomic and cultural 'disadvantage', and 'inadequate' teaching, it is mainly those from 'good' homes and 'good' schools who seek out and/or acquire this label.

Peter tells me that his dyslexia affects the ways that he learns best, although 'it's not that different to normal people, I guess. Coz obviously I don't have much comparison. But it does take me longer to learn something and it takes me longer to get good at something'. This has implications for maths because 'a lot of the things in maths . . . you learn a sequence. And I'm really bad at learning sequences . . . and it takes me a long time . . . to learn a sequence. So usually what I just do is I don't learn the sequence I learn [where] it came from and then in the exam I can work it out as I go along. And it just, it works out quicker'. Since Peter works slowly he finds doing repetitive exercises 'a waste' and 'annoying'. They are time consuming and he finds that he gets the idea after a few questions. However, he is aware that working fast is normally associated with 'mathematical ability'. At the start of the interview Peter describes a typical GCSE maths lesson: 'There were about two people that were always ahead. Always, always ahead because they were really quick and, so most of the time, I was a little bit behind because I'm dyslexic and it takes me longer to do stuff'. But the exams were another story and 'I was always like either ahead of them or even with them'. Here Peter has no problem in asserting that he is better at maths than those who raced ahead in class. His dyslexia enables him to reverse the usual associations between speed and 'mathematical ability' and to position himself as a mathematician despite his slow pace. Related to this are his feelings about competitive as against collaborative activities. He feels that maths is often taught competitively and he disliked this aspect of his GCSE class 'continuously competing and always trying to get ahead of everyone'. His dyslexia legitimated his opting out of this.

Peter also connects his maths likes and dislikes to his being dyslexic. He likes visual maths, such as graph work and algebra. He dislikes and has difficulties with 'simple' mental arithmetic and singles out tables ('I learnt my fives but that was it'), factorizing, and manipulating sequences of numbers as particularly problematic. So although he does worse than others at numerical problems again his dyslexia is read to mean that this is not a judgement on his 'mathematical ability'. His emphasis on the how of maths (mentioned earlier) is a case of making a virtue out of a necessity. He asks, at the end of his discussion of whether maths is about understanding why rules work, or simply learning rules, 'but, I mean, why rules work is much more interesting, isn't it?' This allies him culturally with mathematicians. However, it is not just his dyslexia that enables his positioning as a mathematician despite his deficiencies at calculation. For: 'To be thought of as calculating is not complementary. Calculating is often what the other is: women; scheming; wheeling and dealing bargainers. The refined mind reasons, but does not calculate. Indeed, witness the oft-told joke that mathematicians cannot add up' (Walkerdine 1997a: 57). Here I am not suggesting that Peter is consciously aware of all these associations. However, I am suggesting that his positioning is in part made possible by a sociocultural slippage between the binaries:

> Reason/Calculation
> Reasonable/Calculating
> Masculine/Feminine

This links back to the ideas about maths, and the ways that it is tied to gendered binary structures of thought, introduced in Chapter 1, and links forward to ideas about the gendering of reason discussed later in this chapter. It is reliant upon the discursive construction of 'routine calculation' as inferior to and opposed to 'real understanding' and on a series of associated, unequally valued, oppositional binaries. In Saldon's story, to which I turn now, the rejection of routine, repetitive calculation in favour of problem-solving takes on aspects of a quest as he uses/is used by the oppositions:

> Independent/Dependent
> Active/Passive

Saldon's Story

Saldon is studying for AS levels in biology, chemistry, maths and further maths. He is Bangladeshi and his mum is a primary schoolteacher and his dad an underground supervisor. He came to Westerburg because, 'It's quite a good school' that is 'mainly for A levels so I thought it would be more focused'. Maths is his favourite subject and although 'my parents obviously want me to [be a] doctor, so that's why I chose chemistry and biology', he has other ideas and thinks that medicine's 'very competitive, and also it's very stressful and so I'm not sure if I actually want to do that'. Instead he is thinking of 'maybe going into either the IT area, or the financing area' or even, as he later reveals, into engineering. His choice of engineering is motivated by its problem-solving orientation, something that is also what he likes most about maths.

Saldon's active, independent, problem-solving approach is the basis for his identification as a mathematician. This is evident when he reminds me that his teacher, 'Rudolff, he talked [about] how true mathematicians always look for problems in real life, and like to solve those problems ... that's what mathematicians like to do, and that is what I agree with, that we like to look for real problems in real life and solve those ones'. Through the pronoun 'we' he names himself as a mathematician. In this statement he also claims teacher validation for this identification and for his interpretation of mathematicians' activities. He tells me that his summer holiday reading has helped him to understand what mathematicians do: 'what I noticed mainly was, um, they, mathematicians, have gone deeply into small details which I never knew existed. I mean, they've given names to like lots of different graphs, like surjective graphs, bijective graphs, and so on. And just because one might have two values for x, and they've given it a whole new name. That's what's quite surprising because they've gone into such detail and explained everything, every aspect in such detail.' His use this time of third person rather than first person pronouns to refer to mathematicians suggests that he is in a process of becoming, analogous to an apprenticeship.

What Saldon dislikes most about maths is working through a series of repetitive questions, and what he enjoys most is investigating, as he explains in the quote at the start of this chapter, where he again emphasizes doing things independently and learning actively. Regarding his independent approach, he explains that 'I probably learn best ... not when teachers tell me, but when I figure it out and if I get it wrong, then they tell me'. He tends to work individually in class because he sees maths as 'something that you think about', something you construct for yourself. Whereas 'in science there are some times when I do group work because sometimes it's not a matter of working it out, it's a matter of remembering or something you can't do, so sometimes yeah we tend to ask each other how this works or "do you remember how this is done?"'

His success in maths GCSE came when he took it independently in Year 10. I ask, 'So you didn't do the GCSE through the school. Why was that? 'Mainly because I wanted to do it early', he pauses and continues, 'yeah, and the thing about maths is that sometimes when they do the parts we have to do loads and loads of repetitive questions, that I tend not to do so well in because often I find, I often lose interest after a while, so the thing is with puzzles I'm doing it myself, I'm building it myself and so everything is new and different.' He suggests that 'maybe the school thought I wasn't ready for it and so I took it privately and got the A*'. This speaks of a confidence in his 'ability' in the face of contrary assessments.

As with Peter, Saldon feels that his enjoyment of and success in maths make him different. Notably, he feels that his active approach makes him different from other people, because 'most people might remember the text they saw in a book', but 'what I do is I have an active diagram of what it's like, in my head'. Later he tells me that what other people, not doing maths, 'don't like the most is the part where you actually have to think about it. They find that a lot of hard work. When you have to work out and actively think. They find that very tiring'. So they 'rely more on their natural talents, like most of them who don't like maths are extremely good at languages, like foreign languages, and English, and they're sort of like naturally good at that'. He cites the example of a friend of his who 'did alright in maths, he got A, which is quite good, but he didn't like it at all because he found it was too hard', he prefers languages. He is constructing this opposition as natural. So maths and languages represent 'two probably opposites'. And science is related to maths because 'they've got like algorithms, they depend on theories ... you have problems ... they're constantly changing and improving and that's what we're doing in maths, constantly like finding out new theories and new problems, and new ways to solve problems'. In contrast, English 'stays like more or less the same all the time', and 'there hasn't been much change in English now, apart from in language, than it was, like a hundred years ago, whereas maths is constantly new'. Here the static, passive picture of English is contrasted to the dynamic, active picture of maths. Maths is an active discipline and Saldon and other mathematicians are active disciples of it. Saldon is clear about which side he is on, being more comfortable with and better at, the precision of maths and its numbers than with the vagueness of English and its words. In this comment, about geography, he expresses some of his frustration when working with words: 'I know the answer, but when I write it in and the teacher marks it, she says "well you didn't actually put that sentence in or that", which I would have thought it naturally implies'. However the teacher insists, ' "You have to write that part in". And so I kept losing marks like that, so I was never very good at that English part'. So in constructing this opposition Saldon draws on several interrelated oppositions:

Mathematics/English
Dynamic/Static
Numbers/Words

When I ask Saldon about why boys and girls tend to choose different subjects, his discursive opposition of maths and English becomes explicitly gendered. He tells me that girls are better 'at expressing themselves and tend to have more viewpoints'. Whereas 'boys are probably a bit more superficial about things. But that's about it. Erm, yeah I think, erm, boys also are probably more interested in challenges like a boy will probably be like very interested, more interested in playing a sport like football or basketball, or probably doing something like chess or something, whatever, whereas girls will probably prefer talking and friendship and actually socializing'. It is interesting to see how Saldon transforms boys' superficiality, with which the passage starts, into their more positive interest in challenges, by the end of the passage. Also Saldon reads masculinity both within the physical challenges of football and basketball and within the intellectual challenges of chess (the discourses that support this are discussed later in this chapter; also relevant is my discussion in Chapter 7 of the ways that the further maths classroom practices connect challenge with competition).

To sum up, Saldon tells a similar story to Peter, drawing on the discourses of mathematicians as naturally different, of his independence and confidence in his talents in the face of others' disbelief, and of a dislike for routine and repetitive calculation in favour of investigational work and problem-solving. However, while Saldon and Peter both draw distinctions between mathematicians and nonmathematicians, they go to considerable pains to stress that these are complementary and equally valuable groups. Often students' stories of difference are imbued with unequal value judgements. Some attach associations of superiority and some of inferiority to being a mathematician. Graham does the former and, because he includes himself in this group, he does a lot of discursive work in an attempt to avoid looking arrogant.

Graham's story

Graham, a white, middle class young man, is studying for AS levels in double maths, physics, computing, that is 'maths, even more maths, further maths, physics, which is just another name for maths, and computing, which is just maths on computers', and psychology. When I ask Graham why he chose physics he tells me: 'I'm good at physics, I was probably the best in the year at physics'. He knows this because he got the highest test marks and his teacher 'didn't really like physics and she always got me to like tell the whole class some new concept'. Regarding computing he recounts, 'I've been interested in computing since I was about 10 or 11, properly interested, not, I mean, most kids if they're given a computer will like computer games, but interested in mucking about with computers, without games'. He then tells me how he did GCSE Information Technology (IT) outside school in eight months and got the top A* grade. Psychology offers him a break from his other mathematically oriented subjects and relates to the way 'I usually find I can', he pauses and then continues, 'see what people are thinking and why they're thinking, quite a lot. I can usually help my friends sort their lives out if they're, you know, if they've got problems and stuff'. This is an impressive range of skills to which he lays claim, but to claim 'mathematical ability' he has more to negotiate.

I tell him, 'I want to know if you have any idea what people not doing maths think about maths and further maths'.

He begins, 'They think it's unenjoyable, sometimes. And sometimes I could have not chosen maths, I could have chosen biology, chemistry or anything I did well at … I usually find if someone doesn't work hard early on, then if they leave it too long without working, then they find they're behind and then they think they're stupid, which gets into a kind of cycle.'

Although in my question I set up a distinction between Graham, who is doing maths, and others, who are not, Graham's answer speaks of similarities between himself and those imagined others. Immediately after telling me that they do not enjoy maths, he imagines himself in their position. He then posits a psychological mechanism whereby early experiences of failure produce defences against the possibility of future failures. However, difference, in the sense of 'natural ability', is reintroduced when he concludes that: 'depending on the ability of the student to start with, it will depend on how long they can leave it before they can sink or swim'. This brings in the opposition:

Naturally able/Hard working

It is an opposition that is central to the identity work that Graham does in the interview.

This interaction of 'hard work' and 'ability' in determining success is also evident in Graham's description of his GCSE maths experiences with which the interview begins. His group had four teachers. 'The first teacher I had was pretty good, looking back on it' but 'sometimes the class mucked about so I don't know, didn't get a vast amount of work done'. This teacher left and their next 'wasn't very good at all' because 'the class didn't respect her, really, and therefore not many people did much work'. Once again Graham 'must confess I didn't do much work during then'. Their third teacher was 'brilliant' and 'she got the class under control' with her 'dynamic kind of teaching', although she too left, this time a few weeks before their exams. He summarizes the situation: 'we got through a lot of teachers … I think we had a bit of a reputation as being a pretty bad class'. He continues that teachers found it 'shocking' that a higher maths group did not behave because 'they think intelligent people should, I dunno, want to work harder, which I think is quite illogical because how intelligent you are does not mean how hard you want to work. It's purely just how good you are'. He ends by constructing two types of academic success: 'there are going to be some people who are going to be less intelligent and got into the higher group by working hard … but there's always the people who just find maths easy and then didn't have to work hard to get into the higher group, and never did work hard'. 'Hard work' is the province of the 'less intelligent' and opposed to 'effortless achievement' (Mac an Ghaill 1994: 67).

Throughout the interview Graham is positioning himself within this 'authentically intelligent' group he has marked out. For example, he chose to come to Westerburg for practical reasons of accessibility and because 'they do have a grade limit to get in so I'd probably end up with … people with more of my kind of level'. Then, when discussing what he likes about his pure maths teacher, he explains: 'He'll go through loads of clever little shortcuts … which reinforces your learning. But the problem is, I think, that if anyone couldn't, if anyone was less able, and they might not be able to cope and they would fall behind'.

However, claiming 'authentic intelligence' means he must carefully negotiate the role of 'hard work' in his own academic success, something he defines as necessary but that always threatens his performance of 'effortless achievement'. In the passages relating to the sequence of GCSE maths teachers, Graham repeatedly tells me that he did not do much work. I now look at the places where he says that he did work hard.

After telling me that he got the top A* GCSE grade in maths, I suggest, 'the end really helped, I guess, the last teacher'.

'Yeah', Graham says and then qualifies this, 'I probably could have done it without. I worked hard on my own I actually revised a fair bit, not, not a vast amount I suppose. I actually tried to understand the concepts in the lesson, so I found that if … I understood what was being said and understood it at the beginning of the lesson it was fine … I didn't work for the rest of the lesson, which really annoyed some teachers'.

In asserting his independence from the teacher Graham concedes that he did work for his exam. He then immediately withdraws this since it threatens to align him with those he dismissed earlier as 'less intelligent', only in the top set through 'hard work'. This illustrates his continual balancing act in which all admissions of effort are accompanied by evidence that this was not the norm. For example, 'I actually finally worked in Year 11 for my GCSEs to pull them up', and the shift from primary to secondary school was 'about the first time in my life I actually tried hard', he pauses, 'for a bit, even though to most people that's still mucking about'.

Five further oppositions play their parts in establishing Graham as 'mathematically able' within the space of the interview:

Independent/Dependent
Fast/Slow
Active/Passive
Reasoning/Calculating
Thinking/Writing

These are all present in his discussion of investigations: 'I really still do love maths challenges or investigations because ... most maths teachers, almost all of them, teach you, if you see what I mean. Whereas maths investigation, you're really left to yourself which is more of a challenge'. He recalls how quickly he was able to complete a particular investigation: 'I really enjoyed that one and I did it in a day, I think ... I didn't write it up though. I'm quite lazy about writing it up. I enjoyed thinking about the problem. I'm quite good at seeing patterns in stuff. But the bad thing is I'm terrible at mental arithmetic. I was probably the worst in my class at mental arithmetic'. Here the process of writing is constructed as peripheral to the mathematical thinking, which is essentially about spotting patterns and rising to challenges. Not writing up is linked here to his laziness and difficulties with mental computation. There are important distinctions inscribed in his talk about these. While he describes himself as 'very, very lazy', he does not want a lazy mind and values a teaching style that 'doesn't just let the brain get lazy and passive ... it makes you actively involved in the lesson'. Similarly when given an investigation he looked at 'how visually it would fit together whereas some people just played round with actual numbers', the 'just' in this sentence relegating numerical work to a secondary status.

Graham aligns himself with maths as a signifier of 'natural intelligence'. In addition to the oppositional constructions examined above, it is the sociocultural myth of the 'mathematical genius' that underlies this identification. In the next section I explore the stories of those who deny being 'good at maths', despite their excellent results in the subject. In these stories this myth of 'genius' has negative consequences, setting up a figure who defines what being 'good at maths' is but with whom identification is impossible.

Doing 'not good at maths'

This section draws on the stories of the remaining further maths interviewees: Ling, who was born in Macau and moved to Portugal when she was 6 years old and to England only a year and a half before I met her, Rachel, Desmond and Darren, and Yasser, who although not in the further maths class is working through the further maths syllabus in his own time with the assistance of his teacher.

Turning first to Yasser and Ling, it is clear, from their thoughts on other people's views of maths, that they do not see being 'good at maths' as making you different:

Ling: When I tell people that I do two maths, they say, they always say, 'then you must be very clever' or something. And so I think, um, they must think that to do two maths the people need to be very clever or intelligent, but that's not, I don't think that's the case.

Yasser: They think that it's hard, and it's just for brainy people. That's what they think usually. However, it's not true. As our teacher always says, you need just to persevere and that's it. It doesn't need you to be really clever or whatever.

However, while Yasser sees no essential differences between those who do maths and those who do not, and as a result seems to find being mathematically successful unproblematic and easy to incorporate into his identity, Ling's response is more complex. While Yasser jokes that perhaps the idea of maths being 'hard' was started by some maths student wanting the kudos, Ling tells me that she does not know why they say that 'and I feel a bit like embarrassed because I'm not, I'm not clever'.

'Why are you not clever?' I immediately ask.

'I just don't feel I am', she replies, 'they ask me some questions like, the, the tricky questions like, and I can't answer them'.

I inquire as to whether she knows anyone who she thinks is clever and she tells me, 'I don't know anybody who says that they are clever themselves', but that there is one person 'not in this maths, it was in the other school. So like he can solve all the problems, I don't know how but'. Here Ling is projecting onto her classmate the phantasy 'mathematical genius'. Projecting 'involves feelings which cannot be tolerated being evoked in someone else, where their fate can be observed from a safer distance' (Segal 2000: 66). The power of this phantasy helps us to understand the strength of another denial of her 'mathematical ability' that comes when I ask for her GCSE grade. She replies: 'Um, A*. But erm that was the, a re-take, like, I took one in Year 10 and I took one in Year 11 as well'. Here Ling finds a way of immediately denying that her top grade implies that she is 'really good at maths'. The suggestion is clearly that being really good would imply not having to retake the exam but getting an A* first time, although Year 11 is the usual year in which to sit the GCSE and being selected to enter for it a year early could be seen as evidence of her talent in the subject (especially considering that she had been in the country for only a few months at that point). It is interesting to think back to and contrast this with Saldon's reaction to his school's decision *not* to enter him for his GCSE in Year 10.

Rachel's denial of her own 'ability' is even stronger than Ling's. Early in the interview she identifies the private tuition she receives from Bradley, a friend of her father, as pivotal for her decision to continue with maths: 'Bradley was really nice, just like finally realizing that it [maths] actually made sense after all. Coz I came out of Year 10 thinking "yeah, at the end of Year 11 I can give it up" and, um, hopefully I might even get a C and I was going to ask to do the intermediate paper, and then, and now I'm not just doing A level, I'm doing two A levels'. So for Rachel maths is not independent of the teacher. She describes her lessons with Bradley as 'where he sits down and very, very, very patiently, um, sits down and explains everything even though it must feel so much like pushing water uphill'. Rachel constructs herself as a dependent learner; she clearly ascribes no brilliance or talent to herself. Both her 'ability' in and enjoyment of maths began with her tutoring by Bradley and there is the possibility that that is also where they will end. This makes them tentative and context dependent; it also introduces contradictions. For example, after protesting how vehemently she hates physics, she reflects: 'If I'd had a teacher like Bradley for physics, I probably would have really enjoyed it and done it at A level. But I didn't, so'. This story of the teacher being intrinsic to her enjoyment and success in maths, since 'I don't do anything myself', is very different from the versions of maths as person-independent drawn on by Graham, Saldon and to a lesser extent by Peter.

Like Ling, Rachel explicitly denies a position as clever, this time when discussing possible careers. She tells me that her 'dad thought I should do accountancy or law, but I haven't got, I'm not going to get the A levels for law'. First she explains that she is doing the wrong subjects, 'I'm doing English, but I think you need history and stuff for law', but then she adds, 'I wouldn't like it anyway, because it's too difficult'.

'What, what would make it difficult?' I ask.

'Coz it is. All the people that I know that do law are really, really, really clever'.

'And', I pause and then pursue this, 'so why aren't you really, really, really clever?'

'Coz I'm not. I'm me'.

'How do you know?'

'Because I just aren't', she insists.

Thus, regardless of however brilliant her academic results may be, Rachel will not be able to use them as evidence of her own intelligence since there are people out there who are 'really, really, really clever' and 'I'm me'.

Darren and Desmond complete the picture of the further maths participants at Westerburg. Desmond identifies with a competitive, problem-solving maths: 'I just like solving things. Like if no one else can do it, it's even better. If no one can do it and I can do it, that's the icing on the cake ... So I push myself [on investigations] so that I could go a step further than other people to get the top grade, because investigations is intriguing. They're nice. That's what mathematicians really like, I think.'

However, Darren, of the five male further maths interviewees, gets closest to a denial of his being 'good at maths'. After telling me that he got an A*, he continues: 'I don't know how though. I see other people in my class and they are all so much better than me'.

'They were better than you?' I ask.

'They seemed like they were better than me ... They just seemed to get what they say before me'.

'That's really interesting, so you thought they were all better than you?'

'It seems like it, yeah. Coz they just seemed to go "oh yeah, got you". And they asked them questions, and they know the answer'.

Darren's interview contained many such ambiguous exchanges. On a first reading, this passage, like those I quoted from Ling and Rachel's interviews, seems haunted by the myth of 'mathematical genius'. However, his response here is inseparable from the context in which it occurs, as part of a joint interview with Desmond (the other students discussed in this chapter chose to be interviewed alone) and this exchange comes immediately after Desmond's discussion of how upset he was at not getting an A*. In addition Darren does not actually say that he thinks those other students who 'seemed' better than he is actually are and perhaps the exam has led him to revise his earlier view of his and these other students' relative 'mathematical abilities'.

What makes this possible?

Within the student stories I have constructed here learners' identifications with maths are fragmented, contradictory and fluid. Patterns of sameness and difference are central to the ways these identifications are constituted: the samenesses and differences between maths and *other* subjects, and between mathematicians and *other* people. Key features of this are the ways that students position themselves/are positioned within a series of interrelated binary oppositions. Collecting together all these oppositions produces the following list:

> Maths people/Non-maths people
> Mathematics and sciences/Languages and arts
> Ordered and rule-based/Creative and emotional
> Numbers/Words
> Thinking/Writing
> Fast/Slow
> Competitive/Collaborative
> Independent/Dependent
> Active/Passive
> Dynamic/Static
> Naturally able/Hard working
> Real understanding/Rote learning
> Reason/Calculation
> Reasonable/Calculating
> Masculine/Feminine
> Really good at maths/Good at maths

This list, of course, is not exhaustive, to it can be added the entries discussed in earlier chapters and more entries will be added before the end of this chapter.

In Chapter 1, I suggested that instead of asking, 'Why do girls engage in specific practices?' the question be reversed to ask, 'How do specific practices do girls?' (Flax 2002). So, in the rest of this chapter, I interrogate the sociocultural practices that make such imaginings a central feature of young people's relationships with maths. This is not a new approach. Valerie Walkerdine (1990) argued, before the 'reversal' in gendered patterns of mathematical attainment, that the issue was never about girls' and boys' 'real' performances but the stories we tell about them, the discourses in which they are inscribed and the positions these make available to learners. She warns us to 'avoid getting caught in the empiricist trap in which we are led to attempt to prove the mathematical equivalence of girls' (1990: 135). In order to avoid this trap, I now move to the wider context in which they make meanings. Below I describe three clusters of sociocultural stories. These tell of:

- Enlightenment rationality
- Socially incompetent mathematicians
- Heroic mathematicians

I have selected these because they help to make sense of the patterns of discourses in the talk of the further maths students. They are stories that organize the student stories narrated above, stories that are a part of their conditions of possibility.

Unreasonable women

The binary oppositions that organize the stories in this chapter draw on the gendering of rationality and reason as masculine and irrationality and unreason as feminine. Feminist writers have traced the ways in which this truth has been produced through the history of Western Enlightenment thinking.

The historical analyses of Genevieve Lloyd (1993), Mary-Jayne Fleener (1999) and Anne Oakley (2000), focusing on the fields of philosophy, maths and science respectively, demonstrate science has always been imagined as a gendered project to know and conquer nature. For example:

> The intellectual virtues involved in being a good Baconian scientist are articulated in terms of the right male attitude to the feminine: chastity, respect and restraint. The good scientist is a gallant suitor. Nature is supposed to be treated with the respect appropriate to femininity overlaid with long-standing associations with mystery – an awe however which is strictly contained.
>
> (Lloyd 1993: 17)

So masculine reason's goal was to have control of and power over feminine nature, a goal perhaps prompted by a fear of the Other: chaos, disorder, women. The pattern of oppositions runs:

> Science/Nature
> Order/Disorder
> Masculine/Feminine

Valerie Walkerdine's (1990) work supports these ideas through a detailed examination of the links between the production of the oppositions:

> Reason/Unreason
> Rationality/Irrationality
> Masculinity/Femininity

She traces how the Enlightenment turned its scientific gaze on the human body and produced a 'truth' about women's nature as outside of rationality. Since the gendered body was the basis for explaining the mind, gender is 'internal to, and productive of, the means by which we understand reason' (1990: 68). Women could fail to fit the stereotypes and could resist the power of the truth established by the dominant scientific discourses:

> But the necessity to struggle and the form that struggle took was completely bound up with determining that truth. And because the account was located in women's bodies, it immediately placed them as naturally external to a capacity for reason. It is important not to see this as a distortion or a simple mistake, but as a productive force which had effects.
>
> (Walkerdine 1990: 68–9)

The result of this, 'the way in which femininity is read as a constellation of signs that mark it off as antithetical to "proper" performance to an incredible degree' (1990: 134) is not only evident in teachers', parents' and peers' constructions of young men and women's 'abilities', but also, in young women, like Ling and Rachel's views of themselves.

Certainly rationality is a powerful thing to which to lay claim in contemporary society and maths is an effective way of making such a claim. However, there is another side to the label 'mathematical ability'. Suzanne Damarin (2000: 74) points out that although much work on gender and maths is 'based on the reified idea that mathematical knowledge and skill is a sufficient condition for enhanced power and prestige within Western society ... this is a minority view which is countered every day in the press and other media'.

Geeks and nerds

Within popular culture, the dominant image of mathematicians depicts them as boring, obsessed with the irrelevant, socially incompetent, male and unsuccessfully heterosexual. Even a 'quality' newspaper described the two mathematicians who solved a puzzle, earning a £1,000,000 prize, as posing 'for pictures resplendent in patterned jumpers and sensible haircuts, seem[ing] to typify a certain academic type renowned – to put it diplomatically – more for their fluency with numbers than for their acquaintance with the cutting edge of dance music' (Burkeman 2000). In another typical example from the recently deceased and widely mourned cult television series, *Buffy the Vampire Slayer*, Buffy, Xander and Willow are discussing how straight-laced Giles, the librarian, is. Imagining him as a teenager, Xander comments, 'Giles lived for school. He's still bitter that there were only twelve grades'. Buffy adds, 'He probably sat in math class thinking. "There should be more math! This could be mathier" '. They complete the stereotype by asserting that his diapers were tweed (Batali and DesHotel 2002: 6*).

Such figures are closely related to the computer nerds/hackers, discussed by Deborah Lupton. They:

Are invariably male, usually in their late adolescence or early adulthood ... are typically portrayed as social misfits and spectacularly physically unattractive: wearing thick, unflattering spectacles, overweight, pale, pimply skin, poor fashion sense. Their bodies are soft, not hard from too much physical inactivity and junk food ... According to the mythology, computer nerds turned to computing as an obsession because of their lack of social graces and physical unattractiveness. Due to their isolation from the 'real' world they have become even more cut off from society.

(Lupton 1995: 102)

There is an opposition between the softness of their bodies and the hardness of the maths they do.

These images did play in the words of the young people I talked to. For example, three students are discussing a group of boys in their class whom they label as both 'good at maths' and 'nerds', when AJ asks: 'Do you think socially they're lower?'

Maryam laughs and says, 'yes'. AJ continues, 'because ... they're really fast in maths and everything, but they have no social skills whatsoever'.

Imran agrees, 'It's true. That's true'.

'That's true, actually, I'd rather be like medium stage in maths, and have social skills. I wouldn't want to be like them', concludes Maryam, suggesting that one cannot be good at both maths and social skills. Mathematicians are other here, part of 'them' rather than 'us'.

However, in popular culture, in addition to the other-ing of mathematicians as nerds there is the more flattering other-ing of mathematicians through their idealization as adventurers and as geniuses. These discourses are present in the student stories narrated earlier:

- Peter, Saldon and Graham identify with mathematicians as adventurers. Seeing both mathematicians and themselves as active, dynamic, problem-solvers.
- Ling and Rachel fail to identify as mathematicians, even though they do not think you have to be different to do maths, because their idea of the intuitive, mathematical genius stops them from thinking of themselves as '*really* good at maths'.

I now move on to the popular cultural sources of these versions of mathematicians.

Madmen and geniuses

'The mathematical genius' was at the centre of the recent films, *A Beautiful Mind* (2001), *Enigma* (2001), *Good Will Hunting* (1997) and *Pi* (1998). The plots of these films interweave conventional storylines, for example, of generational change, finding love and espionage and counter-espionage, with narratives that depend on maths. I focus here on two such mathematical storylines each of which is central to three of the films. These are tales of the pursuit of quests for rationality and tales of the costs of pursuing these quests.

In *A Beautiful Mind* and *Enigma*, love stories are central. In both films the main characters start with the social unease of the nerd and end as heterosexual heroes. In *A Beautiful Mind*, based very loosely on Sylvia Nasar's (2001) biography of the mathematician John Nash, our hero conquers his mental illness and wins the Nobel Prize. In *Enigma*, set in Bletchley during World War II, he uses his mathematical skills to triumph over German codes and his action hero skills to triumph over British spies. In both films our hero gets the girl; *Enigma* includes no reference to Alan Turing, the gay real life hero of Bletchley, and *A Beautiful Mind* leaves out John Nash's bisexuality, first family and marital problems. The images they present of mathematicians are flattering. Mathematicians are puzzlers/problem-solvers, active, independent thinkers; they follow their own road and triumph in the end. These are stories of masculinity, of separated rather than connected ways of relating to the world (Gilligan 1993), of the love of a good woman and, above all, of the determined pursuit of a quest.

Quests, notwithstanding Jo Boaler's (1997) appropriation of the word to describe girls' mathematical activity as a 'quest for understanding', are usually masculine enterprises, look at *Lord of the Rings*. In the novel *To the Lighthouse*, Virginia Woolf uses an interesting metaphor for her character Mr Ramsay's philosophical progress. She describes how he uses his 'splendid mind' (Woolf 1994: 57) to range across all the letters from A to Q one by one, but he cannot reach R:

> Qualities that in a desolate expedition across the icy solitudes of the Polar region would have made him the leader, the guide, the counsellor, whose temper, neither sanguine, nor despondent, surveys with equanimity what is to be and faces it, came to his help again. R – ... Feelings that would not have disgraced a leader who, now that the snow has begun to fall and the mountain-top is covered in mist, knows that he must lay himself down and die before morning comes, stole upon him, paling the colour of his eyes, giving him, even in the two minutes of his turn on the terrace, the bleached look of withered old age. Yet he would not die lying down; he would find

some crag of rock, and there, his eyes fixed on the storm, trying to the end to pierce the darkness, he would die standing. He would never reach R.

(1994: 58)

In this passage Woolf connects mental challenges with physical ones and so makes explicit the masculinity of Mr Ramsay's intellectual project. However, Woolf's account is critical and heavily sarcastic. There is a sense here of a boys' own adventure and her writing highlights the linearity of the imagined quest and its futility and narrowness. That the rational thought processes demanded by maths impose restrictions and that these have consequences is another theme of films about mathematicians.

In all four films the central mathematician has mental health problems. In *Good Will Hunting* and *Enigma* the suggestion is that these are only indirectly related to maths, instead being due mainly to experiences of childhood abuse and romantic abandonment. However, in *Pi* and *A Beautiful Mind* the character's madness is directly linked to maths. In both films this connection is made in the way that the process of doing maths is presented as individual, fevered, mysterious and intuitive. In *A Beautiful Mind*, John Nash is shown scribbling formulas on every available surface, in a state that is indistinguishable from his later insanity. His original work on game theory, the only one of his maths results mentioned in the film, is presented as the result of a flash of inspiration brought on in an attempt to maximize his and some fellow mathematicians' chances of 'success' with a group of women they encounter in a bar. The women serve as mute muses in this scene.

The connection between maths and madness is more striking and more disturbing in *Pi*. Mental chaos and instability are conjured through the use of high contrast black and white film, a fast paced dance soundtrack and the rapid intercutting of visual sequences. The main character's unusual and reductive 'philosophy of life' is repeated in voice-over at various points in the film: '1: mathematics is the language of nature; 2: everything around us can be represented and understood through numbers; 3: if you graph the numbers of any system patterns emerge. Therefore there are patterns in nature'. He also repeatedly recounts details of how, as a 6-year-old child, he stared at the sun for a very long time: 'The doctors didn't know whether my eyes would ever heal. I was terrified alone in that darkness. Slowly daylight crept in through the bandages and I could see. But something else had changed inside of me. That day I had my first headache'. He is seen self-medicating, injecting drugs to control his headaches and seizures. The final scene comes immediately after a breakdown and shows him as now unable to do maths and seemingly having found the inner calm denied him while he was mathematically active.

Good Will Hunting initially looks rather different from *Pi* and more like the other two mainstream films. It too is a love story, telling of a socially awkward young man who overcomes his own background of childhood physical abuse and poverty, to find his true love and his true self. However, like *Pi* it is a story of the costs of rationality and of the pain of maths that ends with the central character, Will, abandoning the subject. Although this time leaving behind maths in order to 'go see about a girl' is Will's choice, the logic of the film presents this choice as inevitable because of the nature of maths. It does this through a series of oppositions:

> Mind/Body
> Separation/Connection
> Theory/Experience
> Reading books/Living life

Maths is attached to the first terms in these oppositions and Will's relationship with his girlfriend Skyla is associated with the second terms. At first, Will, who lives the life of the mind absorbed in books, refuses the emotional connection and experience offered by his relationship with Skyla. He lies to her and, when they begin to get close, denies his love for her and ends the relationship. When, through counselling (in a series of vomit-inducing scenes with Sean played by Robin Williams), Will becomes ready for this emotional connection, he abandons maths. The idea that maths requires such separation is reinforced in the film, for example, by the actions of the professional mathematician who takes Will under his tutelage. This man relates to women only as conquests and not as partners. Since Skyla is the only female character who gets to say more than one line in the film, femininity too is associated with bodies, connection, experiencing and living. The film presents these as more valuable ways of being but as ones that exclude maths.

Overall, the stories of mathematicians discussed above help to maintain rationality as masculine and being 'good at maths' as a position that few men and even fewer women can occupy comfortably. They do widen a little the range of behaviours that might be considered to be part of the 'mathematical personality' to include heroism and madness along with social incompetence (a pattern that fits with the recent trend towards 'geek chic' on the small screen, see Winters 2005). However, they persist in constructing the mathematician as masculine and as something you are or are not 'naturally'. Thus they support key features of the nerd stereotype. So while literacy is seen as an essential part of being fully human, 'in contrast to this framing, arithmetic is not naturalized as genetically human, but as *genetically determined within humans*' (Damarin 2000: 76, original emphasis).

Conclusions

In this chapter I have looked at the way that students position themselves as 'good at maths' or 'not good at maths', something that is intimately connected with whether they experience pleasure or pain when doing maths. Peter, Saldon, Graham, Yasser, Ling, Rachel, Desmond and Darren's words illustrate the rarity and complexity of occupying a position as 'good at maths'. They demonstrate that the gendering of maths is not only a matter of teacher and peer stereotyping and discrimination, or of the difficulties of combining a career in maths with the family responsibilities that still disproportionately fall to women. Much more than this, it is about the gendering of maths itself, the gendered phantasies of rationality and of genius, and the ways these work with the construction of masculine and feminine as oppositional categories.

In this chapter I put to use the poststructural approach to gender and 'identity' that I outlined in Chapter 1, showing how students write themselves/are written by competing discourses. Beverley Skeggs (1997: 261) suggests that poststructural approaches 'provide a way of examining structuring absences'. Popular culture is a structuring absence within maths education. Despite a growing recognition of the need to 'ponder the role of school in the "age of desire" … to contemplate the purposes of schooling if the distinctions between advertising and entertainment diminish' (Kenway and Bullen 2001: 7) and to wonder where maths would be in such a scenario, there seems to be a resistance to doing so. I end this chapter by considering reasons for this resistance to the idea that maths is a social practice that is inseparable from the realities and phantasies of the worlds in which we live.

One of the main points I want to make in this book is that we need to get away from the valorization of mathematical reasoning as the ultimate intellectual achievement. And it is helpful to use a psycho-analytic thought experiment to explore the denials and fears contained by this investment in reason. Using this approach the psychic investment is seen to derive from our terror of its Other: 'the loss, the object desired, [which] exists waiting in the wings, in the external reference suppressed in the discourse. The Other of mathematics is uncertainty, irrationality, out of control, madness and so on' (Walkerdine 1988: 199). We need such thought experiments because, as I have shown in this chapter, our current investment in reason is gendered, and to imagine ways that maths might be otherwise, ways that might create more spaces for women, and men, to engage successfully and pleasurably with the subject, we have to see our practice of 'pure mathematics' and our desire for certainty as phantasies based on the exclusion of women (and other Others) and to relax our tight hold on reason. The student stories in this book are perhaps best thought of as examples of such thought experiments.

Summing up, through the stories in this chapter, I have shown that:

- Within the binary system, which structures our words, thoughts and actions, maths is aligned with masculinity.
- The masculinity of maths is maintained through powerful fictions about rationality and genius; these are both historically rooted and active in contemporary culture.
- We need to re-make maths starting by recognizing that it is a social activity, and is negotiated not absolute.

This raises questions about what becomes of students, like those discussed in this chapter, who like the certainty and black and white-ness of maths, those who find safety in numbers. This is a matter that I return to in Chapter 9 when I focus on the pedagogic implications of 'relaxing our tight hold on reason'. Before that, in the next two chapters, I shift from considering the ways maths is gendered as masculine through discourses that associate it with rationality, to considering how it is gendered as masculine through discourses that associate it with high status, and financially lucrative positions in the labour market. I am concerned to trace the impact of these masculine constructions of maths for learners of maths, particularly young women.

chapter / **four**

Proving something to others

Maths teachers and researchers frequently report that students describe the subject as being useful throughout their everyday life but then cannot give any concrete examples of this usefulness. They might mention adding up the bill in the supermarket or checking a bank statement (neither of which I, or I suspect most people, actually do) but can't come up with anything beyond this (for one example of such research see Stanic and Hart 1995). In this and the next chapter I tell stories of seven students whose relationships with maths help to make sense of this apparent contradiction. The four students in this chapter all question the utility of maths in terms of its relationship to 'real' life (as did many of the participants in this study) but are simultaneously *using* maths to prove things about themselves to *others*. They are:

- Simon, who chose maths, in spite of the way its curriculum violates his notions of 'common sense', in order to prove his worth to potential employers.
- James, who also chose maths as a way of securing his future within the labour market.
- Michael, who chose maths because he wants to use its reputation as a hard subject to prove his intelligence to those around him.
- Toni, who chose maths because she wants to be respected as intelligent and to be able to influence others.

The three in the next chapter are all using maths to prove something about who they are to *themselves*.

These stories emphasize the role of human relationships, particularly with friends, family members and teachers, and of emotions in the learning of maths; they illustrate how maths is disconnected from their current lived experience and from their imagined futures; and, through them we can see the ways the phantasy of the absoluteness and objectivity of maths impacts on learners. I pick up on all these themes later in the book. However, what I want to develop here (and in the next chapter) is the idea that choosing maths is one way in which these students do gender, and when this is combined with the gendering of maths as masculine and the social power that attaches to the subject, it is a significant source of inequity.

So, in these stories, I want to look at how maths becomes part of each student's gender identity project. In them I put into practice the approaches to gender identity developed in Chapter 1. What I said there was that identity in general, and gender identity in particular, both play a central role in organizing our experience and are unstable and fragmented. Identities are always stuck in a process of becoming and are never completed; we need to be continually working on them. Gender is a verb not a noun, something that we *do* (and are done by) rather than something that we *are*.

So identities are insecure things and this applies, above all, to masculine identities: 'Masculinity is something that we have to be constantly trying to prove. It isn't anything that we can feel easy or relaxed with because we have to be constantly vigilant and on guard to prove, for instance, we are not "soft" or "sissies"' (Seidler 1997: 39). In this chapter I look at four students' talk about their experiences of maths, viewing these as performances of a masculinity that para-doxically, you can never have *and* you are always afraid of losing. Three of these students are male and one of them female. The central question considered in this chapter and the next is: *How is this threatened loss of masculinity different for women than it is for men?* It is commonly said that the masculinity of maths makes it more difficult for girls and women to choose and succeed at the subject than for boys and men. However, my aim here is to use an unusual approach to imbue this idea with new meanings and understandings so that different responses to it become possible.

Simon's story

Simon's mother is an English housewife. His father arrived in this country 'on a boat' from Hong Kong and then worked in nightclubs. Simon is studying business, geography, IT and maths at Grafton School. Simon's interview was the longest individual interview I did, he appeared very relaxed and discussed all the topics I asked about at length. In this story I look at the way he positions himself as a business-oriented representative of 'common sense' in his views on maths teaching, and his subject choices. I show him performing a masculinity tied to the new vocationalism within the curriculum.

I begin with his views on maths since these mark out clear

differences for him between it and his other subjects. Simon's favourite maths lessons are those where 'you go in there knowing nothing and you go out knowing much more about that' topic. He enjoys the buzz of understanding. His experiences, more than those of any of the other interviewees, resemble those of the girls in Jo Boaler's (1997) study who found their 'quest for understanding' frustrated within procedural maths lessons: 'They wanted to locate the rules and methods within a wider sphere of understanding. Thus they wanted to know *why* the methods worked, *where* they came from and *how* they fitted into the broader mathematical domain' (Boaler 2000: 33, original emphasis). Simon wants, 'to understand like, not just the answer's this because it's this, or *e*'s infinity because of this, whatever yeah. It's better to understand why it is like that. Coz when you understand why it is like that, not just know that it is that, then you can learn easier'.

He links this explicitly to the pace of the lessons, and the way one topic rapidly becomes another and then another. He insists, 'you've gotta make sure that everybody understands yeah, the whole topic yeah, before you move on, because when you move on and people get left behind yeah, I think that's when you start getting problems'.

He has a very clear agenda about how to improve maths teaching and speaks authoritatively about it. His agenda, which is also reminiscent of the girls Jo Boaler interviewed, includes not just a slower pace to lessons but also more participation and connection to real life. This latter point comes out most strongly in his response to my question: 'What do you think other people, not doing maths, think about it?'

'They think to themselves that it's a really boring, pointless subject ... But to be honest you won't never use it in your life, like if you're gonna be an accountant after maths, you might do a bit of maths but it's not gonna be nothing near the stuff, like there's a lot of pointless stuff ... I reckon people view ... maths being really difficult. And that's why they think it's boring, because they don't understand it. That's why they've got a lot of bad experiences because the teacher just said '3 + 3 = 6' and that's it ... and "the sum of the triangle", I mean "Pythagoras" theorem is a plus b equals c squared. And they, they just don't know why, why you're doing that. You know what I mean? Does it work in real life, have you checked it out or got a real life example? Have you got a triangle that you've actually measured and that you can tell that it's actually right? ... You could be lying. Coz generally a lot of what the maths teacher says you don't understand anyway, so they could just go on and on yeah something that's completely lies, and they will think to themselves it's maths, "obviously I don't understand it coz it's hard".'

Simon clearly wants many shifts in maths teaching including a move to a more democratic classroom in which students can challenge teachers. The changes he wants to make suggest that he sees mathematical truths as less absolute than most people do. However, this is complicated by his belief that discussion does not work in maths, because, 'well you do the discussion, but if you know the answer you know the answer, and then there's nothing to discuss'. He feels this even though he finds discussion in other subjects useful, as he puts it 'when you're talking with someone else you get ideas so it's better'. So for Simon, introducing real life and 'common sense' into maths classrooms will displace the power and authority of the teacher but not of the maths itself.

Simon feels there are fundamental things that mark out maths from other forms of knowledge and so affect the way it is best communicated. Looking in more detail at the way he talks about these differences, he describes geography as 'not really a hard intellectual subject', while of business, he says: 'It's not that much, it's not that really demanding, I think, I think maths is more really demanding. It's more, you can either get it right or wrong, but in other subjects, it's more of a grey area, you know what I mean ... [Business] is not something that can be put in a textbook, I don't think. You couldn't teach someone how to be a good businessman'. He connects studying geography and business, the subject that he enjoys the most and his intended career, to the kind of person he is. With geography, 'it's the way that I think, it's really straightforward ... because it's more like real life'. While business is like law, which he wishes he had taken, because 'I can understand that stuff ... I understand why it's gotta be there and why, I don't know, I just find it's interesting and I just wanna know about it'. It is clear from his interview that it is what Simon reads as the 'common sense' aspects of business and geography (and law) that enable him to identify with them, and it is their absence from maths that prevents him from identifying with it.

The tenuous nature of his affiliation with maths is evident in the extrinsic motivation for his choice of the subject: 'I chose maths because I think it sounds good when you say you're doing maths. And also because it's, it's the most challenging subject ... that and physics I reckon, and chemistry. They're like the most challenging subjects and, [he pauses] generally if you can do something like that you are an intelligent person ... Also because in maths, when you're applying for jobs, if you say you got maths, they always automatically assume that your common sense is good and that you're generally smart. Not just that you know how to work out an equation or whatever. They generally think you're smart and they think you're hard working coz they know that maths is a hard subject. So I thought that, in terms of getting a job, that it would be a good idea to take it.'

Simon constructs himself as a doer rather than a thinker; someone concerned with the concrete rather than the abstract. He fits a pattern identified by Mairtin Mac an Ghaill (1994: 63), in his study of masculinities and schooling, that he named the 'New Enterprisers': 'Working within the new vocationalist skilling regimes of high-status technological and commercial subject areas, the New Enterprise students were negotiating a new mode of school student masculinity with its values of rationality, instrumentalism, forward planning and careerism'. It is interesting how Simon works geography and maths, both traditional academic disciplines, into his story. In the case of geography, Simon sees it as vocational, pretty much on the same terms as business or IT. I think this is due to the very dynamic and practical way it is taught at Grafton. However, with maths, something that Simon clearly sees as disconnected from real life, it is the earning power in the labour marketplace that he will get by succeeding at it that enables him to tie it to his view of himself. This pattern of the discourse of the possibility of economic empowerment through studying maths, overriding discourses of maths as irrelevant and uninspiring, recurs in a slightly different form in James' story.

James' story

James is in the second year of his postcompulsory education at Grafton. He is repeating his maths AS level and is also in the second year of his A levels in physics and sports studies. This year he has supplemented his original subject choices with a fourth subject, performing arts. James is white. His mother is a housewife and his father a fire engineer. From his interview it seems that James takes a highly pragmatic approach to life. The centrality of this to his identity is apparent in his answer to my question: 'What do you think other people who are not doing maths think about the subject?'

'Yeah, a lot of people ask me, um, like, "Oh what A levels are you doing?" and I sort of say maths and physics and they go, "Ooh, tough" sort of thing ... "You must be clever" sort of thing. So I mean I think there's a general consensus that it's very hard. But I don't actually think it's that hard. I mean it's just, if you listen, take the notes and just make sure you learn everything and revise a lot, I mean it's not that hard. And I think that's the same for most subjects, as long as you listen, do the work and revise, then, then you can probably do any subject'. Here he describes other people's views of maths as being very different from his own; he rejects an academic identity based on being clever in favour of one founded on working hard. (The contrast with the performance of 'effortless achievement' in Graham's story in Chapter 3 is very striking.) There is no mystery to doing well at maths for James. It is just a matter of applying yourself, something he demonstrated in his GCSE approach. This consisted of getting the notes in class and then working through past papers, 'I mean I had a folder like that fat basically of past papers', he is holding his hands horizontal, one above the other and separated by about ten centimetres as he says this, 'of every question that had ever come up sort of thing and I just gone through every single one'.

James' pragmatic approach is very different from the 'laddish' behaviour that researchers (for example, Epstein 1998; Francis 2000; Jackson 2002, 2003) have found in their studies of compulsory schooling. Within this boys' anti-school culture, hard work, far from being extolled as a virtue, is equated with effeminacy. Status is gained through a range of competitive and aggressive behaviours tied to sport, particularly football, and disruptive behaviour; a studious identity becomes a difficult one for a boy to occupy, carrying with it the risk of being labelled as a 'boffin', as 'gay' or as a 'girl'. The only acceptable way for a boy to succeed is through 'effortless achievement' (Mac an Ghaill 1994: 67). However, Mairtin Mac an Ghaill also found a small group of boys, whom he labelled the 'Academic Achievers', who had a 'positive orientation to the academic curriculum' (1994: 59). They were 'in the process of equipping themselves for social mobility and a middle-class post-school destination' (1994: 62) based on a traditional working class work ethic.

Moreover, the work on masculinities in post-16 education suggests that such positions become more secure for boys who continue beyond compulsory education. The move into sixth form 'marks a key cultural transition that involves young people in new social relations (in particular those of the labour market) and requires new forms of identity to handle them' (Redman and Mac an Ghaill 1997: 169). Sally Power and her colleagues (1998: 143) also relate this to an evolution in the lived relationship between school and work: 'it may be that, at this level, as career aspirations begin to take on more substance and significance, "hard work" is an acceptably masculine attribute because it becomes more closely connected to entry to male professional status'. Bob Connell (1989: 295) explicitly connects this shift to the way power operates within society, since hegemonic masculinity, the type of masculinity that is the repository of social and economic power, is not aggressive, anti-institutional and macho, but is tied to rationality and technical/scientific knowledge. Technical expertise is central to advanced capitalism, and men, through 'the mechanism of academic credentials' (Connell 1989: 296), can invest time and accept a subordinate position within training, in return for a secure employment future.

I think that James's investment in technical rationality and achieving qualifications is apparent in his commitment to hard work. It also helps to explain his preference for 'traditional' chalk and talk methods of teaching, when 'we talk about a topic and then the teacher does, works through an example on it, and then you've got a worked example that you can apply to every other question, sort of thing. I like that'. And for learning individually: 'I always work by myself. I mean if I'm stuck I talk to someone else, and then and talk through it, and, but generally I just work on my own. I find it easier that way'. For James, 'the central themes of masculinity here are rationality and responsibility rather than pride and aggressiveness' (Connell 1989: 297). Bob Connell's (1989: 1995) work suggests that this is the default position for middle class boys who construct their life course through their family's relationship to the educational system (work, such as Plummer 2000; Walkerdine et al. 2001, demonstrates that these class differences also apply to girls). However, such an identity is less secure for working class pretenders, such as James, than it is for the middle class boys who inhabit it. This perhaps explains why his investment in rationality and qualifications translates into subject choices based on instrumentalism rather than enjoyment. I conclude my story of James by looking at these in greater detail.

Academic subjects, except perhaps for sports studies, do not seem to be a source of pleasure for James. When asked for a maths topic, lesson or anything that he has enjoyed this year, he selects, after a long pause and a prompt from me, that morning's lesson, because 'it's just that everything seemed to click, I seemed to remember everything and it all just went really well'. Subjects seem to be almost entirely a means to an end for James. This is clearly demonstrated in the explanation he gives for his decision to take physics and maths: 'My form tutor basically said to me a good A level to take would be physics. It's really hard but . . . if I come out of it and I pass, I would think that like I worked really hard to get that pass coz it's so hard. So he said it's quite rewarding, so I thought 'OK'. But he said it would be wise to take maths with physics because there's so much overlap and it would be, it would just be very helpful'.

As a result of this James had to drop the more vocational media studies in favour of the more academic maths since they clashed. When I ask him how he felt about leaving media studies, he recalls: 'I was happy in the subject but I was looking at more in the long run, as in I'm not interested in the media either anything like that, so I thought maths. And maths is more sort of, you can apply it to more than you can with media. Maths is sort of used everywhere like sort of thing, whereas media is really specific. I thought maths it's more of a benefit in the long run.'

Although James speaks of maths being more applicable and widely used than media studies, he combines this with a strong dislike of questions that require him to apply his knowledge in 'realistic' contexts. This is part of his explanation as to why he prefers maths to physics: 'I don't like the real life situations coz it clouds your judgement. You think about irrelevant things and you, you're talking about bridges and whatever. Clouds, clouds your brain really and you can't really think. Whereas maths you just', he pauses, 'do maths'. This could represent a rejection of the very contrived nature of what passes for a 'realistic' context in examinations (Boaler 1994; see the examples in: Cooper and Dunne 2000; Verschaffel 2002). However, his interview does not contain any criticism of this, simply a statement that 'they'll relate it to a real life situation', while his use of phrases like 'physics they'll give you a shape, but indirectly' and it 'clouds your brain' lead me to think it more likely that he dislikes the way these contexts make it more difficult for him to recognize the specific piece of technical knowledge being tested. So I think his reference to the wider applicability of maths than media studies indicates the way that maths can guarantee access to a wider range of careers, rather than a sense that he will have greater opportunity later in life to use the actual mathematical skills he is studying. This orientation around the future even affects his selection of sports studies as his favourite subject, because 'that's obviously what I want to do most, so that's what's my favourite'.

James has built a masculine identity project around considerations of what is 'more of a benefit in the long run' and around his participation in the traditional goals of schooling, working hard and following an academic trajectory. However, this is a path that, as mentioned earlier, is far from a perfect fit; maths did not work out for James the first time around and in fact he did not return to Grafton after the summer holidays, having found himself a job with training. The way in which working class boys and girls attempting complicity with the goals of a middle class educational system often experience failure is also a theme of Michael's story.

Michael's story

Michael, a working class African-Caribbean Grafton student, is studying for AS levels in geography, IT and maths, as well as re-sitting his GCSE in English in order to improve his grade D. Michael has struggled with maths this year and plans to repeat the AS level course next year rather than progress to the A2 modules. He has had problems making the step up from GCSE (where he got an intermediate grade C) to AS level. He highlights particular problems with the pace of the work, the amount of material that has to be memorized and with negotiating the variety of methods available for tackling each problem. When I ask him what he has enjoyed least about maths this year he says, 'only just loads of writing and equations and having to remember most of it and copy it'. Here, as elsewhere in the interview and in my classroom interactions with Michael, I get a strong sense of how frustrating Michael has often found the process of learning maths. This is a frustration that he nicely captures in his explanation of the connection between 'learning what' and 'understanding why' in maths: 'you have to learn what you're doing before you can understand it, but if you learn it and don't understand it there's no point, so it's just a catch-22'.

He has very different feelings towards maths than towards geography and IT, differences that illuminate the nature of his identification with maths. For Michael, geography and IT relate more directly to his experience of everyday life, there is 'just more thinking about normal situations than with maths ... But maths, more', he pauses, 'it depends what you're going into after school with maths, but when you're actually doing it you don't think you're going to need it further on. So that's why, it's just different'. I ask if this makes maths more difficult or less interesting. Michael opts for the latter, seeing the disconnection of maths from everyday life as very demotivating, 'it's probably just that that makes you lose your interest and, which makes you wanna just give up and stop working'. Another difference that Michael raises in his interview relates to why he chose these subjects. While he speaks of enjoying geography and IT, his motivation for selecting maths is more extrinsic: 'It's coz GCSE, throughout all of my lessons I was on the C/D borderline so I had to work hard to get my Cs and I thought if I could do A levels, like I could even prove more that yeah I've done maths, something that's really hard and no one likes doing, and passed it, so it would be like I've achieved something. And it hasn't happened, but at least I tried, I know I have tried, so it's not that bad'. So, while Michael speaks of enjoying the challenge of doing maths, this is very different from enjoying doing maths.

This is clear when I ask: 'So did you prefer doing GCSE or do you prefer doing A level?'

Michael pauses before replying, 'Probably A level coz it's much more of a challenge. Although that's a problem, the challenge can be too great and you fall behind, like in the other class [the original class before the setting was introduced] that's what happened to me so. It's just a good challenge, that's why I chose it, I thought it would look good first, in my CV, or anything to have A level maths, and also it'd be a challenge to prove everyone wrong'. Certain aspects of Michael's identification with maths are apparent in this answer. He is aware that maths has a reputation as a difficult subject and it is this that leads him to identify it as a challenge; he is using this status of maths as 'hard' as a way of gaining personal power, providing him with the external validation of his 'ability' that he needs to prove wrong those who do not believe in him (this hard/easy opposition is hetero/sexualized, gendered and classed, see Chapter 7). Thus it is the societal valuation of maths that makes an A level in the subject the object of Michael's desire. It will enable him to prove himself. When I ask for whom this proof is required, he says 'everyone' and then elaborates, 'most of the time some of the teachers, some of my friends, coz some of them think you know I'm not too bright at some subjects', and 'even my parents sometimes just to say I've tried, well I've tried it. Just showing that you can have tried something, even though I haven't done it I've tried and know, you see, I can try something else'.

'Is the omission of yourself from the list of people to whom you are proving yourself significant? Are you also proving anything to yourself?'

'Yeah, I am proving it to myself, as [Michael pauses] I'm trying to build up myself more, but, sometimes I think I have to prove it to myself, but sometimes I know say, "yes, I may not be good at it but I know what I know". But people don't know what I know, so it's to really, it's like, um, if you know it all in your mind and you don't have the [he pauses] GCSEs and A levels then people don't think you are that bright, so it's really having it down on paper that counts so that's what I was trying to prove to them. And once again it didn't work.'

These passages conjure up an image of Michael against the world. Competition, as Vic Seidler (1997: 173) points out, is a central part of many masculinity projects: 'The competitive institutions of advanced capitalist societies mean that men are locked into competitive relationships with each other. Often we can only feel good about ourselves at the expense of other men'. However, the deep way in which Michael internalizes other people's views of himself, transforming them into action, is perhaps also a response to his experience of racism and the objectification and othering that are a part of racism's psychic assault on black people (Fanon 1986).

In what follows I break Michael's struggle down into three aspects, highlighting the identity work that he does through each. First, Michael constructs himself as aware that he is not academically brilliant but that he is confident and comfortable with his own understanding and 'ability'. This sense of 'knowing his place' surfaces when I ask how he felt about the 'ability' setting that took place at the start of the year: 'I can understand why they split us up in the first place. Because, um, they either work at a different pace to us or not or try more challenging, because they got higher grades … it's really common sense really to have the brighter people doing much harder work than us, even though we are going for the same thing, if we're doing different methods then we'll probably get the same, so it's really no biggy to me'.

However, beneath the happy contentment that Michael expresses here there lurks a quiet resignation. This resignation is clearer in this next statement where he reflects on his future: 'I was hoping to go on to university but that looks like a grim outlook right now. So I'll probably just start working.'

Second, there is a gap between his and other people's views of him. Michael believes strongly that he is better academically than all his significant others – friends, family, teachers – think he is. We can see this in his transformation of the question, 'What do other people not doing maths think of the subject?' into, 'What do they think of you for doing the subject?'

He replies, 'They think it's one of the most difficult lessons that you can do in A level and what makes it worse is that when they hear what I got in GCSE, they go "oh you're mad for doing it coz it's so hard". So people's impressions of maths A level is just, a subject you don't wanna take coz it's so hard'. The way he personalizes the issue of the public image of maths demonstrates how important it is to his self-construction. Finally, he has a passionate desire to gain the kind of external validation necessary for other people to see Michael as he sees himself.

There seems to be an odd combination of success and failure within Michael's account of his mathematical career. There is a sense that his scheme for proving himself, based on doing well in A level maths has failed, but that, despite this, it does not affect what he knows about himself, and also that it was being brave enough to try that really mattered. However, his conflation of examination success with 'ability', his morphing of people with 'higher grades' into 'brighter people', quoted above, suggests how difficult it is for people like Michael who accept the terms of the conventional schooling project, along with its definitions of success and failure, to maintain confidence in themselves when, in those terms, they fail. It is in stories like Michael's that the structural failure of schooling to meet the needs of working class and African-Caribbean boys is individualized; the political is made personal.

Toni's story

The final story in this chapter is Toni's. Although she is female, her relationship with maths has much in common with those of Simon, James and Michael. In this story I look at this and then consider the impact of her being female on this pattern of identifications. First I discuss how she labels herself. Before we start the formal interview, while we are waiting for her Sunnydale College classmates to leave the room, Toni considers the different names that she can take on within my research writing, but without coming to any conclusions. She would ideally like the name of a Black female scientist or doctor. It is awful that I cannot think of any. Instead I have settled on Toni after the Nobel prize-winning African-American writer and feminist, Toni Morrison. Attaching a label to her ethnicity is also complicated and involves much discussion. She ponders my question thus: 'Me? Well, well, well'.

'She is [a] mixture of every country in the world', explains Natasha, her Nigerian classmate, who is also a participant in the interview.

Toni was 'born here. But then I moved to America when I was like 5. So I came back in June and my mum is from Africa, in Gambia. My dad is half Jamaican. So I don't know what to really call myself. And my mum is half Nigerian and half Gambian. So it's all kind of mixed up. But I was born here so I guess I'll just call myself a British'.

After a short discussion I suggest, 'Mixed heritage?'

Toni sounds pleased: 'There you go. All right there you go. It's really mixed'. Mixed heritage young people like Toni are often unhappy with a simple classification as black (Alibhai-Brown 2001).

Toni lives with her aunty, her brother and her sister. Her father died nine years ago and her mother is a flight attendant. 'My mum comes like always. She was just here like last, last two weeks or so. She always comes and go[es] anyway. Always flying'.

Toni is studying for AS levels in biology, chemistry, maths and science for public understanding. She explains to me that she took this last one because: 'It's just the key skills I guess'. The other three, of which biology is her favourite because 'it deals with cells and you know the human body and all them things', were chosen because of her desire to be a doctor, 'I just like curing people you know' and 'prescribing things, you know. Telling them: "take this and you'll feel better!"'

'Yeah, she does that all the time', agrees Natasha.

'Basically I just wanna be the person that knows everything. Like when you're sick yeah, I wanna be the one to tell you that, "OK take this thing yeah and when you take it you'll feel better and stuff". I just like, just helping people I guess ... Just helping people, that's what I want to do. And I like working with kids also'. Toni mentions several reasons for wanting to be a doctor in this passage, but her desire to control others seems to be the central one (the more traditional feminine roles of helping others and caring for children seem to be afterthoughts). She wants the status, respect and influence that come with medical qualifications. The presence of these motivations in her relationship with maths led me to include her among the students who chose the subject to prove something to others rather than among those who selected it for career purposes (although I am aware that my clean cut categories of Chapter 2 are dissolving into a mess of complex and contradictory motivations). I now look at this relationship.

Toni has little to say about a typical maths lesson, she mentions only the length of the lesson and the grades that she got: 'It was great. Besides the timing was really short. I mean it was really quick. You know that was the only thing. But it was all right. I mean I had good grades anyway so, I was OK'. One way in which Toni uses maths to position herself as powerful is through obtaining good grades. She displays a strong orientation around getting the qualifications necessary for her future plans. This is the reason that she gives for studying in England rather than in America: 'When you have like your, um, degree or certificate that you get for taking your AS, it's really good when you go back to America because you can easily get a university ... That's why I'm here'. Just a few weeks into her AS levels, she already knows the grades that she needs to secure a place in her chosen course at her chosen university.

However, it is not just the good grades that Toni gets that enable her to use maths to feel powerful. She is also using the status of maths as a signifier of intelligence. This is most obvious in the discussion of what other people, not doing maths, think of the subject: 'They think maths is so hard. And whoever's doing maths is so brainy. That's what everybody thinks'.

We then go on to talk about subject stereotypes more generally and I ask, 'Where do you think they come from?'

'Experience', suggests Natasha.

'Some of them don't even come from experience', says Toni. 'I think they come from when people, OK someone like me I'll go and I'll be, "I want to be so smart" or, "I want them to think that I'm so smart" and I'll go, "Oh my god, maths was so hard! You should see, look at this x, x, x". Just to make them think that I'm so smart you know. And then they'll be like "oh my god she's smart!" You know, something like that'.

As with the other students in this chapter, Toni's recognition of the power of maths is coupled with scepticism about the subject's utility. In the interview she asks: 'What's the use of maths?' She explains, 'when you graduate or when you get a job, nobody's gonna come into your office and tell you, "can [you] solve x square minus" you know ... it really doesn't make sense to me. I mean it's good we're doing it. It helps you to like crack your brain, think more and you know, and all those things. But like, nobody comes [to] see you and say, "can [you] solve this?" The basic things I think you have to know about maths is like [she pauses].'

'You have to calculate and stuff', interrupts Natasha.

'Yeah, and subtract, divide'.

'That's why they provide calculators'.

'Yes. Exactly. So why do we have to go to all this? What was we doing today?'

'Differentiation'.

'Differentiation: $x \, dx$. What's all this? I mean really, come on. I just don't, I don't know, I don't see the use of it ... It helps you to think definitely, but apart from that.'

The account above demonstrates that Toni's identifications with maths have many similarities with those of Michael, James and Simon. I have read all these students' stories as evidence that they are using maths to do masculinity, where masculinity is understood as something that is simultaneously desired and unattainable. However, this is something with which I have more difficulties and discomforts in Toni's case because she 'is' female. In order to make sense of how masculine performances are affected by living on the female side of the gender divide I borrow the term 'gender category maintenance work' from Bronwyn Davies (1989: 29).

Davies (1989: 29) devised this concept to make sense of children's actions, including 'what adults often see as incomprehensible nastiness on the part of small children', to maintain the categories of male and female against deviancy and to confirm the social competence of those doing it. She explains their thought processes running:

> I may feel sorry for you, I may even have a fascination with the way you are doing your masculinity [or femininity], but my aggression is essential in defining what you do as a transgression and clarifying for myself that I have got it right. One might say that the "deviants" are necessary for making stronger boundaries. Thus deviation does not change the category, but is used as an opportunity to shore the category up.

My use here is a little different from (but in the spirit of) Davies's in that I apply the term to adults' (as well as to children's) behaviours and think of it as applying to the policing of one's own actions as well as to those of others.

For example, there is evidence that people who make non-gender traditional subject choices, in general, have more conservative views on other aspects of gender roles (Thomas 1990; Whitehead 1996). It is as if their gender category maintenance work demands such conformity to compensate for their 'transgressions' in the area of subject choice. In the rest of Toni's story, I want to consider how she compensates for the gender transgression of doing maths and so to explore the tensions between doing masculinity and 'being' female. I do this by looking at her contradictory experiences of femininity.

Although Natasha's experiences in male dominated sports studies give her a unique take on the effects of the gendered patterns of subject choice, Toni has more to say about gender when I broaden the issue out and ask, 'Is there any other ways in which being female affects your life apart from the ones you've told me?'

'No, not really. I love being female. I love being me', says Natasha.

'Sometimes I wish that I was a boy', begins Toni, 'Coz you know why? Boys are really easy going. They, like basically I say that because like, girls are really, they take too much time first off, like making their nails doing their hair ... Like for example, if I was going to a party tonight, I would've been planning it since last week or even last month talking about, "Oh what dress shall I buy? You know that silver one?" Or talking about "Oh my nails, my hair". You know, boys just cut their hair, take some trousers, any kind of trousers, some nice shirt, it don't even have to be nice, some full shoes, and they are gone. Nothing else. Nothing else. But us it's just too much work, sometimes.'

Natasha provides another example, 'When my aunt was doing my hair', her uncle said, ' "God you spend too much time doing that, why can't you just like, just pull your hair in a bunch?" and she was going like, "Well you've got to look good" and he was like, "Well, what's the point?" '

'If you think about it', begins Toni, 'there's no point to it, because like, OK you just want to feel good, you know. But it's not like you coming to school to attract anybody. So somehow it doesn't make any sense, you taking your time dressing, but you know, trying to look good. But in some other way, you're trying to just feel good about yourself. So it's really different. It's two different things. People dress for boys, some girls, and some girls just dress because they feel like dressing that way and some people just wanna look good. But some people say, "Oh she ain't got no money" or something like that, "she's poor" or something.'

Toni describes the huge amount of time she devotes daily simply to getting ready for college. She finds this draining and questions its necessity but feels obliged to continue. This is reminiscent of the white working class female college students in Beverley Skeggs's (1997) research, who found their physical presentation constrained by the powerful notion of 'respectability'. Skeggs (1997: 4, original emphasis) describes how:

> They operate with a dialogic form of recognition: they recognize the recognitions of others. Recognitions do not occur without value judgements of real and imaginary others. Recognition of how one is positioned is central to the *processes* of subjective construction.

Along with one of the women in Skeggs's study, Toni evokes 'a sense of being caught up in something which is beyond her control'. Perhaps, as Skeggs suggests, the risks of getting out are too great, hazarding 'cultural stigmatizations in her local situation; a challenge to all her friends who collude in femininity; a sign of difference' (1997: 102).

In this discussion we see that, while being masculine carries an appeal for Toni, she is also, and understandably, heavily invested in producing herself as female, both in her own eyes and in other people's. In order to do this she draws on the discursive practices that produce people as masculine or feminine. The tension in these passages between wanting to dress recklessly like a man and wanting to be recognized through her dress as a woman, suggest that we could understand there being similar tensions contained in her desire, discussed earlier, for masculine control and mathematical success within education and employment and her desire to be recognized through her actions in these fields as a woman. Thus, while Toni's desire for and envy of masculinity are tangible, there are conflicts with the demands placed on her to maintain her position within the category 'woman'. Among other things these tensions and conflicts make it more difficult for her to consistently and comfortably inhabit a position as mathematically successful. I continue my exploration of the tensions that are experienced by young women studying maths in the next chapter but first I draw some preliminary conclusions.

Conclusions

Simon, James, Michael and Toni show us how they negotiate their educational choices, using the available discourses on maths and other subjects to construct identities, so as to feel powerful. For these young people (and the others in this group: Mika, Jean, Lee and AJ, see Table 2.4) maths is a powerful choice because its social construction allows it to function in their identity projects as a way of proving their 'abilities' to a range of others, from friends to future employers. This raises three questions:

- Why is maths a more powerful proof of 'ability' than other subjects?
- How is this need to assert one's intellect and forge a high status employment trajectory gendered?
- And, what are the implications for maths teaching and learning?

Below I look at the first two, while I address the final question later in Part 3.

Taking a poststructural approach, the power of maths as a subject and hence its authority in saying something about oneself, is not something fixed and natural but is a contingent product of the discourses through which it is constituted. These discourses produce it as objective, absolute, abstract, hard, a means of controlling our environment and an essential prerequisite for entry into the economically lucrative fields of science and technology. This builds on the idea I introduced in Chapters 1 and 3 that maths, through oppositional discourses that associate it with pure rationality, social incompetence, challenges and heroic quests, is gendered as masculine. This, together with the discourses that relate maths to wage earning potential (McGavin 1999) and the continued gendering of participation in paid labour in contemporary society (Witz 1997), help to explain why this group of students is male dominated.

However, such ideas can tend towards oppositional Mars/Venus versions of gender or to the idea that gender is natural and part of the essence of a person. Both of which I am keen to avoid. Returning to earlier ideas, we can do this by seeing gender as a social practice rather than as an individual trait. Gender is about doing not being. These students' behaviours are gendered because different contexts elicit different behaviours. Since men and women are exposed to a different set of contexts, the system becomes self-perpetuating (Bohan 1997). Both boys' and girls' subject choices represent attempts by young people to occupy powerful positions, but their gender identity projects make available different ways of being powerful. As Nazima persuasively puts it:

> This is also what I think it is. When you study English, right, you somehow have power [pause] you do. And I think, a lot of girls [laughs] I'm sounding really feminist here aren't I? I think a lot of girls tend to have, like power, coz when you, when you know English you have power over virtually anything, even boys, men. Like when I, when I do English now I say things to boys and they're like [whispered] 'What's she talking about?' ... So it's power, I mean English gives you more power in stuff like that, whereas technology just gives you the brains to do this and to do that. It's not that girls aren't interested in money we are, but we just like the power side of everything.

Moreover, while this group of maths students is male dominated, it does include both girls and boys. In Chapter 1, I outlined how I am using masculinity and femininity in a relational way borrowed from Bob Connell (1987, 1995). So masculinity and femininity are viewed as configurations of practice within a gender regime. Certainly constructions of masculinity and femininity are tied to the reproductive arena via an entrenched system of binary thinking; but this can be subverted by a fluid understanding of gender. Instead of dichotomies we have continua; instead of distinctions we have overlaps. We can find masculinity in the actions of girls and women, like Toni, just as we can find femininity in the actions of boys and men. For example, there are:

- Simon's 'quest for understanding'
- James' conscientious and hard-working approach
- Michael's sensitive internalization of other people's views of him

All of these are characteristics usually labelled as feminine. The stories here (and those in Chapters 3 and 5) also provide evidence for the ways class, race/ethnicity and dis/ability intersect with gender. This too suggests that a binary model of gender difference is of little use in understanding the complexity of social life and raises questions about what is made visible and what invisible when we work within such a model.

Summing up, through the stories in this chapter I have shown that:

- All of these students, male and female, are using the social power of maths as a way of doing masculinity.
- Access to the different available masculine and feminine subject positions, while complex, remains highly dependent on a person's assigned gender.

Through Toni's story I asked questions about the tensions this creates for girls and women doing maths. It is my aim in telling the stories in the next chapter to develop answers to these questions.

chapter five

Proving something to themselves

In the last chapter, I introduced the idea that doing something like maths, which is constructed as masculine, in a body which is constructed as feminine, creates tensions for girls and women and that these tensions then make it more difficult for them (than for male learners) to succeed at and to enjoy the subject. In this chapter, I develop this idea by looking at how these tensions play out in the relationships that three young women have with maths. The young women whose stories I tell in this chapter are, like Simon, James, Michael and Toni in the last chapter, using maths as a proof of their 'abilities'. However, there is an important difference here. These three make up the small group of students in my study who chose maths because they wanted, through success in it, to prove to *themselves* something about who they are and what they can do. They are:

- Julie, who chose maths because it is the one subject that provides her with the challenge she wants now and with the possibilities that she wants for the future.
- Lucy, who chose maths because she wants to prove to herself that she can do this hard subject, but then found that she enjoys it.
- Claudia, who chose maths because she always wants to do the hardest thing possible and she likes the feelings of power she gets when doing maths.

Interestingly, all three students associate feelings of both pleasure and pain with maths. This is in contrast with the stories of Simon, James, Michael and Toni, which contain much about the pain of doing maths and not much about the pleasure that it can bring, something that they share with the maths education literature generally. Tamara Bibby (2001: 67–8) asks: 'What picture of mathematics does pleasure develop? How does it shape those "rational" bits?' These are questions that are interesting to keep in mind during these stories.

Julie's story

Julie is a white working class girl who is studying art, geography and psychology alongside maths. Although she stayed at Grafton in the transition from compulsory to postcompulsory schooling, she found this process difficult: 'I got really stressed out and cried a couple of times ... I was just going mad', but now 'it's not so bad'. Julie was one of the five students, mentioned in Chapter 3, identifying as 'good at maths'; she is the only girl in this group. This identification happens in her account of why she chose maths: 'It wasn't anyone pressurizing me, I just in my, in myself, I knew that if there was any lesson that I'd take that was gonna, that was gonna give me like maybe a better chance in the future and that I was quite good at, it was maths ... I don't know, I just, it's a challenging subject without being boring I think.'

However, Julie's self-positioning as 'good at maths' is not consistently maintained. This becomes clear at the start of the interview when she responds to my request to, 'just describe a typical maths lesson, what you do in it, how you feel' with laughter. 'Why's it funny?' I ask.

'Because like there's three people in our class [Salvador, Zia and Jane] that are really, really clever, and even though I feel like I shouldn't be in that class I should be in another class, coz like, the work's quite difficult anyway and then, when they get it really quickly and it's, I dunno.' She knows that, going on her grades, she should be in the 'top' set but still says that she feels that she does not belong there. As with Ling and Rachel (see Chapter 3), despite claiming to be 'quite good at maths', the myth of mathematical genius prevents Julie from thinking that she is '*really* good at maths'.

This could be why, although Julie enjoys doing maths, she also finds that, 'sometimes I really don't want to go to a maths lesson'.

'How do you cope with that?' I ask. 'That's quite interesting.'

'Um, I make myself go, I think it's because like a Tuesday morning I have to get up really early anyway. It's just the thought of having to go in, and sit in, the first two hours of maths go really slow, and [Julie pauses] especially if you don't understand something, you get really frustrated. But I usually, I usually walk out of maths feeling a bit better, and usually smiling, "oh I understand that". But then when I get home again it's a bit like, "Oops!"'

Julie lacks confidence in her maths 'abilities'. This is also apparent in her reliance on other people's, rather than on her own, judgements of these 'abilities'. For example, when she got a grade E in her first module she was visibly upset. 'A lot of people noticed, going, "Are you alright?" and I was like, "No, not really," "Why?" "Coz I got an E"'. Julie needed external validation to help her cope with her mark of 48 percent: 'I was quite upset coz I thought I did OK on the paper. But the thing is the last question which was 12 marks, I didn't do coz I didn't get to it so I basically lost 20 percent, and me and Salvador were talking about it and that means that I got most of the paper that I did answer right . . . I got about 90 percent of what I did answer right, which really gutted me because if I'd done that question I wouldn't be on an E'. Salvador, acknowledged by his peers and teachers as the best maths student in the year, seems to fill the role of an authority on maths exams for Julie. In the rest of this story I am going to explore the ways that Julie's lack of confidence is gendered.

When asked about the difference that being female makes to her life, Julie chooses to talk about the intimacy of her friendships with other girls: 'I think emotionally girls are probably a lot more, they're better off because they can talk to their, like it's easier for us, to say talk about sex with our friends openly. Coz like me and my friends are really open with anything we have to say. Maybe with boys, they wouldn't be able to admit it if like they were still a virgin, they'd get bullied, or they'd get stick for it, whereas a girl wouldn't. It would be like, "oh well that's your decision". And I think . . . that's why a lot of men turn out the way they do like butch and masculine, coz they can't show any emotion, coz then they look like a girl.' This answer suggests an open communication with her friends that Julie really values.

So it is not surprising that Julie takes 'other people' to refer to her friends when I ask: 'What do you think other people who are not doing maths think about the subject?'

'They think I'm stupid, for doing it. Because it's really hard', she begins. Typically she is clear that her friends think maths is 'really hard'. However, before this, her first instinct is to personalize the question and to see it as being about what people think of her. Julie continues, 'and a lot of the people I know didn't do as well in their, the people that I know that did well are in the maths class, so it's, kind of like the people that I do talk to, they'll say, "Oh, why did you take maths? I think you're really silly". Or if they look at [your work they] say, "What the hell is that?" and, "That's too complicated for me, why did you take it?" But I, um, I used to say, "I don't know really" just because, because a lot of them take lessons that ain't so complicated.'

In this passage she vividly recaptures instances of her friends telling her she's 'really silly' and asking her why she chose maths. Her answer to them is a noncommittal, 'I don't know really'. This contrasts with the answers of many other participants who use the divergence of views as a chance to position themselves as more knowledgeable about maths, to say, for example, that while 'others' think it's hard it's not because really it's about the way it's taught or about how you apply yourself. Julie's resolution of this difference through a performance of ignorance seems to contradict the openness she claims for her friendships. It is clear from her talk elsewhere in the interview that she does know why she opted to do maths. Her answer (which I quoted earlier) when asked directly about this suggests both a clearly considered decision and a quiet determination to choose the subject.

Perhaps Julie censors these reasons in conversations with friends in favour of, 'I don't know really' in order to erase the differences between herself and her friends by positioning herself with them, also at a loss to explain why she has opted for such an impossible subject. The paradox of female friendship is that beneath the smooth surface of pretended equality there lurk suppressed differences. Valerie Hey (1997: 65, original emphasis) captures the psychic costs of this for the girls she studied:

> One outcome of the pressure on girls to convert the wider loyalties of friendship into the exclusivities of best friendship is an implosion of individual power. It is not that girls ... did not experience differential *feelings* of power through their ability to access other dimensions: being clever; being pretty; being good at games. They did. It is more that all of these other forms of cultural capital were incessantly evaluated within the domain of their friendships. Importantly therefore, in setting their alliances girls had to position themselves very carefully, lest their success in these other dimensions was perceived as disadvantaging one's peers.

There is a sense here of how a position has to be negotiated between the individual and the collective, a process in which Julie must act to silence feelings which in other contexts she can express.

The interview contains other instances of this silencing, for example in Julie's description of her choice of geography. This was a subject that Julie speaks of having always enjoyed. But, as she says: 'There was another reason behind me choosing it, which was I was doing physics and having physics and maths wasn't a good idea. I couldn't, I couldn't cope with it. And the teacher as well, I couldn't, he, it was like I couldn't, he would not let me leave the lesson and one of the ways I could get out of physics was by doing geography. By taking up geography and I, because there wasn't a geography course available first, and everyone wanted to do it. So they started up a course during like, into like the first month, and so we started doing geography and dropped physics, coz I couldn't do 5 AS levels.' The conflict here is between Julie's opinions and those of the teacher, an authority figure who has taught her since she was 13. She describes him as being very strong willed: 'If he believes in you then he will not let you disbelieve in yourself ... And he would say, "You're doing physics," not, "Oh are you gonna choose physics next year?" He's, "You're doing physics next year ain't you?" and it was intimidation to say "yes." '

Julie was clearly in a difficult situation. She was unhappy in physics lessons, something she elaborates on later in the interview. Again it is her resolution of this that is interesting. She escapes physics by taking geography. In this way she avoids confronting her teacher and removes from herself the responsibility for the decision. This reminds me of Amy in Carol Gilligan's (1993) research on moral reasoning. Amy is given the dilemma of whether Hans, whose wife is dying, should steal the drug he needs to save her but which he cannot afford. Instead of reasoning abstractly, as traditional moral philosophy says that she should, Amy rejects the goal of objectivity and searches for a solution based in relationships. She refuses to accept the problem as it is presented, asking whether Hans cannot persuade the druggist to give him the drug more cheaply on humanitarian grounds, and considering the possibility that should Hans steal the drug, he may be found out, and end up in prison, leaving his sick wife alone. Julie, like Amy, seems to be interested in solutions based on connection.

However, such instances can also be read as an expression of Julie's lack of confidence in and ambivalence about her experiential knowledge. In another example, she says 'I think that I learn best, especially at ... home, when I've got music on. But it's been proven by my psychology teacher, that that's wrong, and it's a distraction, and you should do it in silence. And I can't do that. But I think I learn better with something in the background'. Her own embodied knowledge is disturbed by her teacher's insistence that she has proof to the contrary. Jenny Shaw (1995: 118–19) nicely summarizes how, in her more recent work with Lyn Mikel Brown (Brown and Gilligan 1992), Carol Gilligan describes a crossroads that girls traverse during adolescence, at which:

> Young teenage girls appear to lose the feisty, self confidence and directness of their middle childhood years and replace it with a self deprecating, assumed and false ignorance. They fear being out-spoken lest the knowledge that they have of relationships, themselves and other people, which comes from their experience to date, wrecks

the idealized relationships that they are beginning to want above all ... Swept up in this ideal image girls lose confidence in or deny what they really know, including the evidence of their own bodies, and become disconnected.

Lucy, in the next story is older than Julie, and presents herself as having now acquired the confidence that Julie lacks. I use her story to look at the problems created by her struggle for autonomy.

Lucy's story

Lucy is a working class student who was born in England to an Irish mum and a Turkish dad. She is the only mature student in her AS level maths class at Sunnydale. She was allowed into this group because of the closure of the corresponding evening class. She started AS maths in the previous academic year but after three months, 'I fell ill. And I really sort of lapsed with the work. And I'm back again. I'm mad'. At school she tells me that she was 'just very, very, naughty', and we both laugh. But since leaving school she has spent a number of years studying. She explains that 'when I grew up ... well matured should I say', she thought, '"I need to educate myself", not, for me, it's for me, not for the rest of the world, or you know getting a job ... I'm realizing at the moment. This is all for me'.

Her journey to AS level maths has been a long one. She originally took GCSE maths twice and got an E both times 'and I was not impressed at all'. She then started a new course, an introduction to computing, and was persuaded to do City and Guilds maths. 'And again I wasn't impressed with, like, "No, no, no, I want to do GCSE". And they was like "no, no, start on the City and Guilds again and there'll be things that you've not learnt and you can go from there". So I was like, "OK" coz it was part of the unit for the course that I was taking'. Lucy progressed from there to a further qualification which included units on calculus and quantitative methods and recalls 'it was like, "This is great" you know "I like this"'. She adds, 'I've always wanted to do an A level maths and that, just wanted to do it. Even though I think it's bloody hard. I've just always wanted to do it'.

The reason for this is found in Lucy's discussion of the reputation maths has. Laughing, she tells me that people think 'you're just very, very intellectual when ... you've got maths degrees and everything. Everyone's like, "Wow!"' Perhaps her laughter here functions to cover her embarrassment about what such a claim implies about her (or even as part of a denial that it implies anything about her). Lucy is clear the reputation of maths is justified: 'Coz it's hard work. It's really, really hard work. Maths is very, very, very hard. And you have to be really, really committed. Not that you don't have to be committed to other subjects and everything, like chemistry, science, and physics and all them. But when it comes to things like, erm, I don't know, this is really, really hard and heavy, English, geography, and everything, you don't, I don't think you have to be that committed, you know … I'm not saying this [to be] nasty, because again if I was to take sort of French or German … they may be really, really hard subjects. But again, when it, when it comes to maths, maths is, it's hard work. It's literally really, really hard work. And you know anyone that actually deals with maths will tell you like, "Whoa, you know, this is deep, this is deep" … Whereas with English, I'm not saying that, at the end of the day you're writing essays and you, you have to do a 5, um, 10,000 essay, like of 10,000 words you know like. Then of course it's gonna, it's using the imagination and that but it's not hard. To me that wouldn't be hard.'

Unusually Lucy conflates 'hard' and 'hard work' in these passages. It is interesting to compare this with other students' talk where maintaining a distinction between these terms is important to how they are constructing themselves, notably, Graham in Chapter 3 and James in Chapter 4.

Lucy tells me that this image of maths as 'hard' and 'intellectual' lay behind her initial decision to take it: 'I wanted to prove to myself, not to anyone else, but to myself, that I could do it. That there was something better inside me. And that's how it started but now I enjoy it for some sick, unknown reason'. In explaining this enjoyment she recalls a mathematical discussion we had during one of my classroom observations. This discussion was an 'Aha!' moment for her, when 'all of a sudden you get, you like, "ah yes". It's great! It's a great feeling. It's great to think, "Yes, I've done it!"'

This obvious pleasure, in her sense of power, combines with some pain in Lucy's relationship with maths. This is evident when, immediately after this exchange on what she enjoys about maths, I ask: 'What about what you haven't enjoyed about learning maths?'

Lucy hesitates, 'Um, ah, what haven't I enjoyed?' Then, laughing, she jokes, 'Everything, I've not enjoyed'. As Sigmund Freud (1991) noted, jokes can reveal things that we would normally keep hidden and give clues to the contents of our unconscious. After this Lucy gives a serious answer to my question: 'I can literally do the whole work' and then a few weeks later 'it's difficult to remember it' and, above all, in the pressured situation of the exam, 'I just go completely blank … and it's trying to defeat that'. The strategies that she has developed 'to train my mind to that sort of level' are based on effort. For each topic 'I will literally go home and I will break it all up into literally tiny, tiny segments. And I'll write each segment down so it's got an understanding to it'.

In spite of this struggle, there has been a change in Lucy's relationship with maths. She started out doing maths entirely for the challenge it provides, in order to prove something about her-self, but now she is also doing maths for the pleasure this challenge provides. There is a parallel between this and another change, the change in Lucy's relationships with her teachers. This is illustrated in her talk about Alex, one of her current maths teachers, who is 'absolutely ace'. She explains, 'I've had him for a couple of years and he's absolutely great, because you're not scared of him. Well I'm not scared of him. I know that at the end of the day he's not actually looking down his nose at me. He never, never did. I s'pose when I was in a vulnerable position, then you know, I can sort of explain from there.'

'OK.'

'Um, when I was in a more vulnerable position ... Alex was cool, calm and collected, and, "Alright, fair enough, yeah, yeah". And you could say to him, "No, no, I don't understand, no, no, no, I don't understand" and he'd just go over and over and over it again. Whereas now I'm not afraid to actually say to a teacher, whether or not he's gonna look down his nose at me or not, "Oh god you stupid cow" or whatever, in his mind. I'm not afraid of that no more ... So I'm free like that.'

These changes demonstrate the way Lucy is constructing herself as having shifted from a position as dependent on (male) others' views to one as independent of them, and having grown in confidence and maturity. Lucy's account feels triumphant; within it she shows how she is now free to be herself. However, in contemporary neoliberal society, being your-self takes constant work. We must: fulfil our potential and take advantage of the available opportunities; whether in work or social settings, we have to fit in with the definitions of what it means to be successful; gaps on our CVs are filled in and choices are rationalized so as to make it look like we have coherent directions to our lives. This is a highly regulated version of 'freedom' and the contradictions are apparent in Renton's discussion of his choice to become a heroin addict in the novel *Trainspotting*:

> Society invents a spurious convoluted logic tae absorb and change people whae's behaviour is outside its mainstream. Suppose that ah ken aw the pros and cons, know that ah'm gunnae huv a short life, am ay sound mind etcetera, etcetera, but still want tae use smack? They won't let ye dae it. They won't let ye dae it, because it's a sign ay thir ain failure. The fact that ye jist simply choose tae reject whit

they huv tae offer. Choose us. Choose life. Choose mortgage payments; choose washing machines; choose cars; choose sitting oan a couch watching mind-numbing and spirit-crushing game shows, stuffing fuckin junk food intae yir mooth. Choose rotting away, pishing and shiteing yersel in a home, a total fuckin embarrassment tae the selfish fucked-up brats ye've produced. Choose life.

Well, ah choose no tae choose life. If the cunts cannae handle that, it's thair fuckin problem.

(Welsh 1993: 187–8)

As Nikolas Rose (1999b: ix) explains in more academic language, within the neoliberal world, 'each individual must render his or her life meaningful as if it were the outcome of individual choices made in furtherance of a biographical project of self-realization'. These new forms of regulation can neither be understood as freedom, since 'the self is not merely enabled to choose, but obliged to construe a life in terms of its choices' (1999b: 231), nor as repression since they 'do not crush subjectivity. They actually fabricate subjects – human men, women and children – capable of bearing the burdens of liberty' (1999b: vii).

Lucy is working to become the ideal neoliberal subject. Key features of this are autonomy and individuality. Lucy performs these in her denial that external pressures affect her choices. For example, when she tells me that she 'wasn't impressed with' her computing teacher she adds, 'that's not the reason why I didn't' continue with computing. She agrees with me that teachers do have an effect but qualifies this, explaining 'not that he made my choices. Because at the end of the day I'm, you know, I know what I want'. Similarly Lucy denies that her choices are affected by the social construction of gender. She points out that there are now more women going into maths because it is no longer a 'male-dominated world . . . And this is maybe a suggestion and a theory that at the end of the day women actually pick maths because they actually enjoy the subject more . . . Whereas with males, they might [be affected by] the macho [image]' suggesting that men's, but not women's, choices are constrained by gender.

Then I ask whether 'thinking more generally, do you think that being female has made differences to your life?'

'No. Because it's, to me it's, I'm a female and that's it. I've not thought of nothing else I suppose. It's just a natural thing'.

Despite this definitive answer, Lucy brings the subject up again, at the conclusion of the interview, when I ask her if there is anything that she wants to ask me: 'No, yeah, the woman issue. You said, um, about, just now, the, um, question about being a woman. Where did that come from?' I explain and she tells me that she asked, 'because it's like to me a strange [question], but, "Whoa! I'm a female but that's it". I can be feminine. I sometimes can't be feminine, depending [on] the situation and that. But to me that wouldn't matter. Personally, you know that would not matter to me . . . other people, and that, other women, you know, they sort of shy away from the male dominated areas. But to me it wouldn't matter'.

Lucy's story illustrates one damaging impact of the neoliberal fiction of the autonomous self through which she is writing herself. At the end of the academic year in which I interviewed her, she failed her AS level maths and she looks likely to do so again at the end of this year. Within such a story of her actions she cannot look to class and gender to help her to understand this failure and so has no alternative but to understand it as the result of personal pathology. The dark side of the neoliberal vision of self, this time for middle class girls, is a theme of Claudia's story.

Claudia's story

Claudia is an ambitious young woman who is interested in becoming a barrister. Her family moved from Algeria to Scotland when she was 4 years old and then later to London. In her interview she distances herself from her childhood. Twice she speaks in the third person about this time, removing herself from it: 'My mum and dad are from Algeria' and 'they lived there till I was four and a half'. She is doing five AS levels, instead of the four that is the norm at Westerburg. She tells me 'if you could do six, I'd be doing six' because 'I don't feel alright, if I'm not doing, if I know I'm not doing the hardest thing possible, I'm not really exerting myself, I don't like it'. When I ask about why she thinks she always seeks out challenge she describes how she coasted along at the top of her class in primary school and the early years of secondary school. Then, in Year 11 and now, 'I'm feeling the need to actually' and here she impersonates a teacher 'achieve my potential'. Her five subjects cut across the whole academic curriculum: sciences, arts and languages. They are chemistry, English literature, French, history and maths. Claudia explains, 'I don't like sort of narrowing down my options'. They represent her desire for challenge as well as how she presents herself as: sophisticated (she prefers to sit at the back and is disdainful of those who are eager to answer questions in class), 'defiant' ('I don't [take] things as they're told to me') and determined. That she also jokingly describes her chosen programme of study as 'self-torture' suggests that her academic work carries some pain with it. This fits with the middle class women in the study by Valerie Walkerdine and her colleagues (2001: 175), who were trapped on an educational 'conveyer belt'. 'What we found in our study was that the middle-class girls' educational lives had been rigidly circumscribed by the expectations of academic success, often to such an extent that quite outstanding performances were only ever viewed as average and ordinary' (2001: 179).

I think that this ambiguity can be read into Claudia's subject choices. For example, with French she clearly wanted a challenge: 'I did French to GCSE and I went to France last year, in the summer sorry, and I realized I wasn't quite as good at French as I always thought I was, so I thought I should take it up'. There is a determination as well as a sort of stubbornness here; she is trying to prove that she is as good at French as she thought she was and clearly thinks she ought to be. However, because of the way that she keeps raising the targets she is aiming for academically, I have doubts as to whether she will ever be able to do enough to prove herself to herself. As such this continual challenge seeking may be destructive as well as productive. This double edgedness is clearer in her talk about maths.

Claudia employs a militarist metaphor to explain why she is doing maths: 'I like the fact that I've got to conquer these numbers'. However, as well as her evident pleasure in the power she gets from such conquests, she explains, 'Sometimes I dread going into [maths], "Oh now I've got maths" but I think that's just because of the, what do you call it, stigma, stigma attached to maths. It's like, "Oh, maths, numbers, er!" I don't dislike it. It's not my favourite subject. I'm doing it, I'm doing maths sort of because I know it will be a challenge to me and it's useful and it's good. I think it's good for your brain to do maths'. These painful aspects of Claudia's identification with maths are also manifest in the way that she froze in her GCSE maths exam: 'I was so scared of not having done enough maths revision'. So when 'I went into the exam, for the first few minutes I was just really scared stiff, I couldn't do anything. I just kept staring at the first page and just reading it and not taking it in at all'.

The terror in these passages echoes the experiences described by Laurie Buxton (1981) in his case studies of maths anxiety and panic. He related these feelings to: the time pressure and competitive performances that are part of the early school maths curriculum and the right and wrong nature of school maths which mean that questions in the subject carry with them a power to confer moral judgement on the respondent. Work on maths anxiety (for example, Tobias 1978; Isaacson 1990; Evans 2000) concentrates on those who fail at maths or who drop out early; and so creates the impression that it is only such people who experience such feelings towards maths. In looking for an explanation of Claudia's 'dread' of maths, her account of when she was sent to special maths classes in Year 8 is important. 'I was like always top in the class, top in the year, and, and', she pauses, 'myself and a couple of other students were selected from the year to go to these advanced maths classes ... And they were really, really hard'. We laugh. The classes covered 'really super, super maths for really clever people, stuff you'd see on sort of Open University [television programmes] or whatever and so me and my friend would just sit there and sort of draw, doodling and so, I think, there's often been times when I've like been inclined to be scared of maths coz of not understanding it'. Claudia's fear here seems to relate both to the myth of mathematical genius explored in earlier chapters and to the constant threat that exists of just 'not understanding it', and so of being judged inadequate/wrong.

Her experience of maths can be read as gendered in two further ways. First, she tells me that while she has always been 'good at mental arithmetic' and 'just thinking in numbers comes quite naturally to me', it is the 'harder maths' with which she has problems. This distinction draws on the gendered opposition between reason and calculation, and contrasts with the positions adopted by Graham and Peter in their stories, told in Chapter 3, as self-consciously bad at tables.

Second, in spite of her negative feelings, she did choose maths. Maths' status as an intellectual challenge is central to this, but so are her past teachers. Her version of maths is a relational one: '[Maths] really depends on the person you have teaching you'. She tells me about how, in GCSE maths, 'the first teacher I had I didn't really gel with him so in the first year, Year 10, I didn't feel I really achieved anything', but in Year 11 a 'really good' teacher took the group over.

'What made this person really good at teaching maths?'

Claudia hesitates, 'I don't know, actually. Um', she pauses, 'what made her good? Odd coincidence was that the teacher who I had for Years 7 to 9 was a lady, and the teacher who I found to be good was also a lady ... I think it was sort of, I don't know, a sense of authority.' She laughs. 'Not a sense of authority over her, but the way she treated us, the way she spoke to us, especially like my little group, was really, it was more personal. The last teacher, it was just like, "You haven't done your homework, why? Detention" and, "You don't get it. That's because you haven't been listening. Why?" Blah, blah, blah.'

'So what sort of things did she say that were, that you describe as "more personal?"'

'She'd talk to you about, like at the time when we were choosing, sort of thinking about A levels and she was telling us all, coz she, she'd had a lot of experience teaching maths, like 15 years, 17 years, or something, and so she would tell us about different situations she'd been in and about things that universities would want, things like why maths would be helpful later on and, it was more like, it made maths more sort of accessible.'

However, despite her relational version of maths and her feelings about the influence of the teacher's gender, Claudia, like Lucy, is reluctant to see gender as part of her educational choices. When I ask her about gender and subject choice, she talks briefly about the possible physiological and sociological reasons for this. Then I ask her: 'So do you think that being female makes a difference to your life in any other ways, apart from in subject choice?'

'I read something about if you're a barrister, female barrister, you have to accept that men will go further than you, which I think is a bit, "Er, no they won't!" I want to be the best.' We laugh. 'Obviously men still get better pay, don't they? Erm, I don't know, I'm not really a feminist. I don't think that, I don't know all about that equality thingy and stuff.'

I pursue this, asking, 'What do you mean?'

'Um, I don't know, I don't think I have understood the question very well'.

'Um, what I'm trying to get at is just to see whether people, what effect people think their being male or being female has had on their own life, and is going to have on their life in the future, and has on other people's lives. That's really what I'm trying to get at.'

'Oh, OK. Mm, mm, mm.'

'Yeah, it's not easy.'

'No it's not.' Claudia hesitates. 'Um, I think if you're male then you have more of a chance of being more career orientated and even if you're not career orientated, coz well women produce children, funnily enough, um, it's sort of split between the two. So men are more likely to become leaders and more important people, have more jobs, and so it becomes a man's world really. And women are still, um, second class. I mean I've heard that said a lot but I don't know how true it is.'

'How true do you think it is?'

Claudia pauses before replying, 'It's becoming less and less true, but I think it is, it is true in sort of, in terms of the hard facts it is. Like figures and stuff. Who has what jobs, who earns what, who owns what, who has power, stuff.'

In these passages Claudia, like Lucy, is reading herself through the neoliberal fiction of the autonomous self. This compels her to resist connecting being female to lacking power and to disadvantage within her own life. Instead she attaches these to generalized others and to the impersonal realm of reports, statistics and theories.

Connecting the stories of Julie, Lucy and Claudia

Like Simon, James, Michael and Toni, in the last chapter, Julie, Lucy and Claudia show us how they use/are used by their educational choices to do their identity work. Once again, maths is a powerful choice. Its social construction allows it to function in their identity projects as a way of proving their 'abilities', not only to a range of others, but, above all, to themselves. In the last chapter, I discussed the reasons why it can do this. In this chapter what I have been exploring through their stories is how this creates tensions for them because, while maths is discursively inscribed as masculine, their bodies are discursively inscribed as feminine, and it is this femininity that they are invested in producing as 'natural'. There are three questions that arise out of these analyses:

- Why is this group of students all female?
- How are the tensions they speak about gendered?
- What is the role of maths in constructing these tensions?

I address these below.

Perhaps it is a coincidence that all these three students are female. In this study I have sacrificed breadth for depth making me cautious about generalizing. Throughout the book I have tackled this by combining the detailed reporting of interviews and observations with the continual linking of these to other studies. In this way I hope that you can assess the relevance of my findings to your own settings. In this case the many studies that demonstrate that boys and men *express* greater confidence in their mathematical 'abilities' than do girls and women, suggest that the female dominance of this group is not simply a coincidence.

In the stories, I have offered various reasons for the gendering of the need to prove to yourself that you are good enough to do maths. These reasons link to a range of experiences – for example, of friendship, of teachers and of bodies – that, in general, differ for girls and boys. I have then related these to the way that, while both girls and boys are required to produce themselves as autonomous subjects, these different patterns of experiences make this more difficult for girls.

Now that girls can, in principle, take the place previously accorded to their brothers, their production as the bourgeois subject is a huge struggle and is never simply or entirely achieved, and certainly not without terrible penalties for body and mind. This view of what happens to the girls is in complete opposition to a simplistic notion of a genderquake as a freeing feminist triumph!

(Walkerdine et al. 2001: 175)

Generally the interviews support the idea that gender is experienced as more problematic by girls than by boys and was talked about in more personal terms by them (although it could simply be that boys find it more difficult to discuss their feelings about being male). These tensions are particularly pronounced in the case of maths because of its key role in producing rational subjects and the gendered ways that it is constructed as absolute and abstract and so as dis-embodied and disconnected.

Conclusions

This chapter has very much built on the earlier ones, to show that:

- Gender is a project and one that is achieved in interaction with others.
- Opting into or out of maths is part of this project.

One of the main tensions that I have experienced in thinking and writing about gender in this chapter is between *equality and difference*. The idea that women are different was the starting point for feminist political struggle. However, it is always double-edged, being prone to political misuse as a defence of discriminatory practices and of the status quo. As discussed in Chapter 1, explanations based in gender difference so easily become self-perpetuating; indeed, when I have presented material from this book I have met the view that work such as mine, which seeks to explain gender differences, is actually part of the problem. Perhaps without all this talk about gender differences there wouldn't be any; and my readings produce differences between boys and girls because that is what I 'want' to do. These are important concerns and, before going any further, I want to tackle them.

Here Michael's response, when I asked him to help me to respond to a comment I had received from a reader of an earlier version of Chapter 4, is a useful starting point. I invited him to explain how *his* need to prove himself differs from similar sentiments expressed by Julie. He was angry about the question and adamant that there was a difference but unable to explain what it was. Reflecting on this, I came up with two possibilities:

- That this difference is 'real' and relates to the way that Michael desires public recognition of his 'abilities' while Julie's desire is more private, she wants to prove something to herself.
- That this difference is 'unreal' and exists only in the way that Michael constructs his own and other people's motivations (and perhaps also in the way that Julie and some other young people construct these).

Reflecting further, I feel that this split is misleading. If we think of an idea as 'real', not because of its power to *describe* the world, but because of its power to *produce* effects in the world, then the second version is at least as 'real' as the first. This means that the difference between Michael and Julie is gendered because Michael thinks it is; his feelings are ones that he experiences and performs as masculine. Everybody performs both masculinity and femininity but only one of these will be felt and *need* to be felt as authentic and natural.

Michael's insistence on difference is an important reminder of the need for progressive research on gender. Stopping feminist research on gender differences is not going to end discussion about them; what it will do is to restrict even further the range of stories through which we can make sense of them. If progressive social theories ignore differences, there is the danger that young people's 'awareness of differences ... lends plausibility to those theories which do base themselves on difference, but explain it in ways which have more pernicious, because determinist, implications' (Henriques 1984: 89). I am thinking here of theories such as 'men are from Mars and women are from Venus' or discussions of the evolutionary bases of a huge range of social behaviours including rape and male sexual infidelity, as well as male superiority in maths. Gender differences have material consequences, and we need to acknowledge this if we are to make decisions that promote equity. For example, since dyslexia is between 75 and 90 percent male, 'any organisation which campaigns for more awareness of dyslexia is effectively campaigning for a better deal for boys' (Shaw 1995: 66).

As Joan Scott (1990) explains, we need to trouble the binary of:

Equality/Difference

First, it is useful to look at the huge variety of positions within each of the two terms:

Equality, for example, can mean anything from the mildest liberal reform (this is piece-of-the-pie feminism, in which women are merely to be included in the world as it is) to the most radical reduction of gender to insignificance. Difference can mean anything from Mary Daly's belief in the natural superiority of women to psychoanalytic theories of how women are inevitably cast as 'the Other' because they lack penises.

(Snitow 1990: 26)

This huge variation makes it meaningless to describe feminist positions in terms of either 'equality' or 'difference'. Second, while difference is often thought of as the opposite of sameness, politically equality has never meant sameness (see Young 1990). In fact:

Demands for equality have rested on implicit and usually unrecognized arguments from difference; if individuals or groups were identical or the same there would be no need to ask for equality. Equality might as well be defined as deliberate indifference to specified differences.

(Scott 1990: 142)

If we are interested in gender equity we need to be strategic using *both* difference, 'our most creative analytical tool', *and* equality, 'to speak to the principles and values of our political system' (Scott 1990: 142). No work takes place in a political vacuum and as a feminist I need to be aware of this and to think about where my work lies and assess its power, 'as a tool for undermining the dense, deeply embedded oppression of women' (Snitow 1990: 29). This is a project to which I hope this book will contribute in a small way.

Summing up, through the stories in this chapter and the last, I have shown that:

- People whose bodies are socially marked as feminine do things that are socially marked as masculine and vice versa. But, the marking of the body as male or female impacts on one's possibilities for acting; not all positions are equally available to all people.
- Given the generally greater social valuation of facets of masculinity, of which maths is one, it is not surprising that these hold out greater appeal for boys and girls than do facets of femininity. This has social justice implications.

Taken together, Chapters 3, 4 and 5 are my answer to the question I started out with: *How do people come to choose maths and in what ways is the process gendered?* My answer suggests that making a wider range of discursive positionings/stories open to a wider range of individuals would be one way of producing a more socially just maths education practice.

As Ken Plummer (1995: 166) advocated (in the rather different context of sexualities): 'It is not an easy option to keep the pluralistic, polyvocal potential of proliferating stories open; but it is probably a very necessary one'. This carries implications for maths pedagogy. It is difficult to link theory and practice, to think through what new insights might mean for teaching. This is something that I attempt in the final section of this book on 'Queering Gender and Mathematics'. The next chapter serves as a bridge between this section and the next, summarizing the ideas so far and setting them in a broader context.

chapter/**six**

Changing directions

This chapter marks a shift in focus within the book. It acts as a bridge between the three chapters just gone and the three that follow in Part 3. All the way through I have been making a case for seeing doing mathematics as doing masculinity so as to challenge both the binary construction of gender and the binary construction of curriculum, and so to open out different ways of doing and relating to maths. In the final part of the book I want to focus on what all this might mean for teachers. I lead into this, in this chapter, by looking to the contexts – historical, political, global, theoretical and practical – for my own small-scale London study. This is in order to make the case for change to map out directions for change, and to look at why change is difficult. I have decided to talk about directions for change, rather than something more definite, because I think that the relationship between research and practice is a complex one and it is impossible to make clear prescriptions from one to the other. The three directions I look to and focus on in turn are choices, gender and maths. But before that, since this chapter builds on previous chapters, particularly the three just gone, I summarize the story so far.

Chapter 3 looked at the way that young people make sense of maths and construct their relationship to it through a series of binary oppositions. The ones discussed in that chapter were:

Maths people/Non-maths people
Mathematics and sciences/Languages and arts
Ordered and rule-based/Creative and emotional
Numbers/Words
Thinking/Writing
Fast/Slow
Competitive/Collaborative
Independent/Dependent
Active/Passive

Dynamic/Static
Naturally able/Hard-working
Real understanding/Rote learning
Reason/Calculation
Reasonable/Calculating
Masculine/Feminine
Really good at maths/Good at maths
Objective/Subjective
Hard/Soft
Mind/Body
Separation/Connection
Theory /Experience
Reading books/Living life

Although I derived this list through making sense of the talk of a pretty select group of students, who both enjoy maths and are academically successful at it, the inscription of maths into binary patterns is more widespread as the stories in Chapters 4 and 5 make clear. Those too are full of talk about what makes maths different from other subjects, what makes the ways of knowing in maths different from other ways of knowing and what makes people who are good at the subject different from other people. *Alternative ways of thinking about maths are the subject of my third direction for change.*

While there are important historical continuities in the ways that individual entries are organized in this list, these entries are also in a continual state of flux. It is not the existence of particular binaries that matter but their underlying logic and pattern, dependent upon polarization and hierarchy, the valorized against the degraded, the masculine against the feminine. This logic structures our thoughts and feelings and marks out the limits of what it is possible to think, to feel and to be. *Alternative ways of thinking about gender are the subject of my second direction for change.*

In Chapters 4 and 5 I went on to develop the central idea in this book. I explored how this binary patterning combines with the socioculturally inscribed opposition of masculine to feminine and male bodies to female bodies, to make identification with maths more difficult for girls and women than for boys and men. Hence they are less likely to choose, enjoy and succeed at the subject. This matters because maths is a powerful resource, a form of currency in the employment and education marketplace. Thus how this resource is distributed, including via the 'free' choices people make, is a social justice issue. *Alternative ways of thinking about choice are the subject of my first direction for change.*

First direction: making choices social

I began this book with a graph showing the gendered pattern of the choice to study maths among 16-year-olds in England covering the past ten years. What is startling about it is how flat it is. Tracing things back further, to the 1970s say, would have shown a clear increase in the proportion of girls choosing to study maths post-16. However, the new fixing, alongside the pattern of a disproportionate rejection of maths by women at every subsequent choice point, is still worrying. In fact in two ways it is *more* worrying than the situation in the 1970s and 1980s. First, because of the way that the male dominance of maths persists even after decades of feminist interventions designed to increase female participation; as Jenny Shaw (1995: 107) says, 'the most striking feature of subject choice is that the freer it is, the more gendered it is'. Second, because there is now a sense in England, as in other parts of the Northern world, that we are into a postfeminist era where the problems of gender inequality have been solved and any remaining differences between men and women are 'real' and/or 'natural' (this is part of the backlash against feminism discussed by Susan Faludi 1992). In England, recent figures suggest that maths is even beginning to get more male dominated with the introduction of AS levels, creating as they do a new structured choice point at 17+ and having a predictably gendered impact (Mendick 2004).

Looking beyond England, the choice to continue with maths is similarly masculine. To give a couple of examples of countries that I have data on:

- In Germany, in 1998/99, 34 percent of female undergraduates chose linguistics or cultural studies (compared with 10 percent of men), 30 percent chose law, economics or social sciences (compared with 34 percent of men), 12 percent chose maths or science (compared with 19 percent of men) and only 7 percent chose engineering (compared with 28 percent of men) (Blattel-Mink 2002).
- In the United States, in 2000, high school and undergraduate take-up of maths courses was gender balanced, being 48 percent female, but participation in doctorates and in maths related career areas was much lower with only 27 percent of PhDs in maths being awarded to women and only 9 percent of engineers being female (Boaler and Sengupta-Irving forthcoming).

Looking beyond maths, many educational and other choices are gender polarized. While climbing and computer gaming are male dominated pastimes, fashion and fiction are female dominated ones.

Yet the gender polarization of subject choices is not a part of young people's lived experience that many of them have noticed. Even after I pointed it out, most of my participants were either unable to come up with a convincing explanation for these gender differences or they put them down to a combination of chance and individual interest, despite my telling them how their local choices fitted into a recurring, nationwide pattern. 'The young people see themselves as individuals in a meritocratic society, not as classed or gendered members of an unequal society' (Ball et al. 2000: 4). It seems that these young people do not have a language with which to speak about the constraints, conscious and unconscious, on choice. In this book I have been working with such a language. My approach to choices starts from the idea that they are inseparable from our 'identity', that is, identity is something that we are constantly producing in and through our choices. Using Judith Butler's (1997, 1999) work I showed how this process turns everything around so that it feels as if it is the self that produces our choices. In other words, it may look like we make our choices but actually our choices make us as much as we make them.

We need such a language because, as is clear throughout this book, discourses of 'free choice' are unconvincing and 'Social regulation can function, not only in a sense through overt oppression, but rather through defining the parameters and content of choice, fixing how we come to want what we want' (Henriques et al. 1984: 219). I now want to look in more detail at why we need this new language of choice by discussing two contexts for this book: educational politics and gender politics.

Within education, the marketization and commodification of learning means that 'choice' is now a powerful signifier (Gewirtz et al. 1995). The media and politicians speak of parental and student choice as *the* way of guaranteeing that each individual gets the most out of what our educational system has to offer and, importantly, contributes the most that they can to the country. The hope invested in education is clear in Tony Blair's (2001) speech after securing victory in the 2001 general election:

> We need to start building the economy of the future based on skills and talents and education and the application of technology, knowing that for this country in the future the forces of global competition and technological change mean that we can only compete on the basis of skill and ability.

These words demonstrate the way that New Labour's stories of educational choice are drawn from the liberal political paradigm in which choices are seen as individual acts, the route to personal autonomy and self-realization, and as deriving from people's 'natural' talents and abilities. Therefore little regard is given to the structures and systems within which these choices and abilities are embedded. Within the pages of this book I have looked at the impact of this on the way we think about ourselves; I have examined the compulsion to choose, and to see each choice as part of a biographical project of self; where everything must be constructed as a success to others and to oneself. The individualizing effects of this means that people are blamed and blame themselves for the effects of social injustices on their lives.

Choice is also central to contemporary gender politics. Liberal versions of feminism, based on liberal political philosophies, which concentrate on removing discrimination against women within the public realm, find it difficult to explain why there remain so few female mathematicians, politicians, engineers and so on, now that the overt barriers to their participation in these fields have been removed (Thomas 1990). It seems that women simply do not want to do these things, we perversely insist on making the wrong choices. This difficulty is manifest not just in the issues of employment and subject choice, but also in arenas as varied as eating disorders, plastic surgery, rape and abortion.

I focus here on just one key example: 'choice' is the rallying cry for the feminist movement's continuing campaign for abortion on demand, and the legal treatment of the issue in North America is illustrative of the paradoxes contained therein. The Roe vs. Wade case was a historic Supreme Court judgement guaranteeing a 'woman's right to choose' on grounds of privacy, in the sense of bodily integrity, the right of an individual to self-expression and self-determination (Schneider 1994). However, as Barbara Rothman (1999) warns, there are problems with superimposing this freedom onto a social structure characterized by inequality. She acknowledges that 'choice' offers an effective starting point for political action, but an ultimately limited one that leaves the status quo unchallenged. This was apparent in the second key judgement on abortion, the Harris case, where the Supreme Court ruled against the requirement to provide state funding for abortions. Catherine MacKinnon (1987: 101), writing from a radical feminist perspective, is clear about the failings of the liberal argument that grants a theoretical right to abortion without providing the resources necessary to make this 'right' a reality:

> The logic of the Court's response resembles the logic by which women are supposed to consent to sex. Preclude the alternatives, then call the sole remaining option 'her choice'. The point is that the alternatives are precluded by conditions of sex, race, and class – the very conditions the privacy frame not only leaves tacit but exists to guarantee.

However, there are problems too with the radical feminist language of choice. Within this framing there is a tendency to see all the breast-implant obsessed 17-year-olds, women who stay with men who hit them and girls who choose literature over physics as victims of 'false consciousness' who need to be shown the truth behind the ideology. The resulting strategies, from banning pornography to scare campaigns to choose maths, are often counterproductive. In this book I have demonstrated the need to take seriously the choices that girls and women (and boys and men) make and see them as making sense in the spaces where they are. It is useful here to compare the perspective on sex and consent within MacKinnon's quote above with that contained in this more ambiguous statement by Elizabeth Wurtzel (1998: 117) on adolescent female sexuality:

> [We] need to understand that when girls misuse or abuse the term 'date rape' it is only because the taxonomy of women's sexual experience has not yet classified all the different perfectly legal and easily available ways that these women-in-training feel themselves being violated – they have no language to express how they had no idea what they wanted until they got what they didn't want.

Thus creating a language that both takes people's choices seriously and engages with the constraints on those choices is necessary. It is also difficult. We all want to believe that our choices are unrestricted expressions of our inner selves and reflections of our underlying abilities. Additionally we all, of course, *do* need to 'own' our choices and take responsibility for them and they *are* the ways in which we are produced/produce ourselves as unique individuals. As well as this, there is another challenge in creating a language to understand the impact of gender on choice: how do we do this without getting stuck in binary versions of gender? This is explored in the next section (Second direction).

Second direction: supporting gender transgression

Using this social language of choice, if choices are viewed as identity work then young people, in choosing or rejecting maths, are telling us stories about who and what they are and are not like, and who and what they do and do not want to be like. In doing so they are drawing on what maths 'is'. For analytic purposes at least, poststructuralism holds that there is nothing beyond discourse. So when examining objects such as maths we look at the discourses in which they are inscribed: maths is what the discourses say it is.

The application of this approach to my data has resulted in coming to understand certain discourses about maths and mathematicians as central to the way that students negotiate their relationships with the subject. 'Real maths' is different from other subjects; it is certain, rational and hard. 'Real mathematicians' are different from other people; they combine the flattering characteristics of geniuses and heroes with the unflattering characteristics of nerds. These discourses are oppositional and gendered; they inscribe maths as masculine. Based on this, boys and girls, and men and women, in doing mathematics are doing masculinity, and so it is more difficult for girls and women to feel comfortable with maths, and so to choose it and to do well at it.

In this book, I am working with a particular model of gender. This model both acknowledges the background of gendered oppositions with and against which we think, and, simultaneously, tries to shift this background a little in directions that will be more productive for social justice. Importantly this model breaks with the dominant pattern of research in gender and education that maps masculinities onto men and femininities onto women so that the binary division of sex is preserved and reinforced, male and female experiences are homogenized, overlaps are excluded and actions that do not fit are rendered invisible. Such work can be useful but should carry a health warning, perhaps:

Warning: Binary Thinking Damages Gender Reform

My model of gender and my use of masculinities and femininities are drawn from the work of Bob Connell (1995: 71). Repeating his definition that I first quoted in Chapter 1, masculinity and femininity: 'to the extent that [they] can be defined at all, [are] simultaneously a place in gender relations, the practices through which men and women engage that place in gender, and the effects of these practices in bodily experience and culture'. However, while stating clearly here and elsewhere that masculinities and femininities are *both* enacted by men *and* by women, Connell includes only men in his detailed empirical studies of masculinities (for example, Connell 1989, 1995). This emphasizes that 'even when the need for an analysis of female masculinity has been acknowledged ... it seems remarkably difficult to do' (Halberstam 1998: 14). However, it also emphasizes how important it is to keep trying to do this. It is as a result of all this that I decided to explore the possibilities of viewing those girls and women, including myself, who do align themselves with maths, as examples of female masculinities.

The most detailed study of female masculinities is by Judith Halberstam (1998). Combining historical, pop-cultural and literary analyses, she points out that while it is often said that it is easier to be a tomboy than a sissy this is not something that carries through into adulthood. In fact in adolescence a lot of work is done in drawing previously masculine girls back within the confines of femininity. Halberstam (1998: 268) argues that while 'excessive conventional femininity often associated with female heterosexuality can be bad for your health' and 'tends to be associated with passivity and inactivity, [and] with various forms of unhealthy body manipulations from anorexia to high-heeled shoes', it is masculinity that is commonly viewed as dangerous for women and girls. She concludes that there is a need

> to make masculinity safe … Although it seems counter-intuitive to suggest that such a project should be necessary in the 1990s, it has been my contention that despite at least two decades of sustained feminist and queer attacks on the notion of natural gender, we still believe that masculinity in girls and women is abhorrent and pathological.

My argument in this book that we need to make a wider range of subjectivities available to a wider range of people fits with Halberstam's. It is about making activities that are differently positioned within the gender regime available to people regardless of their assigned gender. It is about acknowledging the effects of the binary organization of gender on our lives so that we can be less affected by it. Although Halberstam's work is based entirely on lesbian examples of female masculinities, my study makes clear the wider applications of her work. Female masculinities, like male femininities, are neither rare nor freakish but are part of the landscape of everyday gender relations. Despite this everyday-ness, as mine and other research shows, they are sites of difficulties for the women involved.

Additionally, such gender transgressions are more problematic for women than for men. Lisa Adkins' (2001) study of workplace gender relations shows this. Her starting point is male femininity. Originally the meaning of the term feminization, when applied to the labour market, was socioeconomic; it referred to the increased participation of women in the workforce and the decline in traditionally masculine manufacturing jobs. However, 'it is now used to refer to a new sovereignty of appearance, image, and style at work, whose performance of stylised presentations of self has emerged as a key resource in certain sections of the economy, particularly in new service occupations' (2001: 674). A parallel trend is apparent in TV culture: think of all those men on their breakfast TV sofas discussing celebrity 'gossip', health issues and fashion.

However, while both men and women can do femininity in the workplace (or on daytime TV), Adkins (2001: 687, original emphasis) provides evidence that there are two crucial differences between their performances. First, men and women differ in their gender mobility for 'men workers may "take on" (and be rewarded for) performances of femininity, yet women cannot unproblematically "take on" (and be rewarded for) performances of masculinity'; women's gender mobility is restricted '*within* the genre of femininity'. Second, men and women differ in how their deployment of femininity is read. While men's performances are read as exactly that, women's are not. To develop this point Adkins uses Manthia Diawara's (1998: 57) distinction between the position occupied by white actor, John Travolta, in *Pulp Fiction* (1994) and the one occupied by the black actor, Samuel L. Jackson:

> Travolta has literal masculinity, in terms of coolness and language and dress code; no door can be closed to him. But Samuel Jackson has the coolness of his own-immanent-blackness. To me, Jackson, who's a great actor, appears to not be acting; he just appears to be 'a black guy.' Let me give you another example of this. In *Boys N The Hood*, the single mother of Doughboy and Ricky is acting, but she looks so much like a typical welfare mother that she couldn't even be considered for an award for a supporting actress.

So, Travolta as white can appropriate the cultural resources that attach to blackness, while it is much more difficult for Jackson as black to take on those that attach to whiteness. Further, while Travolta's taking on of blackness is clearly a performance, Jackson's is viewed as natural. Diawara contrasts Travolta's transtextual position with Jackson's immanent one. Similarly, as Adkins shows, women are not eligible for the rewards that accrue to men for successful performances of femininity because femininity is immanent to them and so cannot be seen as a performance.

Adkin's (2001) ideas support the need for work such as my own and Halberstam's (1998: 241) that reclaim masculinity for women – 'masculinity does not belong to men, has not been produced only by men, and does not properly express male heterosexuality'. They also highlight some dangers of the flipside of this: making femininity safe for men. Perhaps 'current moves toward the undoing of binaries may involve less of a feminisation and more of an arrangement of gender without women' (Adkins 2001: 692). This warning is important. However, it suggests a need for vigilance rather than a need to abandon the project altogether, a need to keep in mind Judith Butler's (1997: 100) question: 'how can we work the power relations by which we are worked and in what direction?'

Another difficulty with the approach to masculinity in this section is that it has been largely uncritical. Yet femininity and masculinity are not two symmetric sets of practices from which people should be enabled to select at will. Current gender regimes are profoundly unequal and men still secure their 'patriarchal dividend' (Connell 1995). I see the project of supporting gender transgression as a way of transforming the current gender regime and the practices and ways of being that support the oppression of women. After all, it is partly the exclusion of women (and men) from certain practices that allows these practices to function as part of a system of domination.

Transformation, this time of maths, is also the theme of the next direction for change.

Third direction: opening up mathematics

Throughout this book I have argued that in choosing maths students are doing gender; they are also doing class and race/ethnicity, although these have not been my focus. This implicates maths in preserving masculinity, and capitalism and white supremacy, as sources of power and control (see Frankenstein 1995; Shelley 1995). So higher maths remains masculine, not only in the sense that it is numerically dominated by men, but also in the ways that the practices through which it comes into being serve to support the current gender regime, 'the capacity of certain men to control social resources through gender processes – and the kind of society being produced by that power' (Connell 1995: 205). These ideas are based in understanding maths as a social practice, something constructed in and through our actions rather than something 'out there' and external to us.

The question arises as to what futures may follow from a social theory of maths. Here Bob Connell's (1987) discussion of the futures, which can be built on a social theory of gender, is helpful. He sees two possibilities: the abolition of gender or its reconstitution on new bases. The first is a deconstructive strategy that raises questions about whether our current gender relations have any value.

> What would be our loss if they went down the gurgle-hole of history?
>
> It has to be said that a great deal of our culture's energy and beauty, as well as its barbarism, has been created through and around gender relations. A gender-structured culture, and quite specifically sexist sensibilities, have given us *Othello*, the *Ring of the Nibelung* and Rubens portraits, to go no further. Much of the fine texture of everyday life, from the feel of our own bodies, through the lore of running a household, to popular songs and everyday humour, are predicated on gender. Our eroticism and our imagination seem to

be both limited and fuelled by gender. To discard the whole pattern does seem to imply a way of life that would be seriously impoverished by comparison with the one we know. At best it would be so different from the world of our experience that we can hardly know whether it would be desirable or not.

(1987: 288)

Returning to maths, here too the abolition of maths is not only impractical but it is also questionable whether a maths-free world is desirable. My own view is that it is not. It is clear to me that the social and historical practices of maths have resulted in a great deal more than oppression and inequality. A mathematically structured culture, and quite specifically absolutist and sexist sensibilities, have given us the Internet, the central limit theorem and the Mandelbrot set, to go no further. As well as the positive contributions that maths has made to society I have a more personal reason for rejecting a maths-free future. For as long as I can remember I have enjoyed maths and I continue to do so; I value what my mathematical training has made possible for me, while simultaneously mourning the loss of what it has made impossible. This pleasure in maths is shared by many of the students in this study and was the main reason for choosing it for 16 of them and one of the reasons for their choice for a further 12. Just as masculinity is not all bad, and is not fixed in its current form, neither is maths.

This leaves us with the second option, the reconstitution of maths on new bases, the possibility of separating the cultural energy around maths from structures of inequality. As I said in Chapter 3, the starting point for change must be the myth of the certainty of mathematical knowledge, its epistemological status as absolute and untainted by the corruption and messiness of daily life. It is this that gives maths its power and maintains it in its position as the ultimate intelligence test. In this book I have employed various strategies for undermining and subverting this myth. In Chapters 1 and 3, I introduced the idea of psychoanalytic thought experiments that explore the darker side of Reason's dream.

I have also used the metaphors of voice and narrative. By basing Chapters 3, 4 and 5 around students' voices and stories, the 'objective' voice of maths has been put in its place so that other voices can be heard. There are no true voices. However, the idea of 'voice' is still a useful one. It enables me to acknowledge that we feel able to express some things in some places and not in others, that some of these processes feel authentic while some feel like silencing, and that these processes impact on what we can do in different spaces. So an inclusive maths needs a wider range of student voices to be heard in classrooms by teachers, by fellow students and by maths itself. Maths needs to be opened up to different voices with different stories to tell.

This idea of opening up maths may sound appealing but perhaps the idea of abandoning certainty gives you, like it does me, pause for thought, it is a facet of maths that appealed to many of the participants in my study and was a big part of what originally attracted me to the subject. However, my data contain reasons to be optimistic about how people would respond to such a change. Most young people told me that they appreciated the opportunities for discussion and group work in other subjects but felt these to be inappropriate in maths lessons. This was part of Simon's story in Chapter 4. In another example, Phil, who strongly identified with maths, told me that he liked the way in English 'you can sort of have some room to find your own opinion'. He felt that this was not possible in maths 'you need to discuss stuff in English, but you can't really do a lot of discussion in maths'. While initially he found the uncertainty of English, the way 'there's never a wrong or right answer', difficult, by the time of his interview at the end of the second term of Year 12 he told me, 'I'm more comfortable with it now because I can deal with it better, before I couldn't'. Young people cannot be shielded from the uncertainty and ambiguity of the world forever and an overemphasis on certainty in maths 'seems to rest on a misunderstanding about the sorts of knowledge and understanding needed for living well in our sort of society. It risks conveying to pupils a distorted picture of the possibilities and responsibilities of an adult human life' (Bramall 2000: 62). In other words, certainty functions ideologically by closing down what we can think and do, including pedagogically and politically, which is why working against it is so important. These ideas are developed in the final part of the book.

Conclusions

In this chapter I have brought together the findings from my research, combining them into three cross-cutting directions for change. Re-framing them as follows connects these:

- *Making choices social* can be re-framed as unfixing the differences of identity enacted and represented in our choices from their location in the individual.
- *Supporting gender transgression* can be re-framed as unfixing gender differences from the binary straitjacket that, among other things, fixes masculinity in men and femininity in women (and that fixes men in masculinity and women in femininity).
- *Opening up mathematics* can be re-framed as unfixing our ideas

about maths, learners of maths and the kinds of relationships it is possible to have between subject and learner, so as to make room for differences within the subject.

In this way, the idea of unfixing differences brings together my three directions for change. It also provides a way of working productively with the tensions that run through them.

I discussed one of these tensions when grappling with gender in Chapters 1 and 5. As I said there, in one sense doing any research on gender calls attention to the oppositional division into male and female, masculine and feminine, and so reiterates it. Gender is once again fixed in a binary frame. However, the project of unfixing gender from its binary frame requires us first to recognize that fixing and to understand in detail how it works. So, a little paradoxically, it is acts of fixing like the ones in this book that make acts of unfixing possible. There is a parallel tension running through my discussions on maths. In one sense my suggestion that doing maths is doing masculinity fixes the subject in a binary frame, and so sits awkwardly with discussions of unfixing it. But, as with gender, I want to use the fixing of maths in this book as a starting point for unfixing the subject.

Part 3 traces some of the things that teachers might do with the understandings in this book. Each of the three chapters in it roughly follow on in turn from each of the three directions developed in this chapter: making choices social, supporting gender transgression and opening up mathematics. Unfixing what is fixed and disrupting binary frameworks are at the heart of queer theory and practice and so what follows is very much informed by these approaches. Cultural studies, law, biology, theatre studies, film studies, geography, literature, politics, psychology, history, philosophy, computing and health studies, all have chapters devoted to them in a typical edited collection on queering education (Griffin and Andermahr 1994). Maths is absent from this list and from nearly all the work on queer theory that I have read while researching for this book. Why and how that absence has come about are questions worth keeping in mind as I explore, in the final three chapters, how queer approaches can be used in maths classrooms and beyond.

The strategies in the next part of the book are offered cautiously. We cannot escape history and when we resist oppressive practices we cannot be sure that everyone will read our acts of resistance as we intend them. Nothing is predictable. 'My so-called resistant or transgressive actions may simultaneously benefit some and harm others. Every action has ambiguous results' (Morris 1998: 289). Digression is a better way of thinking about things:

To digress from dominant cultural codes is to move away from mainstream discourses. This digression does not guarantee my success or failure. This digression does not necessarily change either micropolitical landscapes or macropolitical horizons, although certainly these are some of my goals. I cannot be sure, either, how others will be affected by my digressions; I cannot be sure how others will read my performances. If anything, digressive moves admit an ambiguous dystopian effect.

(Morris 1998: 280)

In suitably sober mood, it's time to move on …

Part 3

Queering gender and maths

Now, in these first conversations [on queer theory], some of my colleagues ask why such a disparaging term (as they hear it, if not for the ears they imagine) should be claimed. Some consider it as too angry – too oppositional – for what they imagine as the General Public. These folks assume that teachers would never be able to pronounce such a term at school. They wonder if another term could be employed, one more easily exchanged, one that does not boomerang between the utterance and the utterer. Others view it as a new centricity, an attempt to reverse the binary of hetero/homo and to valorize, for a while, the latter term. For still others, it is not polite to call anything queer. Those who seem uncomfortable think the term queer as a noun or an identity. But the queer and the theory in Queer Theory signify actions, not actors. It can be thought of as a verb, or as a citational relation that signifies more than the signifier.

As used in street activism and cultural production, queer politics is meant to disturb and to provoke pleasure.

(Britzman 1995)

chapter seven

Making choices social: refusing essences in the classroom

This chapter takes as its starting point the idea of developing a social rather than an individual language for talking about choice. However, I'm going to sidestep choices a little and concentrate on developing a social language for talking about ability. This is not as much of a sidestep as it might appear. First, because in maths ability is often seen as a proxy for choice, it determines whether you study maths or not: you've either got it or you haven't; if you have then it would be a shame to waste it, and if you haven't then there's no point even trying. A social language for ability is thus a vital ingredient in a social language for choice. Second, whether we are developing a social language for choice or for ability the basic strategy is the same: to refuse essences. To refuse to see our talents, inclinations, interests and so on, as stemming from something inside ourselves, a separate pure bit of us that remains untouched by society so that wherever and whenever we happened to live, we would still ... enjoy adventure, be confident in social situations, hate pink, love chocolate, possess perfect pitch, fancy men, have a special talent for algebra, or whatever else we do that we feel is just part of who we are, and so couldn't possibly be otherwise. Usually there is an acknowledgement that in particular situations, somewhere there is no chocolate or where we never get a chance to learn algebra, these parts of ourself would remain dormant; but there is also the assumption that they would still be there, waiting to be discovered.

I have also chosen to focus on ability because of the powerful stories that circulate about it. There are stories of true genius shining through. For example, Ramanujan was a self-taught Indian mathematician whose genius was discovered when he wrote a letter to Cambridge mathematician G. H. Hardy (the same G. H. Hardy I quoted in Chapter 1). Ramanujan is name-checked in *Good Will Hunting*, another diamond-in-the-rough story that shows how raw mathematical talent will out (see Chapter 3). Beyond maths, there are contemporary talent contests, such as the global phenomenon, *Pop Idol*, where, so the rhetoric goes, those who have the X-factor (and how monolithic that terms makes it look) win out in the end. Linked to this are stories about the biological basis of ability. Indeed, the first research into the possibility of a maths gene is currently underway at Cambridge University, headed up by a professor of developmental psychopathology (Revill 2005). Such ideas are used to support the idea that mathematical ability is unchangeable:

> If a child has had bad teaching in mathematics, it is accepted that the resulting deficiency can be remedied by extra good teaching the following year. But any suggestion that the child's mathematical deficiency might have a genetic origin is likely to be greeted with something approaching despair: if it is in the genes 'it is written', it is 'determined' and nothing can be done about it; you might as well give up teaching the child mathematics. This is pernicious rubbish on an almost astrological scale.
>
> (Dawkins 1982: 13)

Here the evolutionary biologist Richard Dawkins rejects talk of immutable essences, suggesting a socially mediated understanding of biological processes like the one I introduced in Chapter 1. However, in spite of this, throughout maths education and beyond, talk of natural ability is all-pervasive and all-powerful. Throughout Part 2 the impact of these stories on learners' relationships with maths is clear.

So, what would refusing ability as essence mean? First, it is not about rejecting the idea that there are clear differences between what people are capable of doing mathematically in specific situations. Instead it is about refusing to accept that these capabilities are in any way fixed in the person and asocial, that they can and should be used to predict future performance, and that what is relevant to success in maths in any context can be summed into a single ability.

Clearly this would mean a rejection of grouping students by so-called ability (which is always actually prior attainment) whether by setting, streaming, banding, tracking or any of the other systems that exist across the world. However, the pervasiveness of ability within maths education practices, and education generally, goes way beyond these processes for sorting learners into teaching groups. This was a point convincingly made by Stephen Ball (1981) in his classic study *Beachside Comprehensive*. Ball researched Beachside School both before and after it made the transition from banded to mixed-ability teaching groups. In his book he traces how this change in organization solved the behaviour problems that had been associated with the middle ability 'band 2' classes without results suffering. However, he also found important continuities between the two systems. The ranking of pupils by teachers and the separation of students into pro- and anti-school subcultures, which were evident under banding, persisted within mixed-ability environments. Ability continued to operate within classroom practices, through selection, competition, the prioritizing of academic success and so on. In fact, after mixed-ability teaching was implemented there were less 'inappropriate choices' of examination entry level by students at age 14 than there had been under the banding system; so he concluded that, ironically, mixed-ability teaching 'provides a much more "effective" basis for the socialization of appropriate aspirations for this important choice point' than banding, since students better know their place in the 'competitive and hierarchical system of achieved-ability' (p. 278) when in mixed than in banded groups.

Along with Ball, I do not want to say that there is no difference at all between these systems, but that it is not enough to draw clear distinctions between mixed-ability groupings on the one hand and ability groupings on the other. What matters is to trace the way ability plays in and through these systems and to interrupt and refuse this. An important starting point for this is to change our way of seeing what goes on in classrooms, to start *noticing* (Mason 2002) the workings of ability. This is my focus in the next two sections of this chapter that contain case studies of two classes that I observed at Westerburg Sixth Form College. Students feature in these (including some of those discussed in Chapters 3, 4 and 5) but the focus is on teachers and how they construct mathematical epistemology, appropriate pedagogy, and the role of examinations differently dependent, on their ability-based expectations of the two groups, thus making very different spaces and identifications available to learners and inducting them into very different communities of practice. After these case studies I explore how to create alternative stories and then some of the pedagogic possibilities these approaches open up.

Veronica Sawyer's class

Mrs Sawyer has just marked the second homework of a first year AS level group at Westerburg. The homework topic was completing the square although a lot of the errors occurred in the students' manipulation of fractions. As a result she decides to suspend the normal curriculum and spend an hour looking at prime factors, highest common factors, lowest common multiples and then the four operations on fractions. She describes this as a 'very, very simple' topic 'dealing with very, very basic things' and further as 'babyish'. The students progress through the work largely in silence and with few problems. Their teacher interrupts them at regular intervals to offer advice, call out answers, deal with queries and remind them how to deal with the operation rehearsed in the next set of questions. Vicky is one of the first to complete the fractions exercises and has had no problems with them. This surprises her teacher who had commented at the beginning of the lesson that, given the mistakes Vicky made in her work, this lesson will be particularly useful for her. Mrs Sawyer asks her: 'So it wasn't that that was the problem? What was it?' Vicky pleads ignorance and suggests that, 'perhaps it was just a bad day'. Mrs Sawyer simply adds that it cannot be that because she has made these same errors twice, and the discussion ends.

This incident, taken from my fieldnotes, struck me as typical of how, often, the assumptions of teachers about how maths is learnt cannot explain learners' behaviours. The teacher's conversation with Vicky indicates that she has assumed that the latter's inability to apply a skill (in this case, the manipulation of fractions) in one context (in this case, completing the square) indicates a general inability to apply that skill in all contexts, and one that can be remedied by a decontextualized drill and practice of the given skill. This incident shows how, despite evidence to the contrary, maths teachers often continue to act as if they are 'delivering' transferable skills to students with fixed abilities; the parts of their lived experience that cannot be understood within such a model disappear.

The lesson described above is typical of the way students in this class generally work individually on repetitive exercises that practise set procedures, when they are not being taught didactically. Mrs Sawyer's decision to improve the group's skills by going back to basics exemplifies the way she feels that maths has to be done in a particular order. Within this discourse of a hierarchy of knowledge in which she inscribes maths, some topics are located near the top of the scale, as 'hard' and others near the bottom, as 'easy'. Mrs Sawyer often describes 'easy' topics as 'babyish', this association with a younger state being carried through by their being labelled as junior school or GCSE work. Such references draw on and fuel a series of parallel binaries; 'baby' work is 'easy' and is opposed to 'grown up' methods that are 'hard'. These binaries are gendered and hetero/sexualized; the masculine 'hard' opposes the feminine 'soft' and 'yielding'. And, they are classed: certain aspects of middle class 'cultural capital' are taken as signs of mathematical maturity and ability (Morgan 1998).

In looking for meanings in maths classes, researchers and practitioners have discussed the absence of sense-making from overly procedural, competitive lessons. As discussed in Chapter 4, Jo Boaler (1997) reported that many students, but particularly girls, found their 'quest for understanding' frustrated by the fast paced repetition of techniques that dominate top set maths pedagogy. Mrs Sawyer's approach to the 'quest for understanding' is interesting. On two occasions I saw her substitute belief for understanding. For example, her discursive framing of a topic shifts from comments like 'I know this is hard for an afternoon lesson', to 'you've got to believe me, it's not magic, you've got to believe me, I'm not fooling you'. Alternatively she often suggests deferring the quest, 'you've got to be patient with yourself when you're learning'. Understanding will result from time, effort and hard work. This construction of understanding is used as a rationale for stemming the flow of student questions. However, for me, the most important difference between the 'quest for understanding' of the girls in Boaler's study and the one that Mrs Sawyer wants her class to pursue is motivational. She makes clear that it is the examination that defines not only what understanding is needed, but also whether you have understood or not; external authority replaces internally authorized sense-making.

In all the classes I observed there was some mention of the exam. However, the frequency and nature of such mentions varied greatly. In Mrs Sawyer's class the exam itself was discussed often and the teacher used many opportunities to describe exam technique. However, it was largely through the constructed figure of 'the examiner' that the exam made its presence felt. This (assumed male) examiner is sometimes a hard taskmaster rigorously insisting on one form of answer over another and at other times a doddery old man who finds messy work 'confusing'. The examiner guides the choice of methods as when Mrs Sawyer instructs her students to score neatly through each term when expanding brackets so that the person marking your script can still see it and to write 'comparing' when comparing coefficients in order 'to show off to the examiner that you're a logical person'.

That the examiner is also the ultimate arbiter of right and wrong in the eyes of the students is clear from Imran's and Saeed's comments to me during a lesson on inequalities. When I point out to Imran that he has used $=$ instead of $<$, he says twice 'you know what I mean', and then shifts to 'the examiner will know what I mean'.

Saeed, who gets the answer '$-x < -4$', wants to know how to get the answer at the back of the book. After I explain, he wants to know 'will they mark that [his original solution] as right in the exam?'

However exams carry with them constant evaluation, not only against the requirements of the examiner, but also against each other. Martyn Denscombe (2000: 370) found that students saw exams as offering 'the prospects of success or failure which could be used as a "measure of the person" on which to make comparisons with others'. Next I look at the way these processes of producing ability-based comparisons were played out and encouraged in the classroom.

During the 15 hours of lessons that I observed with Mrs Sawyer there were two short tests. These tests are clearly linked to improving student performance in the exam. However, the competitive element goes beyond this, as students are required to declare their marks in front of the rest of the class. Mrs Sawyer also sustains competition between this group and her parallel first-year class, 'my other set, my decision maths set, that you're in competition with'. When several members of the group provide her with the correct answer to the product of $4x^3$ and $3x^2$ she praises them with the words 'you've already beaten my other group'. And while the students are working in silence on a test she describes the errors made by her other group as her reason for doing this test, adding to me, but clearly audible to the whole group, 'I just wanted to see if this lot could beat them'.

Mrs Sawyer emphasizes not only differences between her groups but also differences within them. She draws on two discourses to explain these differences: 'lack of preparation' is used to explain how some are doing less well, and 'natural ability' is used to explain how some are doing better. Although not explicitly invoked to explain failure, the use of a discourse of 'natural ability' to explain success necessarily carries with it the implication that lack of 'natural ability' contributes to lack of success. Yasser (from Chapter 3) is an example of how these positions are lived:

> Yasser is referred to by his teacher as 'naturally able' and is clearly marked out as different. He is sometimes given different work to do and on one occasion is asked to teach the class his method for tackling quadratic inequalities. At first he tries to explain his solution verbally, but this proves difficult so he suggests, 'Shall I write it?' Mrs Sawyer responds, 'Please do'. When Yasser writes up his solution there are many looks from students that combine amusement and bemusement. Imran declares, 'That is so complicated, I've never seen that in my life!' Next to him AJ has his hand up, while Saeed says to his teacher, 'He's clever, isn't he?' then adding, 'He should do further maths'. She agrees with him, 'He should but he's busy doing other things'. Saeed asks her, 'Why don't you encourage him to do further maths?' She responds, 'I've tried, it's his choice'. Yasser has now completed writing up not just his original solution but also the graph that Mrs Sawyer asked him to do when his first approach appeared obscure. AJ asks, 'What is that?' and then repeats the question. Sanjay has a furrowed brow and his

hand up. Then Mrs Sawyer steps in and goes up to the board and explains the graphical method while leaving up Yasser's work because, 'It is worthy of honour'. She further suggests that you could make sense of his diagram by putting numbers in, 'But you've done it theoretically like a good pure mathematician'.

Yasser is constructed here as a mathematician (he eventually does do further maths). However, the manner of his construction as an esoteric being, a curiosity, 'the spectre of mathematical "genius"' (Bartholomew 2000: 4), as *Other*, makes it more difficult for the rest of the group to share this position. This raises the question of what positions are available to them.

I have shown that Mrs Sawyer's classroom, in common with many maths classrooms, is one where the motivational practices promoted are not the intrinsic ones of pursuing a challenge or a 'quest for understanding' or of gaining enjoyment from it. The absence of these practices makes subject positions as a mathematician less available to learners. Instead learners become rule-followers, good or bad students, 'naturally able', bottom or top of the class, among other things, and, above all, exam-passers (or exam-failers). In the next section I explore how the discourses about ability, examinations and mathematicians within the Westerburg further maths class hold out different possibilities of identifications for students.

Alan Rudolff and Jason Dean's further maths class

The further maths students spend ten hours each week having lessons together. The practice of teaching them maths, as well as further maths, as a separate group is part of the discourse of their difference from 'normal' maths students. However, the further maths teaching and learning practices have much in common with those described above. The teacher rehearses techniques at the board accompanied by questions to check understanding, then students work through similar exercises; regular homework is set and marked; and tests are used, for among other reasons, to assess progress and to motivate students. Both further maths teachers, Alan Rudolff and Jason Dean, frequently refer to the exams and to the actions of examiners and I begin with this aspect of their practice.

In Mr Rudolff's lessons I observe one discussion on why Tippex is banned from exams, two on the decision mathematics examination answer booklets and lots on how to present answers clearly to the examiner and use the question format, and the number of marks allocated in order to assess what is required. On more than one occasion he exhorts his students to 'pity the poor examiner' who gets very little money in exchange for deciphering their work. Similarly, Mr Dean emphasizes the important goal of exam performance. For example, when discussing the merits of alternative methods he emphasizes: 'What I really care about is that when you're sat in the exam you do it [in] a way you're happy with and you get the right answer'.

As in Mrs Sawyer's group, students take up this concern about the requirements of the examination/examiner. These concerns surface particularly when they are tackling questions they find difficult. Students ask how many marks such questions would be worth and how long they would have to do them. However, there is an important difference from the attitudes in the other group. These students do not abandon questions that go beyond the exam's requirements. This suggests that alternatives to becoming exam passers are available to learners. Below I consider what alternatives are supported by their classroom practices.

Mr Dean teaches the group pure mathematics. It is his first year at Westerburg and his first time teaching further maths. He thinks the group is different and makes this apparent to the class. After three weeks he tells them they are already over two weeks ahead of a normal maths group and he often begins a phrase with the words, 'You're a further maths group so . . .' Thus these comparisons with normal maths students are related to assumptions about their underlying abilities and to the fast/slow opposition.

They are also tied to the hard/easy opposition. For example, when the group are tackling integrals involving trigonometric substitutions, Mr Dean says, 'You're a further maths lot so you should be able to do this sort of question'. He then recalls giving this question to one group three times and they still could not do it.

Graham asks if they were a further maths group. And, when Mr Dean says that they were not, Graham responds, 'So there is some hope for us'.

In another case Mr Dean relates this to the theory/practice opposition explaining to the group that, 'Again we're doing all the theory. You won't actually be asked in the exam but we should, as a further maths group, know where it all comes from and why it works'. Their abilities and status as further maths rather than 'normal' maths students give them access to a different curriculum and make possible different relationships with maths.

Another way that Mr Dean inscribes the group's difference relates to how he likes to work through material in the correct order and seems disturbed when his plans to do this are disrupted. Sometimes, as when

Peter supplies a full solution of an equation rather than just the next step, Mr Dean re-imposes staged progress. He goes back a step and says, 'I'll do that in a minute, you've got a bit ahead of me'. Sometimes, as in the incident that follows, he lets go of ordered progress:

> When Mr Dean is detailing the three possibilities for the discriminant of a quadratic, Gary asks what the zero case looks like graphically. First, Mr Dean explains they are doing this later. But, after a pause, he asks: 'What do you think?' Gary suggests a straight line, then Ahmed indicates a parabolic shape with his hands and says it will 'be on the x-axis'. Mr Dean works through all three cases graphically. He expresses anxiety at having deviated from his plan: 'I'm a bit worried that we've done it all at once. I was going to stop and let you do a few questions after the formula bit'. He asks: 'Shall we stop where we are at the minute and go back to the graphs later?' The consensus is clearly in the negative, student responses include, 'Let's just get it done now' and, 'We're on a roll!' Mr Dean asks: 'Is there anyone who doesn't want to carry on now?' He tells them that there is nothing wrong with admitting this and, on the contrary, it is a sign that you are 'mature enough to admit it'. They carry on when there is a silent response to this.

Seeing his concerns, I ask Jason about this lesson. He tells me that this was the lesson when he realized the difference between a further and a 'normal' maths group. I then ask him if he would teach this topic differently to another group. He explains he would, going slower and perhaps using the computer, something concrete that contrasts with the abstract presentation described above. His understanding of further maths students as different, and importantly as more able, enables him to teach them less hierarchically and prescriptively but also prevents him from considering shifting the ways that he teaches other people maths.

In addition to comparisons with other groups, tests, evaluations and individual comparisons are standard classroom motivational practices. When Mr Dean returns their first test he tells them that four of the scripts are good and the others need work. Then, while going through specific questions, he provides information on how many people within the group succeeded at each. Another form of competition is embedded in his use of challenges. Jason tells me they are becoming a further maths group because they 'want challenges'. He regularly describes questions as 'challenging' or asks the group to 'test' some equations for him. Competition here is first against maths itself and second against others in the group. Challenges also play a role in Mr Rudolff's interactions with students. However, he links these rhetorically to their being not further maths students but mathematicians.

Mr Rudolff stresses problem-solving and beauty as aims. He praises solutions that are 'beautiful' and sets worksheets where 'the idea is not to find the answer to the problem, it's to find a method to the problem'. He connects these to an identity as a mathematician. For example, he gives two reasons to care which graphs are planar. Mathematicians care because there is a problem/puzzle and so they want to solve it, whether it is useful or not, and others care because of applications to microchip technology.

There are several classroom practices, in addition to his general problem-solving orientation, which are illuminated by reading Mr Rudolff's classes as a mathematical apprenticeship. For example, he uses language like 'theorem' and 'conjecture' and material on the history of maths. He is also involved in coordinating the work of a group – consisting of Apu, Bart, Desmond, Graham, Jacob, Paul and Peter (the same Graham and Peter featured in Chapter 3) – for the Cambridge University *Motivate* scheme. Students have to use maths to tackle problems and then present their solutions to Cambridge lecturers at a videoconference. In one lesson:

> Mr Rudolff gets the *Motivate* group to the front and sets questions for the other students. Mr Rudolff talks to the group very publicly. He stands at the front and uses the board (why can't he sit with them?) He runs through the progress they have made for Wednesday's presentation and summarizes this on the board. Graham and Jacob are writing a computer program. Mr Rudolff records 'constructed–demonstrate–results'. He asks Graham if this program represents a mathematical or a computational achievement. Graham feels that it is both. Since the other two groups have made less progress he suggests that they combine and look at the diabetes issue and arranges times to meet with them. Bart wants advice. Mr Rudolff reads from the sheet: 'Find out as much as you can about Type I and Type II diabetes'. He adds: 'I wouldn't spend too long on that because it's not mathematical'. He suggests they re-read the relevant talk and then he will help them.

Mr Rudolff also tells students that mathematicians are 'lazy', that they 'like to find easy ways' to do things, and 'that as a mathematician you're over the hill at 28'. Importantly: 'good mathematicians tend to find frustrating' the need to show your 'method' and not just find the 'solution' and so they do not necessarily come top of the exam. Through this discourse mathematical ability is separated from exam success and is even constructed as a disadvantage in exams since 'bright students are often impatient and just want to solve the problem', 'you have to go out of your way to show that you have answered the question', and 'this penalizes the best students because they will go straight to the answer'. Thus the alternative to exam passing in this class is based on the idea that those who score highest in maths assessments are not synonymous with the best and the brightest mathematicians.

Seeing ability in action

The stories of the two classes above are about the practices that we engage in within maths education and the meanings these have for learners and teachers. They remind us of the resources the young people in Part 2 of this book have available to them to build their relationships with maths.

These stories show ability in action in maths, the way that ideas about it make possible particular actions on the part of learners and teachers, while making other actions impossible. Ability acts in these classes through the alignment of a series of binary oppositions. In Mrs Sawyer's class we have the following oppositions relating to maths itself:

Hard/Easy
Hard/Soft
Grown-up/ Babyish
A level work/GCSE and junior school work
High/Low

These are tied to a set of oppositions about learners of maths:

Top of the class/Bottom of the class
Naturally able/Badly prepared
Mathematician/Normal maths student
Other/Normal

These constrain, while not determining completely, the identifications that learners can make with maths. Because of the alignment of mathematician with Other, even those at the top of the class find it difficult to identify with this label.

The pattern of binaries looks a little different in the further maths class. In terms of maths itself, we find the oppositions:

Maths challenges/Syllabus questions
Theory/Practice
Abstract/Concrete
Beauty/Utility

Together with the always implied:

Hard/Easy

In terms of learners, we have:

Fast/Slow
Further maths students/Normal maths students
Problem solvers/Rule followers
Lazy/Hard working
Young/Old
Mathematicians /Exam passers
Mathematicians/Other people

In one sense, this is a more productive series of binaries since it allows more spaces for the learners in the group to identify with maths and as mathematicians. However, both sets of oppositions are gendered and constructed through the exclusion of those who locate themselves and are located within the second abject term of each pair. They also both fix maths ability within the person and oppose mathematicians to other people. If we are to make ability social we need to disrupt these binaries. Noticing them is vital to this process. If we can see our assumptions then we can begin to unpick them and to engage in new experiments in thought. We can change commonsense. I continue with some ideas about what these thought experiments might look like.

Essence-less abilities

Since I am interested in disrupting binaries I have turned to queer theory whose raison d'être is binary disruption. There are three collections of queer strategies that I put to work in what follows; they are all, following from Deborah Britzman's invocation at the opening of this part of the book, meant to disturb and to provoke pleasure:

- *Troubling binaries*: if there's a take home message from this book, it's that binaries are trouble and need troubling. This strategy does this by showing how the two sides of a binary are not separate, but actually each term in an opposition requires its other, the one 'only becomes intelligible through the difference to its other ... This definitional interdependence' (Luhmann 1998: 144) threatens the distinctiveness of the more powerful term, and so forms of normalization are needed to protect it from the threat of collapsing into its Other. Making visible these forms of normalization is part of this strategy.
- *Stopping all the binaries lining up*: this strategy undermines binaries by focusing on the relationships between them rather

than on any individual binary. It disrupts 'the desire for the neat arrangement of dichotomous sexual and gendered difference' (Luhmann 1998: 145), disturbing the way that positionings in binaries line up predictably. As Eve Sedgwick (1994: 6, original emphasis) asks: 'What if instead there were a practice of valuing the ways in which meanings and institutions can be at loose ends with each other? What if the richest junctures weren't the ones where *everything means the same thing?*'

- *Telling stories*: the rationale for this approach is that binaries are kept in place by the fiction of the rational subject. This strategy is about refusing this identity, about shifting from assuming and affirming identities to looking at how a reader becomes part of the text, looking at what identifications are possible and using story-writing as a way of intervening in these processes, re-inscribing people and objects and words, opening up possibilities for new identifications and meanings.

These strategies have been implicitly there in everything I have written so far. For example, my methodology is based on the telling stories approach and my idea that doing maths is doing masculinity does a little to stop the binaries of male/female and masculinity/femininity lining up, and to see what happens when these two do not mean the same thing. Making these strategies explicit is helpful. In the rest of this chapter I use these techniques to develop ways of looking at people, and stories through which to make sense of their lives, that do not jump straight from seeing what they can or cannot do mathematically to judgements about their character, intelligence and value as a human being (or vice versa). My starting point is to trouble the binaries:

Ability/Inability
Able/Unable

The way I will do this is to look at what the terms in these oppositions have in common, focusing on the costs of ability and of inability.

Using a psychoanalytic thought experiment, ability, and the knowledge that follows from it, always have a cost; inability becomes evidence of not being able to bear to know something, of a desire not to know. This leads us to not dismiss inability but to ask what we can learn from it: 'in this question, the desire for ignorance is performative rather than cognitive. It is indicative of the incapacity – or the unwillingness – to acknowledge one's own implication in the material studied' (Luhmann 1998: 149). So I am suggesting that we understand 'inability' as a 'refusal of knowledge'. My favourite example of using this idea is Fritz. Fritz was a young child who had problems with doing long division and came to the attention of the psychoanalyst, Melanie Klein. She recounts that Fritz:

> Told me that in doing division he had first of all to bring down the figure that was required and he climbed up, seized it by the arm and pulled it down. To my enquiry as to what is said to that, he replied that quite certainly it was not pleasant for the number – it was as if his mother stood on a stone 13 yards high and someone came and caught her by the arm so that they tore it out and divided her ... He then related ... that actually every child wants to have a bit of his mother, who is to be cut in four pieces; he depicted quite exactly how she screamed and had paper stuffed in her mouth so that she could not scream, and what kind of faces she made, etc. A child took a very sharp knife, and he described how she was cut up; first across the width of the breast, and then of the belly, then lengthwise so that the 'pipi', [*in his imagination, mothers also had penises, it seems*] the face and the head were cut exactly through the middle, whereby the 'sense' was taken out of her head. The head was then again cut through obliquely just as the 'pipi' was cut across its breadth ... He continued that every child then took the piece of the mother that it wanted, and agreed that the cut-up mother was then also eaten. It now appeared also that he always confused the remainder with the quotient in division, and always wrote it in the wrong place because in his mind it was bleeding pieces of flesh with which he was unconsciously dealing.
>
> (Klein cited in Segal 2000: 27–8, original emphasis)

After Klein's analysis of Fritz, he managed to do all his long divisions correctly. (This does not necessarily mean that this is exactly what Fritz was experiencing when he did long division but that it proved useful to him to think of it in this way.)

Other researchers have traced the phantasies involved in doing maths. Robert Early (1992), in his work on experiences of mathematical challenge, encouraged his students to record their phantasies of challenge and then conducted a Jungian analysis of them. Looking for timeless and universal themes, he read their phantasies in terms of alchemical processes through which learners were trying to turn ignorance into gold. One particularly memorable student phantasy was: 'I felt as though I was jumping rope on a razor blade, and with each jump blood trickled onto the blank paper below me' (1992: 15). These phantasies speak about the costs of not knowing, of being unable.

It is easy to find such things in the words of the young people I interviewed. For example Natasha, the Nigerian student at Sunnydale College who was interviewed with Toni from Chapter 6, mused: 'Why do I like it [maths]? You know what I'm saying? Coz like um it's getting difficult for me. But it's good. I like maths from when I was a little kid coz where I come from, I used to, I was a little kid in Nigeria. So maths then was their main priority so it's like you have to love it'. And Analia, a Turkish student at Westerburg College, recalled: 'I remember how I learnt to do my multiplications. My dad told me to bring my marble box and do multiplication, and he had some marbles and he showed me it, and I remember I used to go to the shop with him and he used to find these little subtraction and um adding books, you know, they would be like thick and they'd have like five questions on every paper, 2 + 4, or something. You know, you used to get, you used to do them and take them up to him and he'd go, "Oh, well done! And those others, well done!" and you'd think, "Wow!"'

In both of these passages we get a sense of what Natasha and Analia have invested in being successful at maths and of why it might be a source of pleasure for them. It would be easy to tell stories about how, when doing maths, Natasha affirms her national identity and Analia affirms her relationship with her father (I have written more about Analia in Mendick 2005). These stories disturb ideas about natural ability; they also stop the binaries lining up by aligning the logic and certainty that both these students enjoy about maths with the messiness of emotional commitments and relationships. These ideas return to the questions I raised in Chapters 1 and 3 about from where our attachment to certainty derives and to the psychoanalytic thought experiments I wrote about there. They suggest how many current pedagogic practices are forms of normalization that protect ability from the threat of collapsing into its Other and raise questions about what alternatives are possible.

Pedagogic possibilities

In this chapter, I have begun looking at strategies for intervening into the gendering of maths that follow from the analyses in this book. I have focused on changing the ways we have of seeing learners of maths and the processes of learning, looking at the ways that ability controls these and at ways of reading that undercut ideas of fixed asocial ability. Such approaches are vulnerable to the accusation that they are overly theoretical and no use in practice. This claim draws on the theory/practice binary that was at work in the further maths group and on a related separation between reflection and teaching. However:

Since all practice is imbued with moral meaning and is the explicit exemplification of (someone's) implicit intentions, such a separation must of necessity be incoherent or, if intended, not honest. Teaching is not simply the aggregation of effective techniques: it is a moral activity which integrates practical, cognitive, interpersonal, affective and intellectual aspects of the teacher and requires recognising those aspects of the learner too.

(Povey 1995a: 264)

The position in Hilary Povey's words is that there are no easy distinctions between thought and action and so once we understand people's relationships to maths in the ways that I have within this chapter specifically, and this book more generally, we cannot but do things differently in the classroom and outside of it. This has certainly been the experience with my own practice.

Thus a useful starting point for change is to develop a critical approach to one's own practice. Observing and being observed by others – whether they be teachers, pupils or anyone else – can help in this process. As mentioned earlier, John Mason (2002) has also built up a discipline of noticing. This is a means for people to work on their own practice; it can be used to alter the level of awareness and consciousness that we have of our own actions.

To look at how ability works in practice, observation and noticing need to be focused on two related areas:

- The ways that pedagogic practices compare people, drawing distinctions between them and ranking them, and the ways that these are taken up by learners.
- The ways that pedagogic practices give meaning to classroom activities, ascribing motivations for engaging in them, and the ways that these are taken up by learners.

These are the things that I have explored within the case studies (on page 123) in this chapter. After raising awareness of their current practice, teachers then need to find alternative ways of talking about the differences between learners and alternative ways of giving meaning to activities. Below I offer a few practical suggestions.

First, in terms of differences between learners, teachers can start by assessing work without giving it a grade or a mark. Paul Black and Dylan Wiliam (1998: 6) in a survey of school assessment practice, comment:

The giving of marks and the grading functions are over-emphasized, while the giving of useful advice and the learning function are underemphasized ... [There is much] use of approaches in which pupils are compared with one another, the prime purpose of which appears to them to be competition rather than personal improvement. In consequence, assessment feedback teaches pupils with low attainments that they lack 'ability', so they are de-motivated, believing that they are not able to learn.

Alongside this shift away from grading, practices such as self- and peer-assessment can be incorporated into assessment practice.

Another way that learners compare themselves in maths is through timed tasks. This association of being successful in maths with being fast at maths destroys the possibility for many to have a comfortable relationship with the subject (Buxton 1981) and, as noted in this book, supports the inscription of the subject within gender binaries. The use of closed tasks, which have clear start and end points, and the valuing of product rather than process means activities often become a series of races. This is clear in questioning strategies:

> One common problem is that teachers do not allow enough quiet time so that pupils can think out and offer an answer. Where, as often happens, a teacher answers her or his own question after only two or three seconds, and where a minute (say) of silent thought is not tolerable, there is no possibility that a pupil can think out what to say. There are then two consequences. One is that because the only questions that can produce answers in such a short time are questions of fact, these predominate. The other is that pupils don't even try to think out a response – if you know that the answer, or another question, will come along in a few seconds, there is no point in trying. It is also common that only a few pupils in a class answer teachers' questions. The rest then leave it to these few, knowing that they cannot respond as quickly and being unwilling to risk making mistakes in public. So the teacher, by lowering the level of questions and by accepting answers from a few, can keep the lesson going but is actually out of touch with the understanding of most of the class – the question–answer dialogue becomes a ritual, one in which all connive and thoughtful involvement suffers.
>
> (Black and Wiliam 1998: 11–12)

Paul Black and Dylan Wiliam go on to suggest ways of breaking this vicious cycle such as allowing more time for questions, initiating discussion in pairs and groups around the questions, giving choices of answers and having a vote on them, and getting learners to write down answers some of which can then be read out and discussed. All of these approaches aim to encourage thoughtful reflection and to open up participation. Another alternative to simply asking a question in order to get the desired answer and carrying on regardless of whether it is given or not, is to ask, 'How shall we do this problem? and then ...

follow student contributions to their logical conclusions' (Noddings 1993: 156–7). Yet another approach would be to get learners to ask at least some of the questions.

Incorporating activities that encourage students to take collective rather than individual responsibility for their learning can also disrupt the processes through which pedagogy becomes a race. Once the journey rather than the destination becomes what is important, how quickly you get there (wherever that may be) becomes much less significant. Additionally, in pair and small group work a range of skills come into play that are not always associated with maths, such as explaining, talking, listening and writing, alongside more traditionally mathematical ones, such as calculating, reasoning and justifying. All group members contribute to the task and judgements about who possesses the greatest mathematical ability become both less important and less clear. Of course allowing and encouraging, or even requiring, students to work together is not enough. Students need to 'learn to draw each other out, build on each other's suggestions, and express their appreciation for good ideas and hard work' (Noddings 1993: 156); developing group working needs to be an explicit goal, as important as developing mathematical skills. As well as encouraging learners to work collectively, it can also be helpful for teachers to work with other teachers. This can build critical awareness, model collaborative work and give opportunities for support and sharing.

All these pedagogical approaches change our understandings of learners and of the meanings we have for what people are doing in maths classrooms. Another parallel approach for doing this is to change the words used to talk about the people and practices in classrooms. New words have different associations and connect with different stories so in this way we can switch the discourses that structure our imaginations of learners. There are two main reasons why it is easy to fit learners into the standard stories and discourses. The first is the power of these stories and the second is that teachers often do not know anything about their students that challenges them. By becoming aware of the traps in these stories and by getting to know more about their students, teachers can find information that is surprising and that can be the basis for expanding the range of stories they have about who does maths and why and how they do it. I have been trying to model this process through the analyses in this book. Although the process is potentially richer when teachers have the chance to work with learners over a longer period of time and so to explore their experiences of maths more extensively than I was able to within my research.

To do this, teachers need to become sort-of-researchers in their own classrooms. They need to combine taking a critical approach to commonsense with opening up a dialogue with learners about their relationships with maths. This can be done in many ways, one of which is by getting students to keep journals in which they can record their feelings about maths. Teachers can then read these journals and respond to the issues raised in them. They can also become the basis for initiating dialogue between learners.

Of course all these ideas are easier written than done. Throughout this book I have been interested in the interplay between the social and the individual and in looking at what the possibilities are, within that, for transformation. It is important to be realistic about the many constraints within which teachers' work, which include limitations of time, structures of assessment, wider systems of comparison and sociocultural discourses of natural ability, and stories about the purposes of schooling, to name but a few. However, I do think that teachers and learners can exert *agency* and change the situation in which they find themselves and that is why I have suggested the pedagogic possibilities above. When I use the word agency I am thinking of how an individual, with their always already discursively constituted self, can acquire the ability to catch discourse in the act of shaping them and then engage in a process of 're-naming, re-writing, re-positioning oneself in relation to coercive structures' (Davies 1993: 199). In this chapter, I have put this idea into practice on the discourse of 'natural ability', catching it in the act and intervening via the three queer strategies of troubling binaries, stopping all the binaries lining up and telling stories. In the next chapter I apply these same approaches to thinking about strategies for supporting gender transgression.

chapter eight

Supporting gender transgression: being and acting different in maths

There is a joke that was once, and perhaps still is, popular among mathematicians: 'There have been only two female mathematicians. One was not a woman; the other was not a mathematician' (Henrion 1997: 68). The first half of this is an allusion to Emmy Noether, the German mathematician who was named using the masculine pronoun as Der Noether and eulogized by Herman Weyl with the words: 'The graces did not stand by her cradle' (Henrion 1997: 68). The second half refers to Sofia Kovalevskaya, who despite winning awards for maths is often constructed as *just* a physicist; her identity as a mathematician is polluted by her concern for the applications of maths. This 'joke' presents being female and being a mathematician as two mutually exclusive identities. As this book has shown the situation is more complex than this. It is possible to be a woman mathematician but these two identities do not sit easily with each other. This chapter is about making liveable the gender transgression of doing maths while being female. It is about how those women and girls who are transgressing in this way can be supported and how they can support themselves, what strategies might assist women inhabiting the associated tensions and how they can do the necessary gender category maintenance work. In particular, it is about how to avoid telling these girls and women how they should be and act and instead providing the resources they need to support them in being and acting different.

Feminist work in maths education has long been concerned with the 'missing girls', at each level of education, who are qualified to do maths but chose not to, wanting to intervene so that more women can gain the economic power and social status that maths confers, 'the particular prestige of numbers' (Gould 1996: 58):

> Possibly the most pervasive and persuasive gender reform story of the past decade or so has been that girls and young women should

'multiply their choices' (by succeeding in male-dominated school subject areas), 'broaden their horizons' (by, for example, overcoming stereotyping in planning for paid work) and 'reach for the sky' (through, for example, improved confidence or self-esteem). Within this narrative, a major sub-plot has been the one about mathematics.

(Kenway et al. 1998: 38)

The problem is that the strategies which have been adopted for supporting girls and women in maths, such as using non-sexist resources, providing female role models and raising girls' self-esteem, have been largely unsuccessful. Women *are* doing better overall educationally than they once did but this is far more likely to be the result of wider social and economic changes than of educational interventions (Moore 2004) and they remain under-represented in particular fields. A main reason for the disappointing results of such strategies is that they have attempted to change the girls and women to fit into maths while being happy to leave maths fixed as it is. The idea of changing maths is the subject of the next chapter. It is clearly an important project, but it is also a vast and long-term one. So there is also a need for us to be able to intervene strategically with things as they are now, to think about what is possible for girls and women in maths even if everything else – the maths, the pedagogy, the culture and so on – stays the same. This is my focus in this chapter.

I begin by looking at some of the strategies that have been tried. I use the ideas discussed so far in this book to look at what the problems are with these. I show that, while they were often useful interventions at the time, they have ended up causing more problems than they solve. This is because they imagine a simple relationship between the social and the individual and so either over-estimate the role of individual agency by ignoring the constraints imposed by social factors or under-estimate it by ignoring the possibilities of agency altogether. In both cases they assume that empowerment is something that can be given to someone. I then move on to look at how we can develop strategies that understand people as neither fully determined nor as having unconstrained agency. In the last chapter, I used the idea of someone exercising agency by intercepting discourses, catching discourses in the act of positioning them so that they can re-position themself. In this chapter I stick with this idea of agency, developing strategies for working with girls and women in maths that are based on it. Ones that take empowerment seriously as something that is not a gift that we can bestow upon others but which involves struggle and so may be refused. This means that through such strategies we might end up with results that we cannot predict and of which we do not approve. We might even end up with *fewer* women doing maths.

Commonsense approaches

Many of the strategies that have been tried for supporting female participation in maths have a commonsense feel to them. *Obviously* presenting girls with female role models in maths and running classes to raise their self-esteem will encourage girls and women who are doing maths and make more of them want to carry on with it. Eileen Byrne (1993: 1) shows that such ideas are cases of the 'Snark Syndrome'. She borrows this label from a poem by Lewis Carroll (1910: 3), the mathematician and author of *Alice in Wonderland*:

> 'Just the place for a Snark!' the Bellman cried,
> As he landed his crew with care;
> Supporting each man on the top of the tide
> By a finger entwined in his hair.
>
> 'Just the place for a Snark!' I have said it twice:
> That alone should encourage the crew.
> 'Just the place for a Snark!' I have said it thrice:
> What I tell you three times is true.

In other words, these ideas become commonsense, accepted wisdom, not because of undeniable research evidence, but due to their constant repetition.

I've already discussed the downside of one of these strategies, using non-sexist resources, in Chapter 1. There I mentioned how research has shown that the responses of children to these are not what commonsense might lead one to expect. So readers of feminist fairytales are more often drawn towards the prince who needs rescuing than to the princess rescuer. Given the analyses in this book, which show the tensions around gender transgression, this is not surprising. In returning to this theme here I hope that the research in this book will add depth and breadth to my critiques. I focus on two strategies: intervening to raise girls' self-esteem and presenting girls with female role models. Like the use of non-sexist resources, these approaches have been useful in opening up spaces to talk about gender and education and spaces for feminist interventions, but they are based on simple ideas about how the social and the individual relate and so cannot engage with tensions around gender transgression.

Initiatives to raise girls' self-esteem were 'inspired by a blend of certain American psychological theories with certain feminist theories' (Kenway and Willis 1990: 1). Carol Dweck's (1986: 1040) work typifies this blend. For example, she found that boys are more likely to be oriented towards learning goals 'in which individuals seek to increase their competence, to understand or master something new' while girls are generally oriented towards performance goals 'in which individuals seek to gain favourable judgements of their competence or avoid negative judgements'. Dweck argued that the female pattern of goal orientation leads to challenge avoidance and low self-esteem and is a form of 'learned helplessness'. Since it is found disproportionately among high-achieving girls, Dweck concludes that her work explains why many high-performing girls opt out of maths.

The problem with ideas like these and with so many of the interventions that they have inspired is that they locate the problem in the girls as something that can be solved independently of the context. But discourses about self-esteem cannot be separated from their contexts. Pedagogically, Jo Boaler (1997) found that there were no significant differences between boys and girls in their attitude to and confidence in maths when they were taught using a project approach. However, there were gender differences among those taught in traditional 'chalk and talk' classrooms. As she later commented:

> My main concern with Dweck's analysis is that she attributes certain motivational patterns to girls as though such patterns exist outside the settings in which the girls are taught. This seems to me a fundamental flaw as motivations must surely be highly situated.
>
> (Boaler 2000: 32)

I explored the situatedness of motivation through the examples in the last chapter of how different classroom contexts make different positions available to learners.

Broadening 'context' to beyond the school gates, the self-esteem discourse is individualistic and rooted in liberal understandings of the self (see Chapter 6). These Enlightenment understandings of the self are culturally specific. The painful consequences of these are very apparent in Chapter 5. There, Lucy and Claudia's stories draw out how the impacts of these discourses are gendered and classed. They are also raced. In ignoring the role of racism, access to the English language, respect for mother tongue and teacher stereotyping in determining self-esteem 'it is a model which clearly defines ethnic minority status as a source of disadvantage rather than the butt of discrimination' (Tsolidis 1990: 57). Pat Dudgeon and her colleagues (1990: 79) maintain that, when working with aborigines, 'a community referenced approach is more appropriate and meaningful because it relates to and derives from Aboriginal realities'. These perspectives, along with Julie's story (also in Chapter 5), suggest that an approach based on values of collectivism and friendship may be more effective.

So self-esteem approaches treat their problematic model of the self as unproblematic; they do the same with their model of gender. The interventions ask girls to become assertive, independent and boastful, in other words to become more masculine, *and* to display traditionally feminine traits such as communication and cooperation. This position is riddled with contradictions; there is no acknowledgement of the difficulties for women performing masculinity, which mean, for example, that girls displaying self-esteem are more likely to be labelled arrogant than are boys; as far as feminine characteristics go, 'the self-esteem literature treats them simply as a means to gain access to the very power structures in which such capabilities are derided' (Kenway et al. 1990: 40). Thus, self-esteem approaches endeavour to help girls to have a better understanding of the rules of the game, to accept these rules and to play the game well. As such, they cannot help but view girls as the problem. The same kind of logic underlies the strategy I discuss next, the use of positive female role models.

When looking for positive role models of female mathematicians, many people in the UK think of Carol Vorderman. Carol features in many of our TV shows, but the one through which she first made the leap from engineering to entertainment and for which she is most famous is called *Countdown*. This is mainly a words-based game show, but includes two rounds that involve contestants in using six smaller numbers, combined through addition, subtraction, multiplication and division, to make one larger number between 100 and 999, all within 30 seconds. Carol is the resident 'vital statistician' who steps in to check the contestants' sums and to provide a solution when they cannot. Susan Picker and John Berry (2000), in a recent study that asked children between 12 and 13 years old in the US, the UK, Finland, Sweden and Rumania to draw pictures of a mathematician at work found evidence of a 'Vorderman factor'. In the UK 6.3 percent of boys and 56.9 percent of girls drew female mathematicians, the US was next with 3.1 percent of boys and 30.5 percent of girls drawing a woman, no boys in the remaining three countries drew women and only about 1 in 5 of the girls did, leading the researchers to conclude:

> There is no equivalent program to *Countdown* on television in the United States, but there has been an increasingly well-funded gender equity movement ... Yet for all the programs and money being spent in the United States, it appears that one television program in the United Kingdom, *Countdown*, has been able to accomplish more, showing the effect the media tends to have on children and society.
>
> (Picker and Berry 2000: 74)

So there does seem to be something interesting going on here.

It could be claimed that Carol Vorderman acts as a role model for young women coming into maths. She makes it seem possible and it becomes so. But this idea, like the one that positive images in books will make things better, is based on a very simple cause and effect model of the way that the social forms the individual; education, the media and other social forces are viewed as moulding an inert, but receptive, individual. Eileen Byrne (1993: 92) questions the claims that girls or boys will identify with same-gender role models in such a way as to induce them to change their choices and behaviours:

> We still do not know what the real messages are which reach adolescents and young adults when they see a same-sex role model ahead of them. Does a Grade 12 girl only think that 'women can do that' when she sees a woman engineer or a female University Professor, and not that 'I, Jane can do that'? And what is 'that'? Having a career? Combining a career with marriage? Settling happily for a single life with a rewarding career independence? Or handling machines or management ascribed in her circles as 'male' and therefore being an untypical woman if she follows her model?

We do not know what people see when they see a woman mathematician or how they read that image. We do not know what it means when a young boy or girl draws a female mathematician rather than a male mathematician, whether it makes them more or less likely to continue with maths or how this affects their relationship with the subject. As the dialogue between Maryam, AJ and Imran about nerds, included in Chapter 3, indicates disidentification is likely to be at least as common a response as identification.

There is another question raised by this discussion of role models: Why should gender be a more important basis for identification with another person than anything else? Role models, or better: those with whom we identify, do not have to be of the same gender any more than they have to be of the same class, ethnicity, nationality or sexuality as ourselves. To pick an obvious example: Mohammed Ali was a black, male, Muslim and many people – white and black, male and female, from a variety of religions and none – identify with him; they use his inspirational story (or one of the versions of it) as a resource to narrate their lives. By ignoring the complexities of identification, the idea of using female role models to support female participation in maths reinforces the alignment of gender binaries by suggesting that only women can be role models for other women. This renders irrelevant any considerations of what sort of woman (or what sort of man) a supposed role model is. This is something that Christine Skelton (2001) has discussed in the context of male primary school teachers, where it is often assumed that any man in front of a class is better for boys than every woman.

In one sense, having a woman doing maths does disturb the neat alignment of the binaries. However, binaries are resilient things, their logics are tricky to escape, they are part of the general background of our thinking. Carol Vorderman exemplifies these problems. Although she is a woman, I think that it is too easy to label her a calculator as opposed to a reasoner, playing into the pattern of binaries so important to the identity work of Graham and Peter in Chapter 3. Additionally, her role as game show hostess and her label of 'vital statistician' position her in the visceral half of the mind/body dualism. This is something that she uses to her advantage in marketing a range of detox and other health-related books, videos and other products, the covers of which foreground her body. So we can see all the binaries falling back into neat alignment. Images that might disturb this process are dealt with later in this chapter.

So the idea of role models diverts attention away from interrogating the construction of the women (and men) in question and the tensions that they embody and does not engage with the contradictory way in which people take-up, or not, these images. These were also problems with an Australian based scheme to promote maths to girls. Jane Kenway and her colleagues (1998) used students' responses to this 1991 Victoria-based programme, called 'Maths multiplies your choices', to critique such strategies more generally. The programme in question consisted of advertising in print, and on radio and television, accompanied by packs of posters, stickers and class activities which were sent to schools. These 'exhorted parents not to "pigeonhole your daughter" and told girls that 80 percent of all jobs require mathematics and so they would have 400 percent more choices if they took mathematics' (1998: 38). The visual images used in the television commercials contained 'before' scenes of girls 'curled up in pigeonholes – colourless, confined and almost catatonic' (1998: 40). That year there was a dramatic increase in the numbers of girls, and of boys, continuing with maths courses. The 'Maths Multiplies your Choices' strategy thus had some success on its own terms, but it did this by positioning girls as not knowing what was good for them and by undermining the many girls who felt that their thoughtful rejection of maths was better than others' unconsidered choice of the subject. The vast majority of girls interviewed for that study, to a greater or lesser extent, felt patronized by the campaign and resented it. Again this underlines that interventions cannot be simply about getting more girls or women into maths. I would agree with their conclusion that we need to recognize female agency and help girls 'articulate the constraints – material and social, real and perceived – on their choices ... in the absence of such education, exhortations to "broaden your horizons" and "reach for the sky" are distorted and often even cruel' (1998: 46).

Schemes like this one, together with self-esteem interventions and the use of role models, assume that the problem of girls and maths is one of ignorance and that knowledge brings freedom. As I discussed in the last chapter, there are serious absences in this idea of the relationship between knowledge and ignorance (and that's before we even start on what freedom is). It is based on a rationalistic model of human behaviour which is challenged by queer theory raising questions that 'render suspect the very basics of pedagogy and its appeal to rational subjects capable of toleration or consolation through accurate representation' (Luhmann 1998: 146). The idea of educating people out of this situation carries an idea of empowerment as something that can be *given* to someone else. But, as Foucault shows, power is a contradictory thing (see Chapter 1). It is both creative and constraining; it is not a commodity to be owned, given or taken by individuals, instead it circulates within interactions and relationships. It is those contradictions around power and how far we can push them that we need to think about if we are to come up with alternative ways of working with girls and women in relationship to maths, and by extension other non-traditional areas. This is what I look at in the next two sections, I investigate what is the room for manoeuvre and how far agency can get us; I explore Judith Butler's (1997: 100) question from Chapter 6: 'how can we work the power relations by which we are worked and in what direction?' The first section explores what use can be made of images of women mathematicians and the second at ways of developing supportive groups and communities.

Using images of women mathematicians

The strategies that focus on non-sexist resources and role models may fail to engage with the complex workings of agency but they do highlight that people need resources to write their own stories, be these images of fictional characters or of other people's 'real' lives. Thus the availability of a variety of potentially progressive/transgressive/ digressive resources is important. I begin by exploring what such resources might look like. Earlier in this chapter I was critical of Carol Vorderman and earlier in this book I was critical of several cinematic images of male mathematicians. Here, I turn my attention to the more difficult task of identifying images that I think are more useful for women in maths.

First there is the figure of Willow Rosenberg in *Buffy the Vampire Slayer*, an image that is queer in more ways than one; she continually slips and slides around the oppositions, confounding binary logics. In one sense, focusing on her is cheating because she is not a mathematician but is a general science/maths/computing whiz, with computers being her strength. However, I cannot think of any maths examples that struggle against rather than glorying in the oppositions in the way she does.

Willow starts series one as a nerd: her appalling fashion sense, fascination with schoolwork and habit of hanging with the out-crowd of Xander and Jesse make this clear in the first episode. Fifty-six episodes later, after helping to save the world a few times and developing her magic skills she goes to university, still intelligent but no longer a nerd. However, there is always a question around this shift because a dream sequence at the end of her first year at university indicates that Willow fears going back into this way of being, suggesting it is still very much part of her sense of self. As this exemplifies, the remarkable thing about Willow is how she always keeps moving. There are many other examples of this that I could cite, perhaps the best is the way the series plays with the character of Dark Willow, but there is not enough space for that one here (if you're a fan then see the discussions in Jean Battis 2003). Instead I will use the example of her sexuality. In high school she is suffering from a bad case of unrequited love for her best friend and then she goes out with a boy who plays guitar in a band. Pretty typical teen TV fodder. However, in her first year at university she has a relationship with a boy and then a girl, slipping beyond the binaries imposed by heterosexuality. Although later in the series she declares herself 'gay now' once again fixing her sexual identity, her attraction to the strong male presence of Dracula means that even then she slides beyond these boundaries, preventing any easy location of her within the straight/gay opposition.

We need more characters like Willow, ones who challenge the ways that we read and write the world in terms of clean cut oppositional categories and the ways that maths fits into these. However, Willow like all resources for narrating the self is contradictory. In one sense she is a traditional, and problematic, pop culture female geek/nerd in that she is not allowed to grow up geek in the way that boys are. The female geek/nerd must be redeemed, usually through the love of a man, who can see through to her essential femininity. She leaves nerd status and enters the world of adult women through becoming the object of the heterosexual gaze. Willow too begins as asexual; her body hidden under shapeless clothes, she reverts to a preverbal, child-like state when she encounters a boy she likes. For men, in contrast, geek/nerd has always been portrayed as adorable, admirable and, in some contexts, desirable; more recently, it has even been pronounced 'chic' (Winters 2005). Male nerds, unlike the female version, do not need to grow out of it or be redeemed by heterosexuality. This is evident in the heroic images of male mathematicians in *Enigma*, *Good Will Hunting* and *A Beautiful Mind* (see Chapter 3) and, in particular, in the ways that these men's ability at and fascination with maths are portrayed as evoking female desire. That even amazing women like Willow are in a more complex position stresses that images themselves are not enough. Also important are the ways that people make meaning out of these images and the resources that they have available for doing this. The next image also illustrates these issues; in this case, what looks like a negative and damaging image becomes useful through the processes by which it is 'appropriated by audiences, which use certain resonant texts, images, and figures to articulate their own sense of style, look, and identity' (Kellner 1997: 96).

The image is a cosmetics bag bearing a lurid depiction of the face of an over-made up young woman surrounded by pink and purple, her large blank eyes stare out at you and the bag carries the inscription, 'I'm too pretty to do math'. In 2005, the image of this bag was circulated to members of the mainly North American Women and Mathematics Education email discussion list where it met with widespread disapproval. Many list members sent emails to the owner of Hippy Chix, the web-based company selling the bag, to complain about the stereotyping. It was like Barbie had once again said: 'Math Class is Tough' (Barbie's 1992 voice chip by Mattell, cited in Leach and Mudry 1998). But she hadn't. The woman on the bag was no Barbie; the ridiculousness of the image suggests a parodying rather than a supporting of the stereotype. And, Hippy Chix (Chavez 2005: online) was no Mattell:

> The Hippy Chix Shop was originally born out of frustration. Frustration in not finding trendy and cool clothes for my daughters to wear to school. I wanted clothes that actually fit their curves and bodies. Frustration in not being able to find funky clothing for myself. Frustration with the corporate world that kept a glass ceiling over my head ... We believe strongly in supporting the aspirations of girls and women. We believe in a diverse world because without diversity imagine how boring our lives would be.

The bag was originally purchased at the request of a group of college architecture students, who obviously did not consider themselves too pretty to do math.

And, most important of all, the sociocultural context of those using and seeing the bag is very different now than it was in 1992. Young people have become sophisticated readers of images. Naomi Klein (2000: 292), in her important book *No Logo* about the anti-globalization movement, has written about the practice of culture jamming, based on how 'marketing affects communities not only by stereotyping them, but also – and equally powerfully – by hyping and chasing after them':

The most sophisticated culture jammers are not stand alone ad parodies but interceptions – counter-messages that hack into a corporation's own method of communication to send a message starkly at odds with the one that was intended ... Many female culture jammers say they first became interested in the machinations of marketing via a 'Feminism 101' critique of the beauty industry. Maybe they started by scrawling 'feed me' on Calvin Kline ads in bus shelters, as the skateboarding members of the all-high-school Bitch Brigade did.

(2000: 281–9)

For example, a section on Barbiology, subtitled 'the art and science of being barbie', on the adiosbarbie website jests, 'We've got theories and actual-factuals about the world's bestselling doll. Math may be hard, but this science is fun!' (Edut et al. 2005). Meanwhile, on an episode of *The Simpsons*, Lisa attempts to introduce a feminist talking doll into the market to counteract the effects of Malibu Stacy saying things like, 'I wish they taught shopping in school' and, 'Thinking too much gives you wrinkles' (Oakley and Weinstein 1994). In one scene in that episode a Stacy doll utters Spiderman rather than Stacy phrases. This is a tribute to a group of real-life culture jammers who, in their own attack on gender discriminatory toys, switched the recordings on GI Joe and Barbie dolls, so that the Joes asked to go shopping and the Barbie's made gut wrenching attack sounds. This speaks of the symbiotic relationship between activism and some parts of the mass media.

In that spirit, I think this image operates playfully and subversively to insert the harmful words into a new context that challenges their original meaning and to trouble the binaries that align maths and masculinity, helping young women to negotiate the tensions involved in doing something masculine like maths while being female. These architecture students are addressing another of Judith Butler's questions: 'Is there a repetition that might disjoin the speech act from its supporting conventions such that its repetition confounds rather than consolidates its injurious efficacy?' (Butler 1997: 20).

This cosmetics bag shows that it is not always easy to distinguish between sexist and non-sexist images. Representations do suggest meanings, but that is all; these meanings are neither inevitable nor fixed. These meanings both inscribe, and are inscribed by their readers, and re-inscription may be the best form of defence. So rather than looking for queer images we need to find ways of developing queer reading and writing practices. This example also shows that such alternative reading and writing practices can be cultivated within supportive groups and communities that provide spaces to negotiate one's own relationship with maths. It is to what such groups and communities might look like and how we might develop them that I now turn.

Developing supportive groups and communities

Suzanne Damarin (2000: 80) points out that biographical accounts of women mathematicians highlight the crucial role often played by a supportive community that is

> multigenerational, affirming and genuinely interested in the mathematical accomplishments of its members, [one that] normalizes the ability, it allows members to experience and enjoy the diversity and humanity of the community, and it can counter directly the totalizing potential of the popular media and discourse.

One way that is often advocated for generating such supportive communities is to provide all-girl learning environments. 'In the single-sex environment, girls can be girlish and at the same time be brilliant. They can giggle and tug on split ends and speak in those sing-song Valley Girl cadences, all the while discoursing on such personal specialties as cognitive psychology, phytoplankton, Parkinson's disease and mother–infant attachment among gibbons' (Freedman 2005). This suggests that all-girl spaces can be places where the tensions involved in pursuing non-traditional subjects are less, where girls' femininity is less in question and so requires less gender category maintenance work.

However, I have some doubts about the other implications of single-sex schooling for girls. I wonder about the impact of forcibly separating girls and boys rather than finding ways to help them interact responsibly and maturely. I wonder why we are 'yet again asking girls to take evasive action, leaving boys to remain unsocialized with impunity' (Byrne 1993: 199). Often the rhetoric is similar to that associated with initiatives to raise girls' self-esteem, as teachers talk about building girls' confidence away from boys. But I wonder about how effective this is, and whether there are perhaps many other women around like the one, educated in a single-sex school, who is quoted by Dale Spender (1980a) as saying that women educated in co-ed environments seem better able to cope than she, once they get to university. And I wonder, what are the psychic costs of the level of surveillance and the drive for success found in so many all-girls schools (Lynch and Lodge 2002)? Jane Kenway's (1990) research in a girls' private school where there is no shortage of self-esteem shows how this is built on pressure to be a certain sort of person and the 'othering' of people, particularly state school students, who do not fit.

Finally, I wonder about how this organization of education reinforces the idea of male and female as two oppositional non-overlapping groups. Teachers who teach single gender classes typically speak of slanting the topics 'to give them a "girly" angle' (WISE 2004), and say that it works because 'boys and girls have common but complementary talents that good teachers will draw out' (2004: 10) and that they need disciplining differently. Dividing up people by gender operates in a similar way to dividing up people by ability, difference is disappeared to create an illusion of homogeneity, as one teacher puts it: 'There is also the additional benefit of "predictability": when you step into the classroom, you know "what you are getting"' (2004: 12). Perhaps, as with ability, you get what you expect because you cannot see what you do not expect.

To sum up, the all-female environments created by single-sex education have some potential for allowing girls and women spaces to negotiate the gender transgression of doing maths but there are also some problems, the main ones of which are the ways that this organization is imposed on girls and how it fixes gender binaries. So what we need are ways of strategically working with all female spaces, while these have something to offer, and of keeping these groupings fluid and based in the needs and improvisations of their members.

There are various possible models around for how such groups can operate and I don't want to advocate one or another but simply to offer a few ideas:

- *Self-help groups*: Suzanne Damarin (2000: 81) advocates that women use these to 'develop their own forms of humor and jokes, and their own causes of celebration'. She borrows from Alcoholics Anonymous (AA) when she suggests that these groups develop a 12-step programme for women in maths. Research into the learning that takes place within AA shows how effective these groups are for allowing people to learn how to write themselves as a non-drinking alcoholic, to learn how to story their lives differently (Lave and Wenger 1991).
- *Consciousness raising groups*: second wave feminist activists in the 1970s formed themselves into groups in which to change their consciousness of what it means to be a woman. Through sharing their experiences in a political context, women came to understand their personal problems as linked to social, cultural and political forces (Oakley 1974; Boler 1999).
- *Anarchist groups*: third wave feminist activists have developed a different model for collective engagement. Riot Grrls and other

groupings, like the ones referred to earlier by Naomi Klein, are based around anarchist principles but often have a similar commitment to direct action to their second wave foremothers. Usually these groups are partly, or even wholly, on-line communities; the Internet opens up a wealth of new ways of bringing people together (Spender 1985; Turkle 1996).

As well as all-female collectives, we need ones that combine men and women and ones that are organized around other marginalized identities including intersectional identities such as working class women and South Asian women. We need groups that are based in temporary alliances over one particular issue alongside broader and longer term ones. Hopefully such groups can be spaces in which people can collectively learn to tell different stories about themselves and their lives and so make different identifications and different actions possible.

All such groups have boundary issues. Recurring ones are: who counts as a woman? Is 'feminist' a better criterion for membership than 'woman'? And can men be feminists? In this case there is also: who counts as a mathematician? We need to keep things open by allowing people to self-identify; there is radical potential in naming oneself and generating understandings of the meanings of that in and for one's life. In this way the division with which I started this chapter, between strategies based on supporting women and girls in improvising around a fixed maths and strategies based on changing maths itself, breaks down. For the spaces of cultural production I have discussed here and the new meanings and understandings generated within them, can and will change maths itself. In particular, they radically undermine the idea of maths as an individual and abstract activity, presenting it instead as collective and socially embedded. Maths becomes a cultural resource (Appelbaum 1995) rather than a fixed body of knowledge and the kinds of reading and writing practices discussed particularly in this chapter, but also in the rest of the book, become a legitimate part of maths pedagogy. Organizations, institutions and teachers have roles to play in encouraging this approach to maths and this is something that links to the pedagogic possibilities discussed in the last chapter and which I develop more fully in the next chapter.

They also have roles to play in acknowledging these groups and developing strategies to catalyze and nurture them. There may be a need to intervene directly, for all groups have their own pattern of power relations and their own exclusions. But there may also be a need to keep out, for often the independence of these groups from official structures is part of their appeal, and because this whole approach is based on the idea that teachers do not have all the answers, on a queering of the teacher/student binary. What is helpful will be different in different contexts and, in particular, will vary with the stage that women are at in their lives and in their relationships with maths. It is necessary to be sensitive to this.

In many contexts, official schemes for networking and mentoring that specifically target women can be useful in building and sustaining supportive communities. However, Helen Colley's (2003) perceptive analysis of mentoring relationships shows that these are not the easy solution that some people present them as. She highlights several tensions around the mentoring agenda. In particular, she points out its individualism, stressing that mentoring interventions work best when they lead on to and are accompanied by 'more collective encounters' and 'group-based educational practices . . . including those that have an emancipatory purpose' (2003: 162). Colley's discussions also draw attention to the contradictions between the business case (the economic argument for promoting women in maths) that usually drives and defines mentoring schemes and the goals of social justice. In a similar way to me she is saying that the specific strategy is less important than the ideas about agency and empowerment that motivate it and that infuse the way that it is put into practice. Empowerment needs to figure as something that you cannot do *for* someone else or *to* someone else and also as something with a contested meaning. One person's empowerment is another person's oppression, as women's differing views on everything from pornography to plastic surgery make very apparent. This means that we have to accept that these approaches will not necessarily lead to more women and girls choosing to study maths and, given how things are at the moment, if we are interested in social justice then perhaps they shouldn't.

The idea of seeing doing mathematics as doing masculinity is useful in two further ways. First, it is honest and realistic about the current state of maths, making it less likely that women will blame themselves if they leave it behind. Second, it makes it less unusual to be a woman doing maths seeing it in continuity with a range of other behaviours that might be classed as masculine in society. This hopefully makes maths a more comfortable place for women to be. I do not intend the association of mathematics with masculinity to suggest something fixed but something, which although deep rooted, is open to change. Maths needs to open up, and with Melissa Rodd and Hannah Bartholomew (2006: 48), I want to 'call for more ways of being, including those which can be identified with contemporary femininity, to be recognized as mathematical'. I explore in the next and final chapter of this book how teachers might work directly to change how things are at the moment in maths.

chapter nine

Opening up mathematics: living with uncertainty

The three women all talked about their love of mathematics ending, which caused severe distress for each of them – one described this as causing her relationship with mathematics to 'spiral out of control'.

(Boaler 2000: 38)

I had taken a lot of this material before and I'd sit there in horror. He was slaughtering this stuff. This was stuff I thought I wanted to study [for] the rest of my life and he's sitting there just slaughtering this beautiful math. It was horrible. I just wanted to start screaming in the middle of class, 'No! You're not talking about it right! Make it clear!'

(Herzig 2004: 387)

I am in mourning. I have lost the love of my life. Well I've lost what I thought was the love of my life but with the insight afforded to me in my newly bereaved state I am beginning to realise that I may have been blind to my love's faults and may well be better off without them. I tell myself that I deserve more, I don't have to put up with the casual abuse, the discrimination and not having my needs met by this relationship. How could I have been so foolish? Love does not conquer all – isn't this a pathetically familiar tale? It would be if I were talking about a person but I'm not; I'm talking about physics. The love of my life, all I ever wanted to do, the dream I clung to all through adolescence and sacrificed all manner of things for is science.

(Hawkins 2002)

The first of these quotations is taken from an interview study of women maths undergraduates, the second from an interview with a postgraduate maths student, and the third from an autobiographical piece by a woman who has decided not to continue with a career in research beyond her doctorate in physics. What is apparent from all of them, and from the research examined in this book, is that the relationships that we have with subjects are both complicated and powerful. We relate to subjects as we do to people. We expect things from them, we get used to them, are upset when they change and so do not give us what we want, and we feel let down by them. Subjects are a source of comfort or, if the wrong choices are made, of distress, anxiety and even terror. They function like people, 'they have to be related to and identified with ... one has to "get on" with them' (Shaw 1995: 113). And, like people, academic disciplines have different 'personalities'. In this final chapter I bring together the main strands within this book around the theme of transforming the personality of maths, giving maths a makeover so to speak, so that more people can get on with it and build positive relationships with it.

Although the last two chapters have focused on making choices social and on supporting gender transgression rather than on changing maths, the ideas in them and the suggested strategies also aim to open up maths to difference, opening the subject to a wider range of learners and a wider range of ways of doing maths and of being mathematical. These have aimed to address the issues raised by the research discussed in the second part and, in particular, have aimed to tackle the binary background within and against which we are working. As Susan Hekman (1999: 146) makes clear, and as I discussed at the end of Chapter 6, our strategies must be ones of both connection to and transformation of this background: 'the fundamental beliefs that constitute the Background give us our world; we cannot step outside them and create new worlds out of nothing. What we can do is to work with those beliefs shifting them in a direction more to our liking'.

To sum up, the queer pedagogic possibilities for maths education that I have suggested so far include:

- Taking a critical approach to one's own practice.
- Incorporating the emotional and relational into pedagogy.
- Developing alternative ways of grouping and assessing learners.
- Emphasizing processes rather than products and using tasks that foster this.
- Developing in learners the skills needed for working collaboratively.
- Reading and writing stories about maths and mathematicians.
- Developing supportive groups and communities.

The closely linked ideas of agency, of catching discourses in the act of our own subjectification, and empowerment, expanding our opportunities for exercising agency, have been central to coming up with these strategies. In this way I have been attempting to develop approaches that engage with the complexity of the relationship between the individual and the social and with the contradictory and unconscious aspects of subjectivity that are so apparent in the relationships that the participants in my research have with maths.

All these approaches attempt to open up maths to difference. And all of these possibilities for opening up maths are limited by our views about what maths is. In particular, the idea of maths as a certain, objective, external collection of absolute truths fixes maths as the unchanging, unchallengeable and immovable centre around which we have to work. This plays out in a number of ways. For example, it creates a myth that maths is a large body of knowledge which must be learnt hierarchically and from a young age. This creates the idea that someone's mathematical progress will be damaged even by taking a year out between school and university, let alone by taking a career break when you have caring responsibilities. It leads to supervisors telling their female PhD students that attendance at women and mathematics events is a distraction from actually doing maths; so how much more of a distraction is having friends, other interests or a family? This narrows the range of career trajectories through maths and structures the expectations people have of mathematicians and their pathways through life. It closes maths down and leaves little space for different journeys with different paces and rhythms. It is time to undo such mathematical myths by going to their source.

The ideological functions of certainty

As I said, ideas about the type of people who do maths, about the ways that people learn and do maths and about what maths is, are closely tied together. They bring together ideas about natural abilities and hierarchies of knowledge and are held in place by a pattern of oppositions that define maths and tie it into an oppressive system of gender relations. The most important of these oppositions is:

Certain/Uncertain

This is the one that is my main focus in this chapter (and this book). Certainty as the basis for mathematical truth needs to go, along with the elevation of mathematical proof to the top of the epistemological tree. For knowledge to be certain it must be kept separate from the world, so I am also interested in these oppositions:

Abstract/Relational
Rational/Emotional

Objective/Subjective
Neutral/Political
Separate/Connected

Queering these oppositions involves seeing that the emotional stuff of maths and the politics of maths are not things that can be separated off to reveal maths in its pure form, but instead are things that are messily intertwined with their others, always already present. This brings me back to where I started: the relationships between the social and the biological and between the individual and the social, and the impossibility of ever thinking one without the other.

Those who make claims to mathematical certainty often state some iconic number fact such as $1 + 1 = 2$ and then sit back in their chair looking smug as if there is nothing more to be said. However, as I have shown in this book, there is a great deal more to be said. For a start, this statement does not simply model the real world, one puddle added to one puddle is still one puddle after all, neither does it apply universally in maths, for $1 + 1$ comes to 0 within the base-2 number system used by computers. However, these responses are really cheap tricks and there are more important rejoinders, for even within arithmetical structures where $1 + 1$ does indeed always come out to 2, that is not the end of the matter. Quite the opposite, that is when things start getting interesting. We still need to think about what is being added to what, by whom and why. We need to think about what meanings people give to the adding they are doing and how it changes them and the world. We also need to engage with the ways that the idea of the possibility of certain knowledge acts to steer us away from these and other difficult questions; thus we need to confront the ideological functions of certainty. These ideological functions are political are pedagogic.

Politically, the quest for certainty risks developing in people a desire for the kind of certainties that are impossible and that lead us into wars and other atrocities. How much of the US response to September 11th has been about this need for safety, security, closure and clear lines dividing good from evil, the civilized from the uncivilized, those who are with us from those who are against us, self from other (Butler 2004)? These ideas connect to the psychoanalytic thought experiments I developed earlier in the book that aim to help us abandon our attachment to reason and to the ideas from the last chapter of seeing maths as a cultural resource, of overlapping stories, rather than a fixed body of knowledge.

Pedagogically, possibilities for change to a more open and inclusive maths need a new epistemology: 'As long as the true–false ideology dominates, the [learners] do not need to pay special attention to the communicative aspect of the mathematical classroom – primarily, communication becomes meaningful if it becomes difficult for the [learners] to find a solution to a problem' (Skovsmose 1994: 81). This was evident in the views of many in my study, such as Simon in Chapter 4 and Phil in Chapter 6, who enjoyed discussion in other subjects but saw no role for it in maths where the answer is everything and is either right or wrong. Clearly all innovations in pedagogy are limited unless we find a new way of understanding maths, a thoroughly social one, like the one I have been developing in this book. Similarly all innovations in policy are limited by epistemology. To give just one example, John White (2000: 2) points out that alongside utilitarian arguments, ideas of mathematical certainty are an oft-quoted defence of compulsory maths:

> It is from within this tradition that Fred Clarke, the eminent British educationalist ... wrote that 'the ultimate reason for teaching long division to little Johnny is that he is an immortal soul' (Clarke, 1923: 2). Few of us living in a more secular age could go along with the religious assumptions in this. Yet many more of us are insensibly influenced by other aspects of the Platonic-Cartesian theory.

So to be able to debate fully what place maths should have in the curriculum we need to release it from being thought of as certain knowledge.

So what are the alternatives?

Uncertain futures

Since certainty, in part, relies on all the binaries lining up together, the ideas suggested earlier in Chapters 7 and 8 can be used to move towards uncertain futures. For example, if learners keep maths journals and share the material in them with teachers and peers this brings emotional factors into the classroom and undermines the separation between the rational realm of maths and the emotional realm of feelings. Pushing this idea a bit further, to queer the rational/emotional binary, the feelings have to be seen to spill out beyond the diaries. Too often in maths education emotional responses, such as anxiety and enjoyment, are classified as affective variables and feature in only a very restricted way as stuff that surrounds and affects cognition, stuff that can be removed, rather than as the means through which learning happens, and so as inseparable from it. For example, Douglas McLeod (1992: 588) speaks about 'linking' the cognitive and the affective (as if they are ever unlinked) and assumes that there are topics that can be classed as 'purely cognitive' and 'strictly affective'. This keeps the cognitive as different from, opposed to and prior to the affective. More than this, it legitimates the collective refusal to view emotions and relations as central to the learning of maths and maintains the power relations that undermine feminist and queer interventions into pedagogy and assessment. Hilary Povey (1995b) has developed approaches with her colleagues that escape this trap by refusing to separate the two and requiring students to present all of these elements within their completed assignments. She aims to change the relationship between learners and teachers and between learners and maths, so that they can experience themselves as author/ities:

> An author is one who brings things into being. Who is the originator of any action or state of things. Authority is concerned with power and the validity of knowledge. Linked together they lead us to the construction of an epistemology which recognises each of us as the originator of knowledge.
>
> (Povey 1997: 332)

This is an explicitly political pedagogy. It is not simply about giving learners more ownership of what they are learning, important as that is, it is also about building their awareness of the ways in which knowledge is implicated in power relations. There are many ideas from people working in maths education who, like Povey and myself, are interested in ways of developing learner author/ity. I have space for only two: problem posing and mathemacy.

Deposing and reposing problems is an approach developed by Stephen Brown and Marion Walter (Brown and Walter 1983; Brown 1986; Brown and Walter 2005). The idea here is that when faced with a mathematical object most learners do not even need to be given a question. For example, when given the sequence 9, 16, 23, 30, 37, 44, 51, 58 ... most learners asked for an answer will happily produce the next one or two terms. They may also give you the rule for generating the sequence and perhaps a formula for its general term. But perceiving this sequence as only implying these questions is a very limited and closed way of engaging with maths. By becoming aware of the assumptions you are making about how to work with this material it is possible to develop new ways of working. Thus, Brown and Walter (1983: 23) come up with alternative questions. My favourites are:

> Two numbers of the list given are prime – as you extend the sequence will there be an infinite number of primes? ...
> There is a number in the sequence that is divisible by 2, a number divisible by 3, one by 4, one by 5, but not one by 7. Is 7 the only exception? ...

Do all digits from 0 to 9 occur in the units place? Tens place? . . .
Is there a pattern to the last digits?

The joy here is that 'while we may have explored arithmetic sequences in general, we have not explored this one *in particular*, and every particular [like the particular case of gender and maths] has a world within it that is not covered by the general investigation' (1983: 23, original emphasis). It is mathematical training that closes us down and makes it difficult to ask new questions 'while those who have not studied the subject, or perhaps consider themselves "weak" in mathematics, tend to come up with more robust questions and observations' (1983: 19); enculturation in a specific topic, and in maths generally, leads to a contraction rather than an expansion of what we can do with it.

There is much more to the strategy than this brief example can capture, but the basic idea is that we look at the assumptions within the question and ask: 'What-If-Not' one of them? It is pedagogically sound in that it is based on the idea that 'we understand something best in the context of changing it' (1983: 123, this is also the idea behind my psychoanalytic and other thought experiments in this book); it gives learners autonomy and control and helps to overcome anxiety by getting away from immediate 'right' and 'wrong' judgements. All of this changes the way that people conceptualize maths. There are other approaches that enable this too, such as the work of Stephanie Prestage and Pat Perks (2001). However, unlike Brown and Walter, they stop short of politicizing maths. The 'What-If-Not' approach highlights how other ways of engaging with maths reinforce the status quo, encouraging us to not ask questions and even to not notice that there are any questions to be asked. Thus its significance goes way beyond maths: 'What if we assumed as a society that war was not inevitable? What if we assumed that the most distant foreigners shared the same fundamental beliefs and feelings that we did? Where would that lead us? What would be the implications? What would be our responsibilities?' (Brown and Walter 1983: 126) Using 'What-If-Not' is a way of using maths to cultivate an orientation to the world that the subject usually undermines.

Deposing and reposing problems finds the political in the mathematical. The next approach finds the mathematical in the political. Ole Skovsmose (1994) develops a critical mathematics education. He does this via looking at examples of project-based work that deal with everything from ecology and energy usage to constructions and community issues. For example, in the project Economic Relationships in the World of a Child, learners began by exploring pocket money, looking at how much people got and what they could do with it. They then went on to explore how far child benefit goes. They finished by being given a budget and having to decide what equipment to buy for a youth centre. He calls the interdisciplinary curriculum that results mathemacy, after literacy.

The project structure is important because it involves scene setting via realism, fantasy, activity or another method. Scene setting creates a range of possible meanings for the maths that learners do, provides an alternative language that they can use to discuss it and makes these meanings and this language legitimate within the classroom. Additionally scene setting enables the construction of vantage points, 'hills in the semantical landscape of project work' (1994: 93) from which, even if learners are struggling with individual parts of the task, the whole undertaking can be surveyed and grasped. 'A scene-setting is a way of breaking the "logic of command" expressed by the sequence of exercises along which every child is guided towards an invisible goal' (Skovsmose 1994: 93).

Again, this approach is pedagogically sound, enabling learners to develop a sense of autonomy in their relationships with maths. Discussing the impacts of the project-based intervention, Economic Relationships in the World of a Child, into a normally textbook-based maths classroom, Skovsmose notes how the children were able to do arithmetic with decimals even though they had never been taught this. He writes that normally:

> Each new step has to be explained, each new page. The children expect the teacher to explain. They expect not to know what to do. They have learned this is the way it is to be. Mathematics has to be learned in the 'proper' way. But this 'knowledge' was forgotten during the thematic work, and the children's abilities increased remarkably.
>
> (1994: 69)

Scene setting releases an 'epistemic energy' via the children's knowledge of and involvement in the context, and the meanings connected to it.

Again, like 'What-If-Not', mathemacy is politically engaged. Skovsmose stresses the role of reflective knowing alongside mathematical and technological knowing. This involves reflecting on everything from the adequacy of a particular algorithm to the impact of that algorithm. Thinking about the impact of an algorithm is one way of bringing what Skovsmose calls the formatting power of maths into the curriculum. Formatting power names the way 'that mathematics produces new inventions in reality, not only in the sense that new insights may change interpretations, but also in the sense that mathematics colonizes part of reality and reorders it – just as the Indian social reality was changed after the English conquered the country and took power' (1994: 42). It is the formatting power of maths that gives us the paradox of relevance that 'on the one hand, mathematics has a pervasive social influence and, on the other hand, students and children are unable to recognise this relevance' (Skovsmose 1994: 82). It is this invisibility that allows the formatting power of maths to continue unchecked. A mathematical archaeology makes maths visible through the process of 'uncovering the mathematical roots of an activity' (1994: 96) and highlighting the role of maths in structuring our understanding of the world.

In an example of how to do this, Skovsmose gives an account of a project that develops the work on child benefit already mentioned, asking learners to invent households in an imaginary district and then to come up with an algorithm for distributing a fixed amount of money between them as child benefit. As learners consider the role of formal methods vs. personal judgement and try to take account of a range of social factors while keeping the algorithm simple enough to apply, they come to understand how 'reality has to be rearranged to make it possible to apply mathematics' (Skovsmose 1994: 121). You can change algorithms but you cannot escape entirely the need to format things in this way. Further: 'Once an algorithm for the distribution of money is fixed, a little part of social life is also fixed. The formatting then becomes a frozen reality for lots of people who have no alternatives but to accept the outcomes of the calculations' (1994: 122).

Investigating the formatting power of maths enables us to explore more than how maths constructs reality; we can also explore how to exercise agency and intervene in this process. It calls attention to both the need to critique the ways that maths colonizes our reality and the need to use the formal language of maths for the purposes of critique:

> What would happen if girls were led to calculate the quantity of their exclusion from interaction in lessons or the number of times they were rewarded for neatness? What would happen if the emotional and social costs were introduced to the possibility of their mathematical calculation? Might the smooth running of the patriarchal and bourgeois order not be damaged by a myriad tiny indentations of anger?
>
> (Walkerdine 1998: 166)

The formal language of maths gives us the potential to describe the world in ways, some of them digressive, which are impossible via other forms of language. Like problem posing, mathemacy shows us the possibilities for using maths education to challenge rather than support the status quo (see also: Frankenstein 1989).

Differences and making a difference

These last three chapters have been three tangents along which my thinking has run since completing the research study that is at the centre of this book. I have offered them not to be exhaustive but in the hope that they will help my readers' minds find their own tangents to fly off at and their own grooves to run along. I have been arguing that, if we are to open up maths, to support gender transgression and to make choices social, we need to queer gender and mathematics. In other words, we need to find ways of intervening into the binary discourses that frame our words, thoughts, feelings and actions about gender and mathematics. I guess if I haven't convinced you of this by now, then there's not much I can say here to bring on an epiphany, so I'll keep this concluding section short.

I started this book with the idea that doing mathematics and being a mathematician make you *different* and by questioning the ways that differences of gender relate to this. However, this book is also about difference in a broader sense. In particular, I have been trying to show that approaches that do not try to eliminate difference or render it invisible are necessary for social justice. This is why I have ended by looking at pedagogies designed to open up maths. Although I started with gender I hope that the ideas here will contribute to making maths inclusive of difference more generally. They are pedagogies of *difference*, not of diversity, where difference is understood as 'unequal, uneven, multiple and *potentially antagonistic* identities which do actually articulate in challenging ways, either positively or negatively, either in progressive or regressive ways, often conflictually, sometimes even *incommensurably* – not some flowering of individual talents and capacities' (Bhabha 1990: 208, original emphasis). While diversity is based on liberal notions of tolerance, difference acknowledges that conflicting ways of being do not happily co-exist in a multicultural utopia.

Since difference is difficult, perhaps I am being too optimistic about the possibilities for changing things. Where is there space for implementing any of this within a marketized education system driven by a narrow standards agenda? Can any of this really make a difference when the structures are so overwhelming?

First, I think that there is always some room for manoeuvre; no structure can structure everything; and, wherever there is power there is also resistance. One possibility is to exploit the fact that maths education, in its current form, is so profoundly unsuccessful. There is evidence, for example from Jo Boaler's (1997) comparative study, that when other approaches are used they produce exam results that are just as good as those obtained through more traditional, outcomes-oriented pedagogies. Second, my optimism that we can make a difference is based on what Patti Lather (2003) has called 'the cockroach theory of social change'. This is the idea that if each of us acts locally, working in our own context and with the people around us, then all our small actions somehow add up to more than the sum of their parts. I do not know what, if any, cockroach trails or tiny indentations of anger my book may provoke but I have written it in the hope there will, at least, be a few.

I chose the two approaches in this chapter partly because of their resonances with this book's project. This book is an attempt to depose and repose questions about gender and maths. To ask: what if maths is not certain? What if gender is not binary and oppositional? Like Brown and Walter (2005: 19–20), I want to limit the limitations imposed by my context:

> Many of us are blinded to alternative questions we might ask about any phenomenon because we impose a context on the situation, a context that frequently limits the direction of our thinking ... The ability to shift context and to challenge what we have taken for granted is as valuable human experience as creating a context in the first place.

As well as seeing this book as a collection of 'What-If-Nots', you can also see it as a big mathematical archaeology. Like Skovsmose's project work it is based on exemplarity, using a specific problem, in this case gendered participation in maths, as an entry into the complexity and totality of ways that maths constructs our social reality. It shows the formatting power of maths and so confronts the problem that

> applications of mathematics are difficult to observe and therefore to express an opinion on. If they stay invisible and beneath the technological surface of society they get out of control. When [we] fail to realise that mathematics is in action, [we] do not have any chance to question [our] own opinions about it.
>
> (Skovsmose 1994: 96)

I hope that, once or twice, you have been moved by what I have written to question your own opinions about maths.

What follows unavoidably from all of this is the politicization of maths. The idea that maths is political is controversial. But, without this understanding, all out attempts to make a difference will be limited, closed off by our unchallenged and often unspoken and unrecognized assumptions about what maths is, could or should be. Thus my greatest hope for this book is that it will contribute to changing the ways that we think about maths; that it will play its part in developing a sociology of maths. This may not seem like very much but:

if human practices are inescapably made up in thought, then thought itself can and does play a role in contesting them. To diagnose the historicity of our contemporary ways for thinking and acting is to enhance their contestability, to point to the need for new experiments in thought which can imagine new ways in which we can be and act.

(Rose 1999a: 58–9)

So I hope that this book, like problem posing and mathemacy, makes visible some of the unquestioned commonsense assumptions within the ways in which we think, learn, teach and live, and so will enable new 'experiments in thought'.

This book started life as my PhD (Mendick 2003), in getting to that stage it went through many versions, in my head, in the computer, in conversations with other people and finally printed on paper and bound. In book form it is recognizably connected to the PhD and yet also quite different from it, a bit like myself a few years older or younger than I am now. Since my own ideas about all of this change daily, I do not want this book to be seen as a final version of anything. I hope that your own ideas about why girls choose not to study maths as much as boys will be similarly mobile.

Language is part of an infinite semiosis of meaning. To say anything, I have got to shut up. I have to construct a single sentence. I know that the next sentence will open the infinite semiosis of meaning again, so I will take it back. So each stop is not a natural break. It does not say, 'I'm about to end a sentence and that will be the truth'. It understands that it is contingency. It is a positioning. It is the cut of ideology which, across the semiosis of language constitutes meaning. But you have to get into that game or you will never say anything at all.

(Hall 1991: 51)

References

A Beautiful Mind, film, directed by R. Howard. USA: Universal Pictures, 2001.

Adkins, L. (2001) Cultural feminization: 'money, sex and power' for women, *Signs*, 26(3): 669–95.

Alibhai-Brown, Y. (2001) *Mixed Feelings: The Complex Lives of Mixed-Race Britons*. London: The Women's Press.

Antz, film, directed by E. Darnell and T. Johnson. USA: DreamWorks SKG, 1998.

Appelbaum, P. M. (1995) *Popular Culture, Educational Discourse and Mathematics*. Albany: State University of New York Press.

Ball, S. J. (1981) *Beachside Comprehensive: A Case-Study of Secondary Schooling*. Cambridge: Cambridge University Press.

Ball, S. J., Maguire, M. and Macrae, S. (2000) *Choice, Pathways and Transitions Post-16*. London: RoutledgeFalmer.

Bartholomew, H. (2000) Negotiating identity in the community of the mathematics classroom. Paper presented to the British Education Research Association, Cardiff, Wales, 7–9 September.

Batali, D. and DesHotel, R. (2002) The dark age, in Twentieth Century Fox Film (ed.) *'Buffy the Vampire Slayer' The Script Book: Season 2 Vol 2*. New York: Pocket Pulse.

Battis, J. (2003) 'She's not all grown yet': Willow as hybrid/hero in *Buffy the Vampire Slayer*, *Slayage: The On-Line International Journal of Buffy Studies*, 2(4). Available at: www.slayage.tv/essays/slayage8/Battis.htm

Bhabha, H. (1990) The third space: an interview with Homi Bhabha, in J. Rutherford (ed.) *Identity: Community, Culture, Difference*. London: Lawrence & Wishart.

Bibby, T. (2001) Primary school teachers' personal and professional relationships with mathematics. Unpublished PhD thesis, King's College, University of London.

Billig, M. (1992) *Talking of the Royal Family*. London: Routledge.

Birke, L. (1999) *Feminism and the Biological Body*. Edinburgh: Edinburgh University Press.

Black, P. and Wiliam, D. (1998) *Inside the Black Box: Raising Standards through Classroom Assessment*. London: King's College.

Blackman, L. (2001) *Hearing Voices: Embodiment and Experience*. London: Free Association Books.

Blair, A. (2001) *Tony Blair's Victory Speech*. http://politics.guardian.-co.uk/election2001/story/0,9029,503936,00.html (accessed 16 December 2004).

Blattel-Mink, B. (2002) Gender specificity in subject perception and decision with main emphasis on science and technology, *Equal Opportunities International*, 21(1): 43–64.

Boaler, J. (1994) When do girls prefer football to fashion? An analysis of female underachievement in relation to 'realistic' mathematics contexts, *British Educational Research Journal*, 20(5): 551–64.

Boaler, J. (1997) *Experiencing School Mathematics: Teaching Styles, Sex and Setting*. Buckingham: Open University Press.

Boaler, J. (2000) So girls don't really understand mathematics? Dangerous dichotomies in gender research. Paper presented to the ICME9 Conference, Tokyo, Japan, 31 July–6 August.

Boaler, J. and Sengupta-Irving, T. (forthcoming) Gender dynamics in mathematics and elsewhere: the value of complex analysis, in B. Francis, C. Skelton and L. Smulyan (eds) *Sage Handbook on Gender & Education*. London: Sage.

Bohan, J. S. (1997) Regarding gender: essentialism, constructionism, and feminist psychology, in M. M. Gergen and S. N. Davis (eds) *Toward a New Psychology of Gender*. London: Routledge.

Boler, M. (1999) *Feeling Power: Emotions and Education*. London: Routledge.

Bramall, S. (2000) Rethinking the place of mathematical knowledge in the curriculum, in S. Bramall and J. White (eds) *Why Learn Maths?* London: Institute of Education.

Britzman, D. (1995) Is there a queer pedagogy? Or, stop reading straight, *Educational Theory*, 45(2). Available at www.ed.uinc.edn/EPS/Educational-Theory/Contents/45_2_Britzman.asp

Brooks, R. (2003) Young people's higher education choices: the role of friends and family, *British Journal of Sociology of Education*, 24(3): 283–97.

Brown, S. I. (1986) The logic of problem generation: from morality and solving to deposing and rebellion, in L. Burton (ed.) *Girls Into Maths Can Go*. London: Cassell.

Brown, L. M. and Gilligan, C. (1992) *Meeting at the Crossroads: Women's Psychology and Girls' Development*. Cambridge, MA: Harvard University Press.

Brown, S. I. and Walter, M. I. (1983) *The Art of Problem Posing*, Mahwah, NJ: Lawrence Erlbaum Associates.

Brown, S. I. and Walter, M. I. (2005) *The Art of Problem Posing*, 3rd edn. Mahwah, NJ: Lawrence Erlbaum Associates.

Burkeman, O. (2000) *Who Wants to Ruin a Millionaire?* www.guardianunlimited.co.uk/Archive/Article/0,4273,4083395,00.html (accessed 16 December 2004).

Burton, L. (1995) Moving towards a feminist epistemology of mathematics, in G. Kaiser and P. Rogers (eds) *Equity in Mathematics Education: Influences of Feminism and Culture*. London: Falmer.

Butler, J. (1995) Contingent foundations, in S. Benhabib, J. Butler, D. Cornell and N. Fraser (eds) *Feminist Contentions: A Philosophical Exchange*. New York: Routledge.

Butler, J. (1997) *Excitable Speech: A Politics of the Performative*. London: Routledge.

Butler, J. (1999) *Gender Trouble: Feminism and the Subversion of Identity*. London: Routledge.

Butler, J. (2004) *Precarious Life: The Powers of Mourning and Violence*. London: Verso.

Buxton, L. (1981) *Do You Panic about Maths? Coping with Maths Anxiety*. London: Heinemann.

Byrne, E. (1993) *Women and Science: The Snark Syndrome*. London: Falmer.

Caplan, P. J. and Caplan, J. B. (1997) Do sex-related cognitive differences exist, and why do people seek them out? in P. J. Caplan, M. Crawford, J. S. Hyde and J. T. Richardson (eds) *Gender Differences in Human Cognition*. Oxford: Oxford University Press.

Carroll, L. (1910) *The Hunting of the Snark: An Agony in Eight Fits*. Bungay, Suffolk: Richard Clay and sons.

Chavez, J. (2005) *From the Owner*. http://www.hippychixshop.com/storeinfo.html#3 (accessed 8 June 2005).

Cline, T. and Reason, R. (1993) Specific learning difficulties (dyslexia): equal opportunities issues, *British Journal of Special Education*, 20(1): 30–4.

Colley, H. (2003) *Mentoring for Social Inclusion: A Critical Approach to Nurturing Mentor Relationships*. London: RoutledgeFalmer.

Connell, R. W. (1987) *Gender and Power*. Cambridge: Polity Press.

Connell, R. W. (1989) Cool guys, swots and wimps: the inter-play of masculinity and education, *Oxford Review of Education*, 15(3): 291–303.

Connell, R. W. (1995) *Masculinities*. Cambridge: Polity Press.

Cooper, B. and Dunne, M. (2000) *Assessing Children's Mathematical Knowledge: Social Class, Sex and Problem-Solving*. Buckingham: Open University Press.

Daly, M. (1987) *Gyn/Ecology*. London: The Women's Press.

Damarin, S. (2000) The mathematically able as a marked category, *Gender and Education*, 12(1): 69–85.

David, M., Edwards, R. and Alldred, P. (2001) Children and school-based research: 'informed consent' of 'educated consent'? *British Educational Research Journal*, 27(3): 347–65.

Davies, B. (1989) *Frogs and Snails and Feminist Tales: Preschool Children and Gender*. Sydney: Allen & Unwin.

Davies, B. (1993) *Shards of Glass: Children Reading and Writing Beyond Gendered Identities*. Sydney: Allen & Unwin.

Dawkins, R. (1982) *The Extended Phenotype*. Oxford: Oxford University Press.

Denscombe, M. (2000) Social conditions for stress: young people's experience of doing GCSEs, *British Educational Research Journal*, 26(3): 359–74.

DfES (2004) *GCE/VCE A/AS Examination Results for Young People in England 2002/2003 (Final)*. http://www.dfes.gov.uk/rsgateway/DB/SFR/s000475/index.shtml (accessed 29 September 2005).

DfES (2005) *GCE/VCE A/AS Examination Results for Young People in England 2003/2004 (Final)*. http://www.dfes.gov.uk/rsgateway/DB/SFR/s000586/index.shtml (accessed 29 September 2005).

Diawara, M. (1998) Homeboy cosmopolitan: Manthia Diawara interviewed by Silvia Kolbowski, *October*, 83(Winter): 51–70.

Dudgeon, P., Lazaroo, S. and Pickett, H. (1990) Aboriginal girls: self-esteem or self-determination, in J. Kenway and S. Willis (eds) *Hearts and Minds: Self-Esteem and the Schooling of Girls*. Lewes: Falmer Press.

Dweck, C. (1986) Motivational processes affecting learning, *American Psychologist*, 41(10): 1040–8.

Early, R. E. (1992) The alchemy of mathematical experience: a psychoanalysis of student writings, *For the Learning of Mathematics*, 12(1): 15–20.

Edut, O., Muhammad, I., Guerrero, P. and Tomlin, A. (2005) *Barbiology: The Art and Science of Being Barbie*. http://www.a-diosbarbie.com/bology/index.html (accessed 4 August 2005).

Enigma, film, directed by M. Apted. USA: Broadway Video, Intermedia Films, Jagged Films, Manhattan Pictures International, MeesPierson Film CV and Senator Entertainment, 2001.

Epstein, D. (1998) Real boys don't work: 'underachievement', masculinity and the harassment of 'sissies', in D. Epstein, J. Elwood, V. Hey and J. Maw (eds) *Failing boys? Issues in Gender and Underachievement*. Buckingham: Open University Press.

Epstein, D. and Johnson, R. (1998) *Schooling Sexualities*. Buckingham: Open University Press.

Ernest, P. (1991) *The Philosophy of Mathematics Education*. Basingstoke: Falmer.

Evans, J. (2000) *Adults' Mathematical Thinking and Emotions: a study of numerate practices*. London: RoutledgeFalmer.

Faludi, S. (1992) *Backlash: The Undeclared War Against Women*. London: Chatto and Windus.

Fanon, F. (1986) *Black Skin, White Masks*. London: Pluto Press.

Fausto-Sterling, A. (1985) *Myths of Gender: Biological Theories about Women and Men*. New York: Basic Books Inc.

Flax, J. (1993) *Disputed Subjects: Essays on Psychoanalysis, Politics and Philosophy*. Routledge: London.

Flax, J. (2002) 'Concern for the self': rethinking subjectivity and ethics. Paper presented to the Centre for Psychosocial Studies, Birkbeck College, London, England, 3 July.

Fleener, M. J. (1999) Towards a poststructural mathematics curriculum: expanding discursive possibilities, *Journal of Curriculum Theorizing*, 15(2): 100–5.

Foucault, M. (1972) *The Archaeology of Knowledge*. London: Routledge.

Foucault, M. (1976) *The History of Sexuality (Volume 1): The Will to Knowledge*. London: Penguin.

Foucault, M. (1977) *Discipline and Punish: The Birth of the Prison*. London: Penguin.

Foucault, M. (1980) Prison talk, in C. Gordon (ed.) *Power/knowledge*. Harlow: Prentice Hall.

Francis, B. (2000) *Boys and Girls and Achievement: Addressing the Classroom Issues*. London: RoutledgeFalmer.

Frankenstein, M. (1989) *Relearning Mathematics: A Different Third R-Radical Mathematics*. London: Free Association Books.

Frankenstein, M. (1995) Equity in mathematics education: class in the world outside the class, in W. G. Secada, E. Fennema and L. B. Adajian (eds) *New Directions for Equity in Mathematics Education*. Cambridge: Cambridge University Press.

Freedman, S. G. (2005) Where popular science is called women's work, *New York Times*, 27 April.

Freud, S. (1991) *Introductory Lectures on Psychoanalysis*. London: Penguin.

Gewirtz, S., Ball, S. J. and Bowe, R. (1995) *Markets, Choice and Equity in Education*. Buckingham: Open University Press.

Gillborn, D. and Youdell, D. (2000) *Rationing Education: Policy, Practice, Reform, and Equity*. Buckingham: Open University Press.

Gilligan, C. (1993) *In a Different Voice: Psychological Theory and Women's Development*. Cambridge, MA: Harvard University Press.

Goldin, G. A. (2002) Connecting understandings from mathematics and mathematics education research. Paper presented to the 26th Conference of the International Group for the Psychology of Mathematics Education, Norwich, England, 21–6 July.

Good Will Hunting, film, directed by G. Van Sant. USA: Miramax Films, 1997.

Gorard, S., Rees, G. and Salisbury, J. (2001) Investigating the patterns of differential attainment of boys and girls at school, *British Educational Research Journal*, 27(2): 125–39.

Gould, S. (1996) *The Mismeasure of Man*. London: Penguin.

Government Statistical Service (1995) *Statistics of Education: Public Examinations GCSE and GCE in England 1994*. London: HMSO.

Government Statistical Service (1996) *Statistics of Education: Public Examinations GCSE and GCE in England 1995*. London: HMSO.

Government Statistical Service (1997) *Statistics of Education: Public Examinations GCSE and GCE in England 1996*. London: HMSO.

Government Statistical Service (1998) *Statistics of Education: Public Examinations GCSE/GNVQ and GCE in England 1997*. London: HMSO.

Government Statistical Service (1999) *Statistics of Education: Public Examinations GCSE/GNVQ and GCE in England 1998*. London: HMSO.

Government Statistical Service (2000) *Statistics of Education: Public Examinations GCSE/GNVQ and GCE in England 1999*. London: HMSO.

Government Statistical Service (2001) *Statistics of Education: Public Examinations GCSE/GNVQ and GCE in England 2000*. London: HMSO.

Government Statistical Service (2002) *Statistics of Education: Public Examinations GCSE/GNVQ and GCE in England 2001*. London: HMSO.

Greer, G. (1999) *The Whole Woman*. London: Transworld Publishers.

Griffin, G. and Andermahr, S. (eds) (1994) *Straight Studies Modified: Lesbian Interventions in the Academy*. London: Cassell.

Guardian (2002a) GCSE results 2002. http://education.guardian.co.uk/gcses2002/table/0,12348,778454,00.html (accessed 16 December 2004).

Guardian (2002b) A-level results 2002. http://education.guardian.co.uk/alevels2001/tables/0,10951,774597,00.html (accessed 16 December 2004).

Guardian (2003a) A-level results 2003. http://education.guardian.co.uk/alevels2003/story/0,13394,1018079,00.html (accessed 16 December 2004).

Guardian (2003b) GCSE results 2003: Maths – Technology (including all subjects). http://education.guardian.co.uk/gcses2003/story/0,13395,1026550,00.html (accessed 16 December 2004).

Halberstam, J. (1998) *Female Masculinity*. Durham: Duke University Press.

Hall, S. (1991) Old and new identities, old and new ethnicities, in A. D. King (ed.) *Culture, Globalization and the World-System*. London: Macmillan.

Hall, S. (1996) Introduction: who needs 'identity'? in S. Hall and P. du Gay (eds) *Questions of Cultural Identity*. London: Sage.

Hanna, G. (ed.) (1996) *Towards Gender Equity in Mathematics Education: An ICMI Study*. Dordrecht: Kluwer Academic Publishers.

Hardy, G. H. (1969) *A Mathematician's Apology*. Cambridge: Cambridge University Press.

Hawkins, R. (2002) *The Experiences of Young Women in Science*. http://www.thefword.org.uk/features/womsci.live (accessed 15 June 2003).

Hekman, S. (1999) *The Future of Differences: Truth and Method in Feminist Theory*. Cambridge: Polity Press.

Henrion, C. (1997) *Women in Mathematics: The Addition of Difference*. Bloomington, IN: Indiana University Press.

Henriques, J. (1984) Social psychology and the politics of racism, in J. Henriques, W. Hollway, C. Urwin, C. Venn and V. Walkerdine (eds) *Changing the Subject: Psychology, Social Regulation and Subjectivity*. London: Methuen.

Henriques, J., Hollway, W., Urwin, C., Venn, C. and Walkerdine, V. (eds) (1984) *Changing the Subject: Psychology, Social Regulation and Subjectivity*. London: Methuen.

Herzig, A. H. (2004) 'Slaughtering this beautiful math': Graduate women choosing and leaving mathematics, *Gender and Education*, 16(3): 379–95.

Hey, V. (1997) *The Company She Keeps: An Ethnography of Girls' Friendship*. Buckingham: Open University Press.

Hollway, W. and Jefferson, T. (2000) *Doing Qualitative Research Differently: Free Association, Narrative and the Interview Method*. London: Sage.

Isaacson, Z. (1990) 'They look at you in absolute horror': women writing and talking about mathematics, in L. Burton (ed.) *Gender and Mathematics: An International Perspective*. London: Cassell.

Jackson, C. (2002) 'Laddishness' as a self-worth protection strategy, *Gender and Education*, 14(1): 37–51.

Jackson, C. (2003) 'Laddishness', hegemonic masculinities and self-worth protection. Paper presented to the Gender and Education 4th International Conference: Revisiting Feminist Perspectives on Gender and Education, Sheffield, England, 14–16 April.

Jones, A. (1993) Becoming a girl: post-structuralist suggestions for educational research, *Gender and Education*, 5(2): 157–66.

Kellner, D. (1997) *Beavis and Butt-head*: no future for postmodern youth, in S. R. Steinberg and J. L. Kincheloe (eds) *Kinderculture: The Corporate Construction of Childhood*. Boulder, CO: Westview Press.

Kenway, J. (1990) Privileged girls, private schools and the culture of 'success', in J. Kenway and S. Willis (eds) *Hearts and Minds: Self-Esteem and the Schooling of Girls*. Lewes: Falmer Press.

Kenway, J. and Bullen, E. (2001) *Consuming Children: Education-Entertainment-Advertising*. Buckingham: Oxford University Press.

Kenway, J. and Willis, S. (eds) (1990) *Hearts and Minds: Self-Esteem and the Schooling of Girls*. Lewes: Falmer Press.

Kenway, J., Willis, S. and Nevard, J. (1990) The subtle politics of self-esteem programs for girls, in J. Kenway and S. Willis (eds) *Hearts and Minds: Self-Esteem and the Schooling of Girls*. Lewes: Falmer Press.

Kenway, J., Willis, S., Blackmore, J. and Rennie, L. (1998) *Answering Back: Girls, Boys and Feminism in Schools*. London: Routledge.

Klein, N. (2000) *No Logo*. London: HarperCollins.

Kline, M. (1980) *Mathematics: The Loss of Certainty*. New York: Open University Press.

Lakatos, I. (1976) *Proofs and Refutations: The Logic of Mathematical Discovery*. Cambridge: Cambridge University Press.

Lather, P. (2003) This IS your father's paradigm: government intrusion and the case of qualitative research in education. Paper presented to the Conference Discourse Power Resistance: New Directions, New Moves, Plymouth, England, 6–8 April.

Lave, J. and Wenger, E. (1991) *Situated Learning: Legitimate Peripheral Participation*. Cambridge: Cambridge University Press.

Leach, J. and Mudry, J. (1998) Flawless coverage and thick numeracy: female cosmetics consumers and the rhetoric of mathematics. Paper presented to the The Production of a Public Understanding of Mathematics, Birmingham University, 11 November.

Lloyd, G. (1993) *The Man of Reason: 'Male' and 'Female' in Western Philosophy*. London: Routledge.

Luhmann, S. (1998) Queering/querying pedagogy? Or, pedagogy is a pretty queer thing, in W. F. Pinar (ed.) *Queer Theory in Educaion*. Mahwah, NJ: Lawrence Erlbaum Associates.

Lupton, D. (1995) The embodied computer/user, in M. Featherstone and R. Burrows (eds) *Cyberspace, Cyberbodies and Cyberpunk: Cultures of Technological Embodiment*. London: Sage.

Lynch, K. and Lodge, A. (2002) *Equality and Power in Schools*. London: RoutledgeFalmer.

Mac an Ghaill, M. (1994) *The Making of Men: Masculinities, Sexualities and Schooling*. Buckingham: Open University Press.

MacKinnon, C. (1987) *Feminism Unmodified*. Cambridge, MA: Harvard University Press.

MacLure, M. (2003) *Discourse in Educational and Social Research*. Buckingham: Open University Press.

Mason, J. (2002) *Researching Your Own Practice: The Discipline of Noticing*. London: RoutledgeFalmer.

McGavin, H. (1999) A-level maths equals money, *Times Educational Supplement*, 19 February.

McLeod, D. B. (1992) Research on affect in mathematics education: a reconceptualization, in D. A. Grouws (ed.) *Handbook of Research on Mathematics Teaching and Learning*. New York: Macmillan.

Mendick, H. (2003) Telling Choices: an exploration of the gender imbalance in participation in advanced mathematics courses in England. Unpublished PhD thesis, Goldsmiths College, University of London.

Mendick, H. (2004) Changing teachers, changing subjects: troubling transitions into AS mathematics. Paper presented to the British Educational Research Association, Manchester, 16–18 September.

Mendick, H. (2005) Only connect: troubling oppositions in gender and mathematics, *International Journal of Inclusive Education*, 9(2): 161–80.

Moore, R. (2004) *Education and Society: Issues and Explanations in the Sociology of Education*. Cambridge: Polity Press.

Morgan, C. (1998) *Writing Mathematically: The Discourse of Investigation*. London: Falmer.

Morris, M. (1998) Unresting the curriculum: queer projects, queer imaginings, in W. F. Pinar (ed.) *Queer Theory in Educaion*. Mahwah, NJ: Lawrence Erlbaum Associates.

Nasar, S. (2001) *A Beautiful Mind*. London: Faber and Faber.

Noddings, N. (1993) Politicizing the mathematics classroom, in S. Restivo, J. P. Van Bendegem and R. Fischer (eds) *Math Worlds: Philosophical and Social Studies of Mathematics and Mathematics Education*. Albany: State University of New York Press.

Oakley, A. (1974) *The Sociology of Housework*. London: Martin Robertson.

Oakley, A. (2000) *Experiments in Knowing: Gender and Method in the Social Sciences*. Cambridge: Polity Press.

Oakley, B. and Weinstein, J. (1994) *Lisa vs. Malibu Stacy*. http://www.snpp.com/episodes/1F12.html (accessed 4 July 2005).

Pi, film, directed by D. Aronofsky. USA: Harvest Filmworks, Plantain Films, Protozoa Pictures and Truth and Soul Pictures, 1998.

Picker, S. H. and Berry, J. S. (2000) Investigating pupils' images of mathematicians, *Educational Studies in Mathematics*, 43(1): 65–94.

Plummer, K. (1995) *Telling Sexual Stories*. London: Routledge.

Plummer, G. (2000) *Failing Working-Class Girls*. Stoke-on-Trent: Trentham Books.

Potter, J. and Wetherell, M. (1987) *Discourse and Social Psychology: Beyond Attitudes and Behaviour*. London: Sage.

Povey, H. (1995a) Ways of knowing of student and beginning mathematics teachers and their relevance to becoming a teacher working for change. Unpublished PhD thesis, University of Birmingham.

Povey, H. (1995b) Working for change in teacher education: some first steps for Monday morning, in L. Burton and B. Jaworski (eds) *Technology in Mathematics Teaching: A Bridge Between Teaching and Learning*. Bromley: Chartwell-Bratt.

Povey, H. (1997) Beginning mathematics teachers' ways of knowing: the link with working for emancipatory change, *Curriculum Studies*, 5(3): 329–42.

Power, S., Whitty, G., Edwards, T. and Wigfall, V. (1998) Schoolboys and schoolwork: gender identification and academic achievement, *International Journal of Inclusive Education*, 2(2): 135–53.

Power, S., Edwards, T., Whitty, G. and Wigfall, V. (2002) *Education and the Middle Class*. Buckingham: Open University Press.

Prestage, S. and Perks, P. (2001) *Adapting and Extending Secondary Mathematics Activities: New Tasks for Old*. London: David Fulton Publishers.

Pulp Fiction, film, directed by Quentin Tarantino. USA: Miramax Films, 1994.

Redman, P. and Mac an Ghaill, M. (1997) Educating Peter: the making of a history man, in D. L. Steinberg, D. Epstein and R. Johnson (eds) *Border Patrols: Policing the Boundaries of Heterosexuality*. London: Cassell.

Restivo, S. (1992) *Mathematics in Society and History*. Dordrecht: Kluwer Academic Publishers.

Revill, J. (2005) Twins hold key to unravelling maths gene, *Observer*, 7 August.

Rich, A. (1983) Compulsory heterosexuality and lesbian existence, in A. Snitow, C. Stansell and S. Thompson (eds) *Desire: The Politics of Sexuality*. London: Virago.

Robinson, J. and Burke, C. (1996) Tradition, culture and ethos: the impact of the Further and Higher Education Act (1992) on sixth form colleges and their futures, *Evaluation and Research in Education*, 10(1): 3–21.

Rodd, M. and Bartholomew, H. (2006) Invisible and special: young women's experiences as undergraduate mathematics students, *Gender and Education*, 18(1): 35–50.

Rose, N. (1999a) *The Powers of Freedom: Reframing Political Thought*. London: Routledge.

Rose, N. (1999b) *Governing the Soul*. London: Free Association Books.

Rothman, B. K. (1999) Now you can choose! Issues in parenting and procreation, in M. M. Ferre, J. Lorber and B. Hess (eds) *Revisioning Gender*. California: Sage.

Schneider, E. (1994) The violence of privacy, in M. A. Fineman and R. Mykitiuk (eds) *The Public Nature of Private Violence: The Discovery of Domestic Abuse*. London: Routledge.

Scott, J. W. (1990) Deconstructing equality-versus-difference: or the uses of poststructuralist theory for feminism, in M. Hirsch and E. Fox Keller (eds) *Conflicts in Feminism*. New York: Routledge.

Sedgwick, E. K. (1994) *Tendencies*. London: Routledge.

Segal, J. (2000) *Phantasy*. Cambridge: Icon Books.

Seidler, V. J. (1997) *Man Enough*. London: Sage.

Seller, A. (1988) Realism versus relativism: towards a politically adequate epistemology, in M. Griffiths and M. Whitford (eds) *Feminist Perspectives in Philosophy*. Bloomington, IN: Indiana University Press.

Shaw, J. (1995) *Education, Gender and Anxiety*. London: Taylor & Francis.

Shelley, N. (1995) Mathematics: beyond good and evil, in G. Kaiser and P. Rogers (eds) *Equity in Mathematics Education: Influences of Feminism and Culture*. London: Falmer.

Skeggs, B. (1997) *Formations of Class and Gender*. London: Sage.

Skelton, C. (2001) *Schooling the Boys: Masculinities and Primary Education*. Buckingham: Open University Press.

Skovsmose, O. (1994) *Towards a Philosophy of Critical Mathematics Education*. Dordrecht: Kluwer Academic Publishers.

Skovsmose, O. and Valero, P. (2002) Mathematics education in a world apart: where we are all together. Paper presented to the Mathematics, Education and Society 3 Conference, Helsingor, Denmark, 2–7 April.

Snitow, A. (1990) A gender diary, in M. Hirsch and E. Fox Keller (eds) *Conflicts in Feminism*. New York: Routledge.

Spender, D. (1980a) Talking in class, in D. Spender and E. Sarah (eds) *Learning to Lose: Sexism and Education*. London: The Women's Press.

Spender, D. (1980b) Gender and marketable skills, in D. Spender and E. Sarah (eds) *Learning to Lose: Sexism and Education*. London: The Women's Press.

Spender, D. (1980c) Education or indoctrination? in D. Spender and E.

Sarah (eds) *Learning to Lose: Sexism and Education*. London: The Women's Press.

Spender, D. (1985) *Nattering on the Net: Women, Power and Cyberspace*. North Melbourne: Spinifex Press.

Stanic, G. M. A. and Hart, L. E. (1995) Attitudes, persistence, and mathematics achievement: qualifying race and sex differences, in W. G. Secada, E. Fennema and L. B. Adajian (eds) *New Directions for Equity in Mathematics Education*. Cambridge: Cambridge University Press.

Stanley, L. and Wise, S. (1993) *Breaking Out Again: Feminist Epistemology and Ontology*. London: Routledge.

Thomas, K. (1990) *Gender and Subject in Higher Education*. Buckingham: Open University Press.

Tobias, S. (1978) *Overcoming Math Anxiety*. New York: W. W. Norton & Company.

Tsolidis, G. (1990) Ethnic minority girls and self-esteem, in J. Kenway and S. Willis (eds) *Hearts and Minds: Self-Esteem and the Schooling of Girls*. Lewes: Falmer Press.

Turkle, S. (1996) *Life on Screen: Identity in the Age of the Internet*. Weidenfeld & Nicolson.

Verschaffel, L. (2002) Taking the modeling perspective seriously at the elementary school level: promises and pitfalls. Paper presented to the 26th Conference of the International Group for the Psychology of Mathematics Education, Norwich, England, 21–6 July.

Walkerdine, V. (1988) *The Mastery of Reason: Cognitive Development and the Production of Rationality*. London: Routledge.

Walkerdine, V. (1990) *Schoolgirl Fictions*. London: Verso.

Walkerdine, V. (1997a) Redefining the subject in situated cognition theory, in D. Kirshner and J. A. Whitson (eds) *Situated Cognition: Social, Semiotic and Psychological Perspectives*. Mahwah, NJ: Lawrence Erlbaum.

Walkerdine, V. (1997b) *Daddy's Girl*. Hampshire: Macmillan.

Walkerdine, V. (1998) *Counting Girls Out*. London: Falmer.

Walkerdine, V., Lucey, H. and Melody, J. (2001) *Growing Up Girl: Psychosocial Explorations of Gender and Class*. Basingstoke: Palgrave.

Wallace, S. (2002) No good surprises: intending lecturers' preconceptions and initial experiences of further education, *British Educational Research Journal*, 28(1): 79–93.

Welsh, I. (1993) *Trainspotting*. London: Minerva.

White, J. (2000) Should mathematics be compulsory for all until the age of 16? in S. Bramall and J. White (eds) *Why Learn Maths?* London: Institute of Education.

Whitehead, J. (1996) Sex stereotypes, gender identity and subject choices at A-level, *Educational Research*, 38(2): 147–60.

Wilchins, R. (1997) *Read My Lips: Sexual Subversion and the End of Gender*. Milford, CT: Firebrand Books.

Wilchins, R. (2004) *Queer Theory, Gender Theory: An Instant Primer*. Los Angeles: Alyson Books.

Winters, J. (2005) *Some Kind of Monster: The Evolution of the TV Geek*. http://www.smrt-tv.com/v1–02/feature_nerds.html (accessed 7 June 2005).

Winterson, J. (1985) *Oranges Are Not the Only Fruit*. London: HarperCollins.

WISE (Women Into Science and Engineering) (2004) *In a Class of Their Own? Teaching Science in Single Sex Classes in Secondary Co-educational Schools*. London: WISE.

Wittig, M. (1992) *The Straight Mind and Other Essays*. Boston: Beacon Press.

Witz, A. (1997) Women and work, in D. Richardson and V. Robinson (eds) *Introducing Women's Studies*. London: Macmillan.

Woolf, V. (1994) *To the Lighthouse*. New York: Routledge.

Wurtzel, E. (1998) *Bitch*. London: Quartet Books.

Young, I. M. (1990) *Justice and the Politics of Difference*. Princeton: Princeton University Press.

Index

Page numbers for figures have suffix **f**, those for tables have suffix **t**
Research participants are indexed by their first name, all others are indexed by surname.

Abdi (teacher at Sunnydale), 33
Adkins, Lisa, 112, 113
AJ (student at Westerburg), 39, 63, 126, 145
Alan Rudolff? (teacher at Westerburg), 37, 127, 129–131
Alcoholics Anonymous (A.A.), 152
Alex Harris (teacher at Sunnydale), 31, 33, 94
Alibhai-Brown, Y., 80
Analia (student at Westerburg), 28, 39, 135
Andermahr, S., 117
Andy Rhoes (teacher at Westerburg), 28
Antz (animated feature), 22
Appelbaum, P.M., 153
Ashley (student at Sunnydale), 39

Ball, Stephen, 108, 122, 123
Barbie Doll, 149, 150
Bartholomew, Hannah, 127, 154
Batali, D., 63
Battis, Jean, 148
A Beautiful Mind (film), 64, 65, 148
Berry, John, 144
Bhabha, H., 164
Bibby, Tamara, 87
Billig, Michael, 41
Birke, L., 13

Black, Paul, 136, 137
Blackman, Lisa, 13, 14
Blair, Tony, 108
Blattel-Mink, B., 8, 107
Bletchley Park, 64
Boaler, Jo, 8, 64, 71, 76, 107, 125, 143, 155, 164
Bohan, J.S., 85
Boler, Megan, 12, 152
Bramall, S., 116
Britzman, Deborah, 119, 132
Brooks, R., 40
Brown, Lyn Mikel, 91
Brown, Stephen, 160, 161, 165
Buffy the Vampire Slayer (TV series), 62, 147
Bullen, E., 67
Burke, Colin, 30
Burkeman, O., 62
Burton, L., 19
Butler, Judith, 14, 15, 22, 108, 147, 150, 158
Buxton, Laurie, 97, 137
Byrne, Eileen, 142, 151

Cambridge University, 8, 9, 122, 130
Caplan, Jeremy, 12
Caplan, Paula, 12
Carroll, Lewis, 142
Chavez, J., 149

City and Guilds maths, 92
Clarke, Fred, 159
Claudia (student at Westerburg), 39,
    87, 96–100, 143
Cline, Tony, 48
Colley, Helen, 154
Connell, Bob, 10, 16, 74, 75, 86, 111,
    114
Cooper, B., 76
Countdown (TV gameshow), 144

Daly, M., 11
Damarin, Suzanne, 62, 67, 151, 152
Darren (student at Westerburg), 39, 57,
    59, 67
David, Miriam, 35
Davies, Bronwyn, 10, 15, 16, 17, 82, 83,
    139
Dawkins, Richard, 122
Deji (student at Westerburg), 28
Denscombe, Martyn, 125
DesHotel, R., 63
Desmond, (student at Westerburg), 39,
    57, 59, 67, 130
Diawara, Manthia, 113
Dudgeon, Pat, 143
Dunne, M., 76
Dweck, Carol, 142, 143
Dyslexic, 48

Early, Robert, 134
Edut, O., 150
English education system explained,
    2–3
Enigma (film), 64, 65, 148
epistemic energy, 162
Epstein, Debbie, ix, 35, 74
Ernest, P., 19
Evans, J., 98

Faludi, Susan, 107
Fanon, F., 78
Fausto-Sterling, Anne, 13
Flax, Janc, 18, 34, 60
Fleener, Mary-Jayne, 61
Foucault, Michel, 17, 19, 20, 147
Francis, B., 74

Frankenstein, M., 114, 163
Freedman, S.G., 151
Freud, Sigmund, 93
Further and Higher Education Act
    (1992), 30

GCSE (General Certificate of
    Secondary Education), 3, 92
Gewirtz, S., 108
Gillborn, D., 3
Gilligan, Carol, 64, 91
Goldin, G.A., 19
'good at maths,' 45–68 *see also* ability
Good Will Hunting (film), 64, 65, 66,
    121, 148
Gorard, S., 7
Gould, S., 140
Government Statistical Service, 7
Grafton School, 25, 26–28, 32, 33, 35,
    36, 37, 40, 47, 70, 73, 76, 77, 88
Graham (student at Westerburg),
    53–56, 58, 63, 67, 74, 93, 98, 128,
    130, 146
Greer, G., 11
Griffin, G., 117

Halberstam, Judith, 111, 112, 113
Hall, Stuart, 23, 166
Hanna, G., 8
Hardy, G.H., 19, 20, 21, 121
Harris case (Supreme Court), 109
Hart, L.E., 69
Hawkins, R., 155
Hekman, Susan, 156
Henrion, C., 140
Henriques, J., 14, 16, 102, 108
Herzig, A.H., 155
Hey, Valerie, 90
Hina (student at Westerburg), 39
Hippy Chix Shop, 149
Hollway, W., 40

'identity work' and identification
    defined, 23
Imran (student at Westerburg), 39, 63,
    125, 126, 145
internet, 115, 153

Isaacson, Z., 98

Jackson, C., 74
Jackson, Samuel L., 113
James (student at Grafton), 26, 39, 69, 73–80, 82, 85, 86, 87, 93, 100
Jane (student at Grafton), 88, 145
Jason Dean (teacher at Westerburg), 127–129
Jean (student at Grafton), 39, 85
Jefferson, T., 40
Jingki (student at Sunnydale), 39
Johnson, R., 35, 167
Jonathan (student at Sunnydale), 39
Jones, Alison, 16
Julie (student at Grafton), 27, 39, 47, 87, 88–92, 100, 102, 143

Kanton (student at Sunnydale), 39
Kellner, D., 149
Kenjin (student at Sunnydale), 39
Kenway, Jane, 67, 141, 142, 144, 146, 151
Kiriakos (student at Westerburg), 39
Klein, Melanie, 134
Klein, Naomi, 149, 153
Kline, Morris, 19
Kovalevskaya, Sofia, 140

Lakatos, I., 19
Lather, Patti, 165
Lave, J., 152
Leach, J., 149
Lee (student at Sunnydale), 85
Ling (student at Westerburg), 39, 57, 58, 59, 62, 63, 67, 88
Lloyd, Genevieve, 61
Lodge, A., 151
Lord of the Rings (film), 64
Lucy (student at Sunnydale), 39, 87, 92–96, 99, 100, 143
Luhmann, S., 132, 133, 147
Lupton, Deborah, 63
Lynch, K., 151

Mac an Ghaill, Mairtin, 55, 73, 74
MacKinnon, Catherine, 109, 110

MacLure, M., 20
Mandelbrot set, 115
Maryam (student at Westerburg), 39, 63, 145
Mason, John, 123, 136
mathemacy, 162
'mathematical ability,' 46, 47, 49, 54, 56, 62, 122, 130, 138
'mathematical genius,' 56, 57, 59, 63, 64, 88, 98
Mathematics on the Underground, 29
Matt Delling (teacher at Grafton), 27, 37
Matthew (student at Sunnydale), 39
McGavin, H., 85
McLeod, Douglas, 159
Mei Jin (student at Grafton), 39
Melanie (student at Grafton), 39
Mendick, H., 8–9, 107, 135, 166
Michael (student at Grafton), 27, 36, 39, 41, 69, 76–80, 82, 85, 86, 87, 100, 101, 102
Mika (student at Sunnydale), 39, 85
Moore, R., 141
Morgan, C., 124
Morris, M., 117, 118
Morrison, Toni, 80
Motivate scheme (Cambridge University), 130
Mudry, J., 149

Nasar, Sylvia, 64
Nash, John, 64, 65
Natasha (student at Sunnydale), 39, 80, 82, 83
National Curriculum, 3
National Health Service, 14
Nazima (student at Grafton), 39, 85
Nefertiti (student at Sunnydale), 31, 39
Niamh (student at Grafton), 39
Nick Bennett (teacher at Sunnydale), 32
Noddings, N., 138
Noether, Emmy, 140

Oakley, Anne, 61, 152
Oakley, B., 150

Perks, Pat, 161
Peter (student at Westerburg), 39, 45, 48–50
Pi (film), 64, 65, 66
Picker, Susan, 144
Phil (student at Grafton), 39, 116, 159
Platonic-Cartesian theory, 159
Plummer, Ken, 75, 104
Pop Idol (TV series), 122
poststructuralist theory, 10, 16–17, 67, 85, 171, 177
Potter, Jonathan, 36, 37, 41
Povey, Hilary, 136, 160
Power, Sally, 40, 74
Prestage, Stephanie, 161
Priya (student at Sunnydale), 39
Pulp Fiction (film), 113

Queer Theory, 117, 119, 132, 147

Rachel (student at Westerburg), 39, 40, 57, 58, 59, 62, 63, 67, 88
Ramanujan (Indian mathematician), 121
Reason, Rea, 48
Redman, P., 74
research study, 25–41
Restivo, Sal, 19
Revill, J., 122
Rich, Adrienne, 11
Robinson, John, 30
Rodd, Melissa, 154
Roe vs Wade (Supreme Court), 109
Rose, Nikolas, 46, 95, 166
Rothman, Barbara, 109

Saldon (student at Westerburg), 39, 45, 50–53, 58
Salvador (student at Grafton), 39, 47, 88, 89
Sam (student at Westerburg), 39
Schneider, E., 109
Scott, Joan, 102, 103
Sedgwick, Eve, 133
Segal, J., 57
Seidler, Vic, 78
Seller, Ann, 34

Sengupta-Irving, T., 107
Shaw, Jenny, 24, 91, 102, 107, 156
Shelley, N., 114
Simon (student at Grafton), 26, 39, 69–73, 80, 82, 85, 86, 87, 100, 116, 159
The Simpsons (TV), 150
Skeggs, Beverley, 67, 84
Skelton, Christine, 145
Skovsmose, Ole, 19, 33, 159, 161, 162, 163, 165
Snitow, A., 103
Spender, Dale, 16, 21, 151, 153
Stanic, G.M.A., 69
Stanley, L., 34
Sunnydale Further Education (FE) College, 25, 31–33, 36, 37, 80, 92, 134

Thomas, K., 83, 109
Tobias, S., 98
Toni (student at Sunnydale), 31, 39, 69, 80–87, 100, 134
Travolta, John, 113
Trisha (teacher at Grafton), 27, 28, 37
Tsolidis, G., 143
Turing, Alan, 64
Turkle, S., 153

Valero, P., 33
Veronica Sawyer (teacher at Westerburg), 37, 123–127, 131
Verschaffel, I., 76
Vicky (student at Westerburg), 39
Vijay (student at Grafton), 39
Vorderman, Carol, 144–147

Walkerdine, Valerie, 16, 18, 20, 21, 22, 40, 50, 60, 62, 67, 75, 97, 163
Wallace, S., 32
Walter, Marion, 160, 161, 165
Weinstein, J., 150
Welsh, I., 95
Wenger, E., 152
Westerburg Sixth Form College, 25, 28–30, 36, 37, 45, 47, 50, 55, 59, 96, 123, 127, 128, 135

Wetherell, Margaret, 36, 37, 41
Weyl, Herman, 140
White, John, 159
Whitehead, J., 83
Wilchins, R., 5, 14, 43
William, Dylan, 136, 137
Willis, S., 142
Winters, J., 148
Winterson, J., 38
WISE, (Women into Science and
  Engineering), 34, 152

Wittig, Monique, 9
Witz, A., 85
Woolf, Virginia, 64
Wurtzel, Elizabeth, 110

Yasser (student at Westerburg), 39, 57,
  67, 126, 127
Youdell, D., 3

Zia (student at Grafton), 88